Nikon® D5000
Digital Field Guide

Nikon® D5000 Digital Field Guide

J. Dennis Thomas

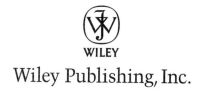

WILEY

Wiley Publishing, Inc.

Nikon® D5000 Digital Field Guide

Published by
Wiley Publishing, Inc.
10475 Crosspoint Boulevard
Indianapolis, IN 46256
www.wiley.com

ISBN: 978-0-470-52126-7

Manufactured in the United States of America

10 9 8 7 6 5 4 3 2 1

For general information on our other products and services or to obtain technical support, please contact our Customer Care Department within the U.S. at (877) 762-2974, outside the U.S. at (317) 572-3993 or fax (317) 572-4002.

Wiley also publishes its books in a variety of electronic formats. Some content that appears in print may not be available in electronic books.

Library of Congress Control Number: 2009929485

WILEY

About the Author

J. Dennis Thomas is a freelance photographer based out of Austin, Texas. He's been using a camera for fun and profit for almost 25 years. Schooled in photography first in high school and then at Austin College, he has won numerous awards for both his film and digital photography. Denny has a passion for teaching others about photography and has taught black-and-white film photography to area middle school students, as well as lighting and digital photography seminars in Austin. His photographic subjects are diverse, from weddings and studio portraits to concerts and extreme sports. He has written several highly successful Digital Field Guides for Wiley Publishing and has another in the works. His work has been featured in numerous magazines and newspapers in the central Texas area and beyond.

Credits

Acquisitions Editor
Courtney Allen

Project Editor
Chris Wolfgang

Technical Editor
Mike Hagen

Copy Editor
Marylouise Wiack

Editorial Director
Robyn Siesky

Editorial Manager
Cricket Krengel

Business Manager
Amy Knies

Senior Marketing Manager
Sandy Smith

Vice President and Executive Group Publisher
Richard Swadley

Vice President and Executive Publisher
Barry Pruett

Project Coordinator
Lynsey Stanford

Graphics and Production Specialists
Ana Carrillo
Jennifer Mayberry

Quality Control Technicians
Caitie Copple
Melanie Hoffman

Proofreading and Indexing
Penny L. Stuart
BIM Indexing & Proofreading

Acknowledgments

Thanks to the whole crew at Wiley and the staff at Precision Camera in Austin, TX.

Contents at a Glance

Contents

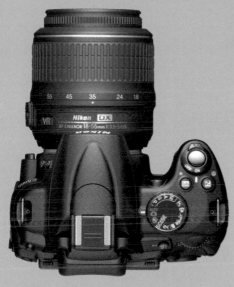

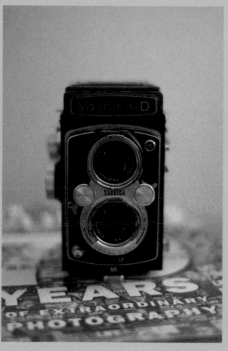

Chapter 3: Exploring the D5000 Menus   47

Chapter 4: Essential Photography Concepts 77

Chapter 5: Selecting and Using Lenses 95

Chapter 6: Working with Light 115

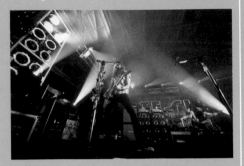

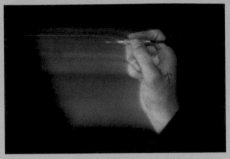

Chapter 7: Working with D-Movie 143

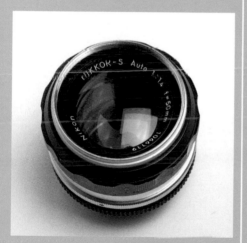

Chapter 8: Viewing and In-camera Editing 153

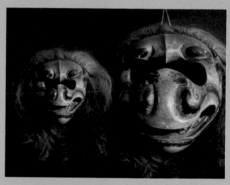

Part II: Capturing Great Images with the Nikon D5000   173

Chapter 9: Action and Sports Photography   175

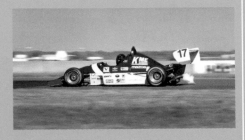

Chapter 10: Flower and Plant Photography   181

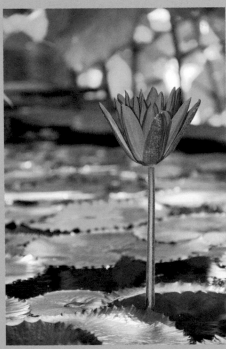

Chapter 11: Macro Photography   187

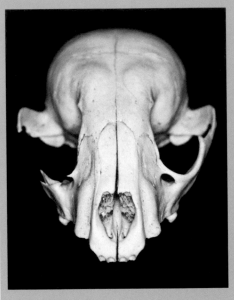

Chapter 12: Night and Lowlight Photography   195

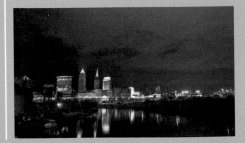

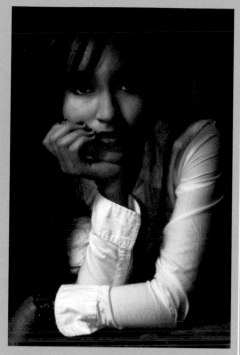

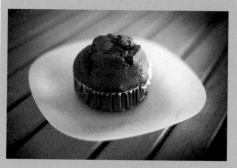

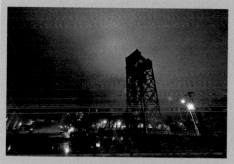

Part III:
Appendixes 223

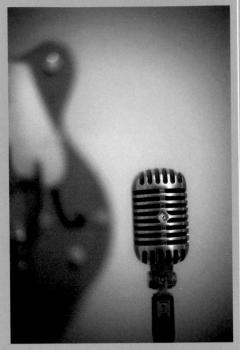

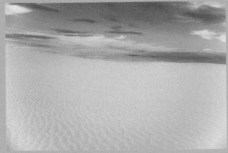

Introduction

Welcome to the *Nikon D5000 Digital Field Guide*. This book is a handy reference for you to get started learning about all of the features and functions of your Nikon D5000 DSLR camera.

This Digital Field Guide isn't meant to replace the user's manual but to be an adjunct to the manual, explaining things in plainer terms and in more detail than the manual. The guide is aimed at D5000 owners that are just starting out in the world of digital SLRs as well as more advanced users with deeper knowledge of photography.

The *Nikon D5000 Digital Field Guide* not only covers the specifics of the D5000, but also covers many other facets of digital photography, from the basics of exposure to lighting and composition. Simply put, there is a lot of information in this book not only about the D5000 but about photography in general; after all, knowing what all the buttons are for is only half the battle. This book's goal is to move you beyond snapshots into well thought-out compositions.

About the D5000

Hot on the heels of its hugely successful D90, Nikon released the D5000: a camera that fits squarely between Nikon's entry-level D60 and the more advanced D90. D5000 users will find that this camera combines the advanced features of the D90 with the ease of use and compactness of the D60. All in all, an amazing little package.

The D5000 inherits most of the features that made the D90 an instant hit. The 12.3 mega-pixel CMOS sensor, amazing high ISO performance, EXPEED image processing, fast response and focusing, Live View with D-Movie mode — the list goes on.

Not content to rest on its laurels, Nikon has added some brand new features to the D5000: namely, the Vari-angle LCD monitor that allows you to move the LCD around for ease of use when using Live View or D-Movie to compose shots in odd angles. Also added are 13 additional Advanced Scene Modes, up from the six on the D90 for a total of 19 Advanced Scene Modes.

Bundled with the D5000 is the highly praised Nikon 18-55mm f/3.5-5.6G VR lens. This lens is a solid performer with a proven track record and will cover most of your basic photography needs. The added bonus of Nikon's Vibration Reduction allows you to handhold the camera at slower shutter speeds without worrying about blurry pictures caused by camera shake. The Silent Wave motor in the lens allows for quick, nearly silent focusing.

Using the Nikon D5000

◆ ◆ ◆ ◆

◆ ◆ ◆ ◆

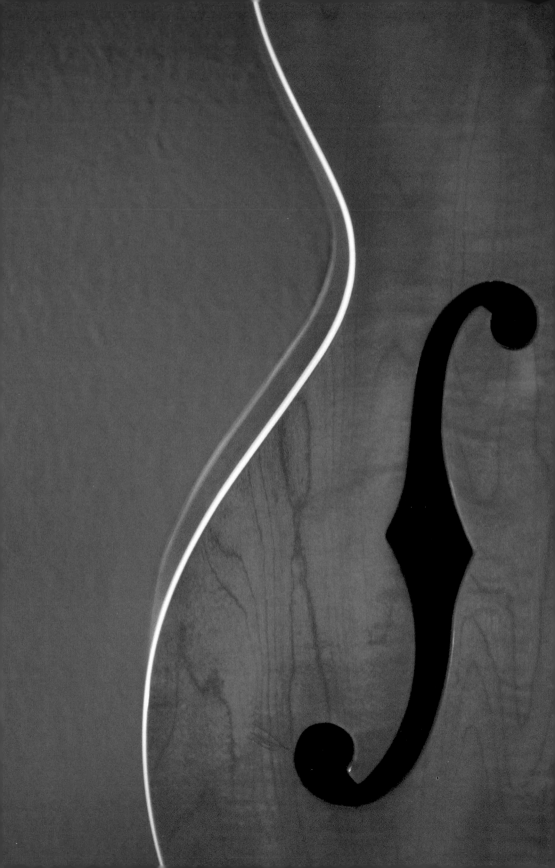

Exploring the Nikon D5000

 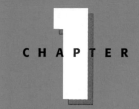
This chapter covers the key components of the Nikon D5000. These are the features that are most readily accessible because they are situated on the outside of the camera: the buttons, knobs, switches, and dials.

If you are upgrading from another dSLR, some of this will likely be a review, but there are some new features that you may or may not be aware of, so a quick read-through is a good idea even if you are an experienced Nikon dSLR user.

If you are new to the world of dSLRs, this chapter is a great way to get acquainted with some of the terms that are used in conjunction with your new camera.

So fasten your seatbelts, and get ready to explore the D5000!

Key Components of the D5000

If you have or are seriously looking at a camera of the Nikon D5000's caliber, you are probably pretty familiar with the basic buttons and switches that you need to work with the basic settings. In this section, you look at the camera from all sides and break down the layout so that you know what everything on the surface of the camera does.

This section doesn't cover the menus, only the exterior controls. Although there are many features you can access with just the push of a button, oftentimes you can change the same setting inside a menu option. Although the D5000 doesn't have the same number of buttons as some of its siblings in the Nikon line, it does have quite a few of them. Knowing exactly what these buttons do can save you loads of time and help you to not miss out on getting a shot.

Top of the camera

The top of the D5000 is where you find some of the most important buttons and dials. This is where you can change the shooting mode and press the Shutter Release button to take your photo. Also included in this section is a brief description of some of the things you will find on the top of the lens. Although your lens may vary, most of the features are quite similar from lens to lens.

✦ **Shutter Release button.** In my opinion, this is the most important button on the camera. Halfway pressing this button activates the camera's automatic focusing and light meter. When you fully depress this button, the shutter is released and a photograph is taken. When the camera has been idle and has "gone to sleep," lightly pressing the Shutter Release button wakes up the camera. When the image review is on, lightly pressing the Shutter Release button turns off the LCD and prepares the camera for another shot.

✦ **On/Off switch.** This switch, which is concentric to the Shutter Release button, is used to turn the camera on and off. Push the switch all the way to the left to turn off the camera. Pull the switch to the right to turn your camera on.

✦ **Mode dial.** This is an important dial; rotating it allows you to quickly change your shooting mode. You can choose one of the Scene modes or one of the semi-automatic modes, or you can choose to set the exposure manually. For a detailed description of all of the exposure modes, see Chapter 2.

✦ **Exposure Compensation/Aperture button.** Pressing this button in conjunction with rotating the Command dial allows you to modify the exposure that is set by the D5000's light meter or the exposure you set in Manual Exposure mode. Turning the Command dial to the right decreases the exposure, while turning the dial to the left increases the exposure. This button also doubles as the Aperture button when the camera is set to Manual Exposure mode. Pressing the button while rotating the Command dial allows you to adjust your lens aperture. Additionally, when pressing this button in conjunction with the flash mode, you can adjust your Flash Exposure Compensation (FEC) by rotating the Command dial.

✦ **Info button.** Pressing this button displays the Information Display on the LCD. This button also doubles as a reset button when pressed and held for 2 seconds in conjunction with the Info button on the back of the camera.

✦ **Focal plane mark.** The focal plane mark shows you where the plane of the image sensor is inside the camera. The sensor isn't exactly where the mark is; the sensor is directly behind the lens opening. This can be useful in determining the exact distance from the subject to the camera. Also, when doing certain types of photography, particularly macro photography using a bellows lens, you need to measure the length of the bellows from the front element of the lens to the focal plane. This is where the focal plane mark comes in handy.

Focal length

Focus ring

Exposure compensation/Aperture button

Zoom ring

On/Off switch

Shutter release
button

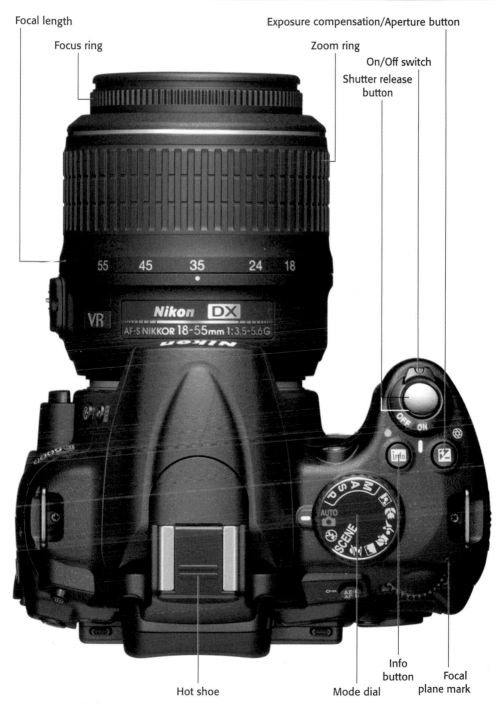

55 45 35 24 18

Nikon **DX**

AF-S NIKKOR 18-55mm 1:3.5-5.6G

VR

Info
button

Focal
plane mark

Hot shoe

Mode dial

Image courtesy of Nikon Inc.

1.1 Top of the camera controls.

✦ **Hot shoe.** This is where an accessory flash is attached to the camera body. The hot shoe has an electronic contact that tells the flash to fire when the shutter is released. There are also a number of other electronic contacts that allow the camera to communicate with the flash to enable the automated features of a dedicated flash unit such as the SB-600.

✦ **Focus ring.** Rotating the focus ring enables you to manually focus the camera. With some lenses, such as the high-end Nikkor AF-S lenses, you can manually adjust the focus at any time. On other lenses, typically older and non-Nikon lenses, you must switch the lens to manual focus to disable the focusing mechanism. With the kit lens, you must switch to manual focus. Rotating the focus ring while the lens is set to autofocus can damage your lens.

✦ **Zoom ring.** Rotating the zoom ring allows you to change the focal length of the lens. Prime lenses do not have a zoom ring.

✦ **Focal length indicators.** These numbers indicate which focal length in millimeters your lens is zoomed to.

> **Cross-Reference** *For more information on lenses, see Chapter 5.*

Back of the camera

The back of the camera is where you find the buttons that mainly control playback and menu options, although there are a few buttons that control some of the shooting functions. Most of the buttons have more than one function — a lot of them are used in conjunction with the main Command dial or the multi selector. On the back of the

camera, you also find several key features, including the all-important viewfinder and LCD.

✦ **Vari-angle LCD.** This is the most obvious feature on the back of the camera. This 2.7-inch, 230,000-dot liquid crystal display (LCD) is a very bright, high-resolution screen. The LCD is where you view all of your current camera settings, as well as review your images after shooting. New to the D5000, the LCD is articulated so that you can move it into many different positions in order to make taking pictures easier in awkward circumstances. The monitor can fold down perpendicular to the back of the camera, and can be rotated 180 degrees to the left and 90 degrees to the right.

✦ **Viewfinder.** This is what you look through to compose your photographs. Light coming through the lens is reflected through a series of mirrors (called a pentamirror), enabling you to see exactly what you're shooting (as opposed to a rangefinder camera, which gives you an approximate view).

Around the viewfinder is a rubber eyepiece that serves to give you a softer place to rest your eye and to block any extra light from entering the viewfinder as you compose and shoot your images.

✦ **Diopter adjustment control.** Just to the right of the viewfinder is the Diopter adjustment control. Use this control to adjust the viewfinder lens to suit your individual vision differences (not everyone's eyesight is the same). To adjust this, look through the viewfinder, and press the Shutter Release button halfway to focus on something.

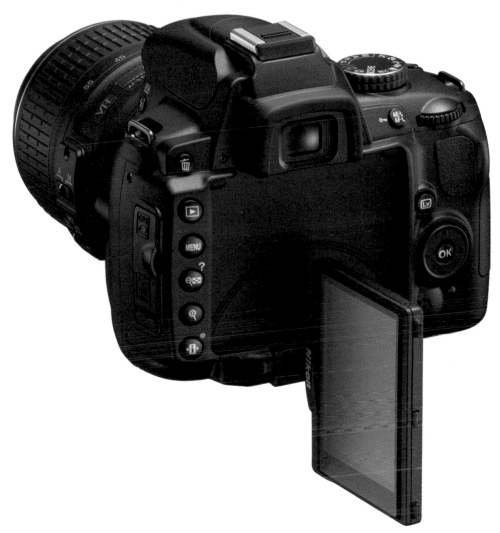

Image courtesy of Nikon Inc.
1.2 Vari-angle LCD.

If what you see in the viewfinder isn't quite sharp, slide the Diopter adjustment control up or down until everything appears in focus.

✦ **AE-L/AF-L lock/Protect button.** The Auto-Exposure/Auto-Focus lock button is used to lock the Auto-Exposure (AE) and Auto-Focus (AF). You can also customize the button to lock only the AE or only the AF, or you can set the button to initiate AF (CSM-12). When in Playback mode, this button can be pressed to lock an image to protect it from being deleted. A small key icon displays in the upper-left corner of images that are protected.

✦ **Command dial.** This dial is used to change a variety of settings, depending on which button you are using in conjunction with it. By default, it is used to change the shutter speed when in Shutter Priority and Manual modes, or the aperture when in Aperture Priority mode. It is also used to adjust exposure compensation and change the flash mode.

✦ **Multi selector button.** The multi selector is another button that serves a few different purposes. In Playback mode, the multi selector is used to scroll through the photographs you've taken, and it can also be used to view image information such as histograms and shooting settings. When in certain shooting modes (P, S, A, or M and certain Advanced Scene Modes), the multi selector can be used to change the active focus point. This is only when the mode allows or you set Single point or Dynamic area AF mode.

Note *The active focus point cannot be changed when in Auto AF mode or Portrait, Child portrait, and Night portrait Advanced Scene Modes.*

✦ **OK button.** When in the Menu mode, press this button to select the menu item that is highlighted.

✦ **Live View button.** Pressing this button initiates the Live view function; pressing the OK button while in Live view starts video recording.

✦ **Speaker.** The speaker is used to play back sound when reviewing video footage.

✦ **Memory card access lamp.** When the light is lit or blinking, the camera is writing data to the SD card. Under no circumstances should

you attempt to remove the SD card while data is being written. This causes you to lose images, possibly damaging the card and/or camera as well.

✦ **Delete button.** When reviewing your pictures, if you find some that you don't want to keep, you can delete them by pressing this button marked with a trash can icon. To prevent accidental deletion of images, the camera displays a dialog box asking you to confirm that you want to erase the picture. Press the Delete button a second time to permanently erase the image.

✦ **Playback button.** Pressing this button displays the most recently taken photograph. You can also view other pictures by pressing the multi selector left and right.

✦ **Menu button.** Press this button to access the D5000 menu options. There are a number of different menus, including Playback, Shooting, Custom Settings, and Retouch. Use the multi selector to choose the menu you want to view.

✦ **Thumbnail/Zoom Out/Help button.** In Playback mode, pressing this button allows you to go from full-frame playback (or viewing the whole image) to viewing thumbnails. The thumbnails can be displayed either four or nine images on a page. When viewing the menu options, pressing this button displays a help screen that explains the functions of a particular menu option. When in shooting mode, pressing this button explains the functions of that particular mode.

✦ **Zoom In button/Info Display/ Quick Settings button.** When reviewing your images, you can press the Zoom In button to get a closer look at the details. This is a handy feature for checking the sharpness and focus of your shot. When zoomed in, use the multi selector to navigate around within the image. To view other images at the same zoom ratio, you can rotate the Command dial. To return to full-frame playback, press the Zoom Out button. You may have to press the Zoom Out button multiple times, depending on how much you have zoomed in.

✦ **Info button.** Pressing this button displays the shooting information. When the shooting information is displayed, pressing this button gives access to the Quick Settings menu. When in the Quick Settings menu, use the multi selector to highlight the desired setting, then press OK to access the options.

Cross-Reference *For more detailed information on the Quick Settings menu, see Chapter 3.*

Zoom Out/Thumbnail/Help button

Playback button   Diopter adjuster

Delete button   Viewfinder   AE-L/AF-L lock/Protect button
Command dial

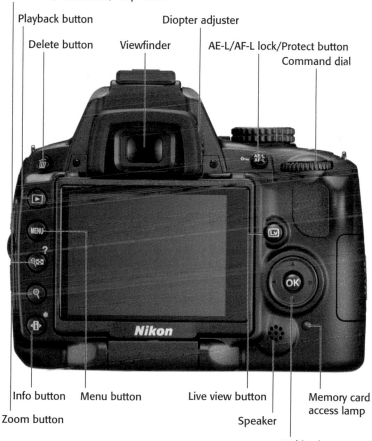

Info button   Menu button   Live view button   Memory card
access lamp
Zoom button   Speaker
Multi-selector

Image courtesy of Nikon Inc.

1.3 Back of the camera controls.

Front of the camera

The front of the D5000 (lens facing you) is where you find the buttons to quickly adjust the flash settings as well as some camera focusing options; with certain lenses, you also find some buttons that control focusing and Vibration Reduction (VR).

Self timer/Fn button

Flash Pop-up/ Lens release
Flash mode/ button
Flash Exposure
Compensation button Autofocus/
Manual focus
Built-in flash switch

Vibration
reduction
switch

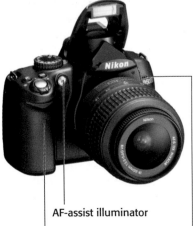

AF-assist illuminator

Infared receiver Microphone

Image courtesy of Nikon Inc.

1.4 **Front camera controls.**

✦ **Built-in flash.** This option is a handy feature that allows you to take sharp pictures in low-light situations. Although not as versatile as one of the external Nikon Speedlights such as the SB-900, SB-800 or SB-600, the built-in flash can be used very effectively and is great for snapshots.

> **Cross-Reference** *For more on using flash, see Chapter 6.*

✦ **Microphone.** The microphone records sound as video is recorded.

✦ **Flash Pop-up/Flash mode/Flash Exposure Compensation button.** Press this button to open and activate the built-in Speedlight. Pressing this button and rotating the Command dial on the rear of the camera allows you to choose a flash mode. You can choose from among Front-curtain sync, Red-eye reduction, Red-eye reduction with slow sync, Slow sync, and Rear curtain sync.

Once the flash is popped up, pressing this button in conjunction with the Exposure Compensation button and rotating the Command dial allows you to adjust the Flash Exposure Compensation (FEC). The FEC allows you to adjust the flash output to make the flash brighter or dimmer, depending on your needs.

✦ **Self-timer/Fn (function) button.** By default, pressing this button activates the camera's self-timer. When the self-timer is on, the camera delays the shutter release to allow you to get into the picture, or to reduce vibration caused by shaking the camera when pressing the Shutter Release button while the camera is attached to a tripod. This button can also be set to provide other functions.

You can set the button to quickly change the release mode, image quality, ISO sensitivity, or white balance through the Quick Settings menu. Pressing the Fn button and rotating the Command dial changes the settings. The Fn button can be assigned to the specific function in CSM f1.

 Cross-Reference *For more information on the Custom Settings menu (CSM), see Chapter 3.*

✦ **Lens Release button.** This button disengages the locking mechanism of the lens, allowing the lens to be rotated and removed from the lens mount.

✦ **Auto focus/Manual focus switch.** This switch is used to choose between using the lens in Auto or Manual Focus mode.

✦ **Vibration Reduction (VR) switch.** This allows you to turn the Vibration Reduction (VR) on or off. When shooting in bright light, it's best to turn the VR off to reduce battery consumption.

✦ **AF-assist illuminator.** This is an LED that shines on the subject to help the camera to focus when the lighting is dim. The AF-assist illuminator only lights when in Single Focus mode (AF-S) or Automatic Focus mode (AF-A).

✦ **Infrared receiver.** This allows you to wirelessly control the camera shutter release using the optional ML-L3 infrared transmitter.

Sides and bottom of the camera

The sides and bottom of the camera have places for connecting and inserting things such as cables, batteries, and memory cards.

Right side

On the right side of the camera (lens facing you) are the D5000's output terminals. These are used to connect your camera to a computer or to an external source for viewing your images directly from the camera. These terminals are hidden under a plastic cover that helps keep out dust and moisture.

✦ **Accessory terminal.** This port is used to connect accessories to the D5000. At present, this port accepts the Nikon GP-1 GPS unit and Nikon's cable release, the MC-DC2.

✦ **USB port.** This is where the USB cable plugs in to attach the camera to your computer to transfer images straight from the camera. The USB cable is also used to connect the camera to the computer when using Nikon's optional Camera Control Pro 2 software, as well as to connect to a printer for direct printing. Using the supplied EG-CP-14 A/V cable, you can also connect the D5000 to a standard TV.

✦ **HDMI Video out.** This connection allows you to connect your D5000 to an HDTV or monitor using an HDMI cable that can be purchased separately from an electronics store.

Accessory terminal

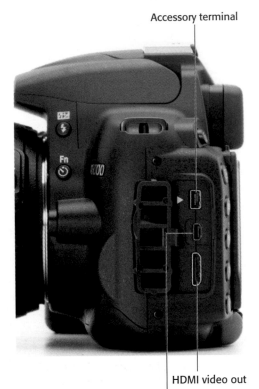

HDMI video out

USB port

Image courtesy of Nikon Inc.
1.5 The D5000's output terminals.

Left side

On the left side of the camera (lens facing you) is the memory card slot cover. Sliding this door towards the back of the camera opens it so that you can insert or remove your memory card.

Bottom

The bottom of the camera has a couple of features that are quite important.

✦ **Battery chamber cover.** This covers the chamber that holds the EN-EL9a battery that is supplied with your D5000.

✦ **Tripod socket.** This is where you attach a tripod or monopod to help steady your camera.

Viewfinder Display

When looking through the viewfinder, you see a lot of useful information about the photo you are setting up. Most of the information is also displayed in the control panel LCD screen on the top of the camera, but it is less handy on top when you are composing a shot.

Here is a complete list of all the information you get from the viewfinder display:

1. **Focus indicator.** This is a green dot that lets you know if the camera detects that the scene is in focus. When focus is achieved, the green dot lights up; if the camera is not in focus, no dot is displayed. When the camera is attempting to focus, the green dot blinks.

2. **Focus point display.** This shows you which AF point(s) is chosen by showing it with a bracket around it. When set to closest subject, no AF point is chosen.

3. **AE lock.** When this is lit, you know that the Auto-Exposure is locked.

4. **Flexible Program indicator.** When this is lit, it lets you know that the exposure has been modified from the original settings defined when using the Programmed Auto Exposure mode. To return to the default settings, rotate the Command dial until this indicator disappears, or turn the camera off.

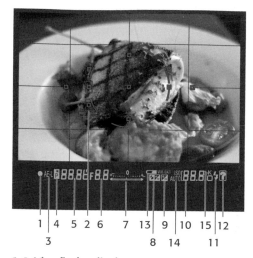

1 | 4   5 2 6   7 13| 9 |10 15|12
3   8 14   11

1.6 Viewfinder display.

5. **Shutter speed display/Noise Reduction indicator.** This shows how long your shutter is set to stay open. When the camera is performing Noise Reduction, *job nr* is displayed here.

6. **Aperture/f-stop display.** This shows your current lens opening setting.

7. **Electronic analog exposure display/Exposure Compensation/Rangefinder.** Although Nikon gives this feature a long and confusing name, in simpler terms, this is your light meter. When the bars are in the center, you are at the proper settings to get a good exposure; when the bars are to the left, you are overexposed; and when the bars are to the right, you are underexposing your image. This feature is especially handy when using manual exposure. When the Exposure Compensation button is pressed, this indicates how much over- or under-exposure is being set.

When the Rangefinder option is turned on (CSM a4), this shows you a bar graph that indicates distance. When the subject is in focus, there is one bar on either side of a 0. When the bars are displayed to the left, this indicates that you are focused in front of the subject; bars to the right indicate that the focus is falling behind the subject. Use the focus ring to adjust the focus. The Rangefinder display is not available when shooting in Manual mode.

8. **FEC indicator.** When this is displayed, your Flash Exposure Compensation is on.

9. **Exposure Compensation indicator.** When this appears in the viewfinder, your camera has Exposure Compensation activated.

10. **Remaining exposures.** This set of numbers lets you know how many more exposures can fit on the memory card. The actual number of exposures may vary according to file information and compression. When the Shutter Release button is half-pressed, the display changes to show how many exposures can fit in the camera's *buffer* before the buffer is full and the frame rate slows down. The buffer is in-camera RAM that stores your image data while the data is being written to the memory card. This area also indicates that the WB is ready to be set by flashing "PRE"; it displays the amount of exposure compensation and FEC when the Exposure Compensation button is pressed; it tells you whether the Active D-Lighting is on or off when the ADL button is pressed; and it also indicates when your camera is attached to a computer.

11. **Flash ready indicator.** When this is displayed, the flash — whether it is the built-in flash or an external Speedlight attached to the hot shoe — is fully charged and ready to fire at full power.

12. **Warning indicator.** When this question mark icon is flashing, the camera is warning you that there may be a problem with your settings. Press the Help button to view the warning.

13. **Battery indicator.** This shows up when the battery is low. When the battery is completely exhausted, this icon blinks and the shutter release is disabled.

14. **Auto ISO indicator.** This is displayed when the Automatic ISO setting is activated, to let you know that the camera is controlling the ISO settings.

15. **K.** This lets you know that there are more than 1,000 exposures remaining on your memory card.

Information Display

The Information Display (also referred to as Shooting Info Display) shows some of the same shooting information that appears in the viewfinder, but there are also some settings that are only displayed here. When this is displayed on the LCD, you can view and change the settings without looking through the viewfinder.

When the camera is turned on, the Information Display is automatically displayed on the LCD monitor. The information remains on display until no buttons have been pushed for about 8 seconds or the Shutter Release button is pressed.

This display shows you everything you need to know about your camera settings. Additionally, the camera has a built-in sensor that tells it when the camera is being held vertically, and the shooting information is displayed upright, regardless of which way you are holding your camera.

The camera also offers a number of options on how the information is displayed. You can choose between Classic and Graphic, and you can also change the color of the Shooting Info Display. You can also choose a different display for the Advanced Scene modes and P, S, A, and M modes. These settings can be accessed in the Setup menu under the Info display format heading.

 For more information on the Setup menu, see Chapter 3.

1. **Shooting mode.** This displays the shooting mode that your camera is currently set to. This can be one of the DVP modes, in which case either the appropriate icon or one of the Semi-auto modes (such as P, S, A, or M) appears, in which case the display shows the corresponding letter. This display changes when the mode dial is rotated.

2. **Aperture/f-stop number.** This tells you how wide your aperture or lens opening is. The terms *aperture* and *f-stop* are interchangeable. Higher f/numbers denote smaller openings, while lower f/numbers mean that the opening is wider, letting in more light.

3. **Shutter speed.** This shows, in seconds or fractions of seconds, how long your shutter will stay open when the Shutter Release button is pressed.

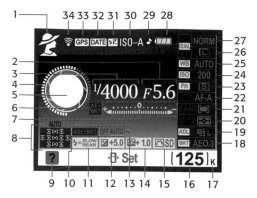

1.7 LCD display wide (landscape) orientation.

4. **Shutter speed display.** When set to Graphic mode, this gives you a visual idea about the length of your shutter speed.

5. **Aperture display.** When set to Graphic mode, this shows you approximately what your lens opening looks like.

6. **Bracketing indicator.** When this icon is shown, auto-bracketing is turned on.

7. **Electronic analog exposure display/Exposure Compensation/Bracketing progress indicator.** This is your light meter. When the bars are in the center, you are at the proper settings to get a good exposure; when the bars are to the left, you are underexposed; when the bars are to the right, you are overexposing your image. This is only displayed when using Manual exposure. When you apply exposure compensation, the bars indicate how much exposure compensation is applied. When bracketing is turned on, this shows where you are at in the bracketing sequence.

8. **Autofocus (AF) indicators.** This area shows you which AF-area mode is in use, as well as which focus point is selected (unless Auto-area is selected).

9. **Help indicator.** When this icon is flashing, there may be a problem with one of your settings. Pressing the Help/Zoom Out button displays information on rectifying the problem.

10. **Active D-Lighting Bracketing indicator.** When Auto-bracketing is set to AD-L and turned on, this icon is shown.

11. **Flash sync mode.** This shows which mode your flash is set to. You can change the flash mode by pressing the flash button and rotating the Command dial.

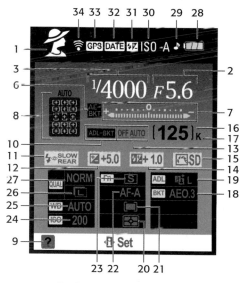

1.8 LCD display tall (portrait) orientation.

12. **Exposure compensation value.** This shows the amount of exposure compensation, if any, that has been set. Exposure compensation is used to increase or decrease the amount of exposure to fine-tune your image.

13. **AD-L Bracketing.** This icon is displayed when auto bracketing is turned on and set to AD-L.

14. **Flash Exposure Compensation.** This shows you the amount, if any, of Flash Exposure Compensation (FEC). FEC is used to make the flash more or less bright. FEC is set by simultaneously pressing the Flash Mode button and Exposure Compensation button, and rotating the Command dial.

15. **Picture Control.** This indicates which Picture Control setting is being used. Picture Controls can be changed in the Quick Settings menu or Shooting menu.

16. **Number of remaining exposures.** This shows you approximately how many exposures can be saved to your memory card. When the Preset White Balance is ready to be set, this blinks "PRE." When the camera is attached to the computer using Camera Control Pro 2, "PC" appears here.

17. **K.** This icon appears when you have more than 1,000 exposures remaining on your memory card.

18. **Bracketing increment.** This shows the EV increments for the auto bracketing feature.

19. **Active D-Lighting indicator.** This shows which setting you have Active D-Lighting set to, or whether it is on or off. Active D-Lighting can be set in the Quick Settings menu.

20. **Metering mode.** This displays which metering mode your camera is set to: Dynamic, Center-weighted, or Spot.

21. **AF-area mode.** This tells you which AF-area mode is selected: Auto-area, Dynamic area, or Single point.

22. **Focus mode.** This tells you which focus mode your camera is set to: AF-A (Automatic), AF-C (Continuous), AF-S (Single), or MF (Manual Focus).

23. **Release mode.** This lets you know what release mode your camera is set to: Single Frame, Continuous, Self-Timer, Delayed Remote, Quick Response Remote, or Quiet Release mode.

24. **ISO sensitivity.** This tells you what your current ISO setting is.

25. **White Balance.** This displays which White Balance setting you are currently using.

26. **Image size.** This tells you the size of the image you are recording.

27. **Image Quality.** This shows the quality or compression of the JPEG, or it shows that you are recording a RAW image.

28. **Battery indicator.** This shows you the remaining charge on your battery.

29. **Beep indicator.** This tells you whether you have the camera set to beep when focus is achieved.

30. **ISO Auto indicator.** When this is shown (ISO-A), the camera is set to Auto ISO.

31. **Manual Flash indicator.** When this is displayed, the built-in flash is set to Manual mode; if a Speedlight such as an SB-400 is attached, this indicates that FEC is applied.

32. **Date imprint indicator.** This is shown when the optional date imprint function is applied. This function prints the date at the bottom of the image as it's being recorded.

33. **GPS.** This is displayed when an optional GPS unit is connected to the camera through the accessory terminal.

34. **Eye-Fi.** This is only displayed when an optional Eye-Fi SD card is being used.

Nikon D5000 Essentials

 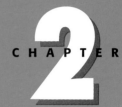

After reading Chapter 1, you should be pretty familiar with the basic layout of the D5000 and all of the various dials, switches, and buttons; you should also find it much easier to navigate to and adjust the settings that allow you to control and fine-tune the way the camera captures images. This chapter covers some of the most commonly changed settings of the camera, such as the exposure modes, metering, AF settings, white balance, and ISO. All of these combined settings are used to create your image and can be tweaked and adjusted to reflect your artistic vision or simply to be sure that your pictures come out exactly as you want, even in difficult lighting situations.

Exposure settings include the exposure modes that decide how the camera chooses the aperture and shutter speed and the metering modes that decide how the camera gathers the lighting information so that the camera can choose the appropriate settings based on the exposure mode.

You learn more about ISO, which also plays into exposure, and exposure compensation is also covered. Exposure compensation allows you to fine-tune the exposure to suit your needs or to achieve the proper exposure in situations where your light meter may be fooled.

This chapter also explains the Autofocus modes, which decide which areas of the viewfinder are given preference when the camera is deciding what to focus on. Discussions of white balance, Picture Controls, and Live View round out the chapter.

Exposure Modes

Exposure modes determine how the different settings are chosen to get the desired exposure. The Nikon D5000 has quite a few options to help you get the exposure that is right for the scene you are photographing.

There are modes that are fully automatic, some that are semi-automatic (in that you choose one aspect of the exposure and the camera takes care of the rest), and a fully manual mode in which you determine all of the settings according to your calculations.

Auto modes

The D5000 has two fully automatic, or Auto, modes that do all of the work for you. These are simple grab-and-go settings to use when you're in a hurry or you just don't want to be bothered with changing the settings. The Auto modes control everything from shutter speed and aperture to ISO sensitivity.

Note *The Auto ISO setting can be overridden using the Quick settings display to change the ISO setting. If the Function button is set to ISO, the Auto ISO can be overridden as well. The override remains in effect unless the camera is changed to P, S, A, or M and returned to one of the scene modes. When changing back to a scene mode from P, S, A, or M, the Auto ISO function is again activated.*

Auto

The Auto mode is basically a point-and-shoot mode. The camera takes complete control over the exposure. The camera's meter reads the light, the color, and the brightness of the scene and runs the information through a sophisticated algorithm. The camera uses this information to determine what type of scene you are photographing and chooses the settings that it deems appropriate for the scene.

If there isn't enough light to make a proper exposure, the camera's built-in flash pops up when the Shutter Release button is half-pressed for focus. The flash fires when the shutter is released, resulting in a properly exposed image.

This mode is great for taking snapshots, when you simply want to concentrate on capturing the image and let the camera determine the proper settings.

Auto (flash off)

This mode functions in the same way as the Auto setting, except that it disables the flash, even in low-light situations. In instances when the lighting is poor, the camera's AF-assist illuminator lights up to provide sufficient light to achieve focus. The camera uses the focus area of the closest subject to focus on.

This setting is preferable when you want to use natural or ambient light for your subject or in situations where you aren't allowed to use flash, such as museums or events such as weddings, where the flash may cause a distraction.

Advanced scene modes

Sometimes the Auto mode isn't going to give you the proper settings to suit your needs, especially when shooting under difficult situations or when you have special circumstances. These scene modes take into account different lighting situations and modify the way the camera meters the light, as well as controlling the focus points, the flash settings, and the aperture, shutter speed, and ISO sensitivity settings.

The camera also determines if there is enough light to make an exposure and activates the built-in flash if there is not enough light. Some of these scene modes, such as Landscape, also make sure that the flash is not used, even in low-light situations.

New with the D5000 are a total of 19 scene modes. Nikon added 13 scene modes to the standard 6 that are available on the D60 and

D90. Some of these modes have been carried over from Nikon's highly popular COOLPIX cameras, so if you were previously a COOLPIX shooter, you will feel right at home. Advanced modes are for photographing specific scene types such as sports or portraits.

The D5000's scene modes allow you to capture the image with the settings that are best for what you are photographing. The camera has the parameters programmed into it, and so you can just rotate the Mode dial to the scene type for the most commonly used scene modes. For example, when shooting sports, you usually want to freeze the action, while when shooting a portrait, you often want a wider aperture to blur out the background.

You can select additional scene modes by rotating the mode dial to SCENE and rotating the Command dial to select the desired mode from the menu. With scene modes, you can simply focus on capturing the moment rather than fretting over what the proper settings should be.

These scene modes take difficult lighting situations and make it easier to get great photos. This can give you a little more flexibility than just sticking the camera in Auto mode and hoping that things will turn out as you want them to.

Portrait

This scene mode is for taking pictures of people. The camera automatically adjusts the colors to give natural-looking skin tones. The camera focuses on the closest subject. It also attempts to use a wide aperture, if possible, to reduce the depth of field. This draws attention to the subject of the portrait, leaving distracting background details out of focus.

The built-in flash and AF-assist illuminator automatically activate in low-light situations.

Landscape

This mode is used for taking photos of far-off vistas. The camera automatically adjusts the colors to apply brighter greens and blues to skies and foliage. The camera also automatically focuses on the closest subject and uses a smaller aperture to provide a greater depth of field to ensure focus throughout the entire image.

In this mode, the camera automatically disables the AF-assist illuminator and the flash.

Child

This mode is for taking great photos or candid shots of children. The camera automatically adjusts the colors to give more saturation while still giving a natural skin tone. The camera automatically focuses on the closest subject and uses a fairly small aperture to capture background details. The built-in flash is automatically activated when the light is low.

Sports

This mode uses a fast shutter speed to freeze the action of moving subjects. The camera focuses continuously as long as you have the Shutter Release button half-pressed. The camera also uses predictive focus tracking based on information from all of the focus areas, in case the main subject moves from the center focus area.

The camera disables the built-in flash and AF-assist illuminator when this mode is selected.

Close Up

This scene mode is used for close-up or macro shots. It uses a fairly wide aperture to provide a soft background while giving the main subject a sharp focus. In this mode, the camera focuses on the subject in the center of the frame, although you can use the multi selector to choose one of the other focus points to create an off-center composition.

When light is low, the camera automatically activates the built-in flash. Be sure to remove your lens hood when using the flash on close-up subjects because the lens hood can cast a shadow on your subject by blocking the light from the flash.

Night Portrait

This mode is for taking portraits in low-light situations. The camera automatically activates the flash and uses a longer shutter speed to capture the ambient light from the background. This balances the ambient light and the light from the flash, giving you a more natural effect. I recommend using a tripod when you use this feature to prevent blurring from camera shake that can occur during longer exposure times.

Night Landscape

This mode is used for shooting photos of skylines and cities scenes at night. Noise reduction is applied and the WB is adjusted to render the color of the city lights better. Using a tripod is best when selecting this mode. The built-in flash and AF-Assist are turned off.

Party/Indoor

This mode is similar to the Night Portrait mode. It is used to take pictures in low-light situations and to adequately capture the background light. The camera uses a wide aperture and a slow shutter speed to capture the background, while the flash is set to slow sync red-eye reduction. The AF point is set to the center. If available, use this mode with the VR on to reduce the effect of camera shake.

Beach/Snow

Light reflecting from sand or snow can fool the camera's light meter into thinking the scene is brighter than it actually is, so when you set the camera to this mode, it overexposes the image slightly to ensure that the sand or snow appears bright. The flash is set to Auto. The camera's AF point is set to the center of the frame.

Sunset

This scene mode captures the intense shades of colors seen during sunset or sunrise. The camera boosts color saturation to enhance this effect. The flash is turned off, and the camera focuses at the center of the frame. A tripod is recommended when using this setting.

Dusk/Dawn

This mode is similar to the Sunset scene mode. This mode is to be used *after* the sun sets or *before* it rises. The color saturation is boosted in order to accent the colors that are less visible when the sun has already set (or has yet to rise) and there is little light available. In this mode, the camera is focused at infinity and the flash is turned off. A tripod is strongly recommended when using this mode.

Pet Portrait

This mode is obviously for taking photos of pets. A faster shutter speed is used to freeze any movement a frisky pet might make. The AF-assist is disabled in this mode.

Candlelight

This mode gives you more natural colors when photographing under candlelight, which can be difficult on standard Auto WB settings. The camera also uses wide aperture settings. The flash is disabled.

Blossom

This mode is for shooting landscapes in which large fields of colorful flowers appear. The colors are boosted for a more vibrant look. The built-in flash is disabled in this mode.

Autumn Colors

When this mode is selected the camera automatically boosts the saturation of the reds, oranges and yellows in the image since those are the most prevalent colors in fall foliage. The built-in flash is also disabled in this mode.

Food

Use this mode when photographing food items. The colors are boosted and the camera attempts to select a fairly wide aperture. When the lighting is low the built-in flash is automatically activated.

Silhouette

In this mode the camera sets the exposure for the bright part of the scene to silhouette the dark subject against a bright background. This option is best used during dusk or dawn.

 Cross-Reference *For more information on shooting silhouettes see Chapter 15.*

High Key

Use this setting when shooting a light subject against a light background. The camera applies some exposure compensation to slightly overexpose and add some brightness to the scene.

Low Key

Use this setting when photographing dark subjects on a dark background. This mode also punches up the highlights just a bit to

get good definition between the shadows and highlights.

Programmed Auto

Programmed Auto mode, or P, is a fully automatic mode suitable for use when shooting snapshots and scenes where you're not very concerned about controlling the settings.

When the camera is in Programmed Auto mode, it decides all of the settings for you, based on a set of algorithms. The camera attempts to select a shutter speed that allows you to shoot handheld without suffering from camera shake, while also adjusting your aperture so that you get good depth of field to ensure everything is in focus.

When the camera body is coupled with a lens that has a CPU built in (all AF lenses have a CPU), the camera automatically knows what focal length and aperture range the lens has. The camera then uses this lens information to decide what the optimal settings should be.

This exposure mode chooses the widest aperture possible until the optimal shutter speed for the specific lens is reached. Then the camera chooses a smaller f-stop, and increases the shutter speed as light levels increase.

For example, when using an 18-55mm kit lens, the camera keeps the aperture wide open until the shutter speed reaches about 1/40 second (approximately the minimum shutter speed needed to avoid camera shake). Upon reaching 1/40 second, the camera adjusts the aperture to increase depth of field.

The exposure settings selected by the camera are displayed in both the LCD control panel and the viewfinder display. Although the camera chooses what it thinks are the optimal settings, the camera does not know what your specific needs are. You may decide that your hands are not steady enough to shoot at the shutter speed the camera has selected, or you may want a wider or smaller aperture for selective focus.

Fortunately, you aren't stuck with the camera's exposure choice. You can engage what is known as *flexible program.* Flexible program allows you to deviate from the camera's aperture and shutter speed choice when you are in P mode. This feature can be automatically engaged simply by rotating the Command dial until the desired shutter speed or aperture is achieved. This allows you to choose a wider aperture and faster shutter speed when rotated to the right, or a slower shutter speed and smaller aperture when the dial is rotated to the left.

With flexible program, you can maintain the metered exposure while still having some control over the shutter speed and aperture settings.

A quick example of using flexible program would be if the camera has set the shutter speed at 1/60 second with an aperture of f/8, you're shooting a portrait, and you want a wider aperture to throw the background out of focus. By rotating the Command dial to the right, you can open the aperture up to f/4, which causes the shutter speed to increase to 1/250 second. This is known as an *equivalent exposure,* meaning you get the exact same exposure but the settings are different.

When flexible program is on, an asterisk appears next to the P on the display. Rotate the main Command dial until the asterisk disappears to return to the default Programmed Auto settings.

 When using non-CPU lenses, the camera must be set to Manual exposure mode.

Aperture Priority

Aperture Priority mode, or A, is a semiautomatic mode. In this mode, you decide which aperture to use and the camera sets the shutter speed for the best exposure based on your chosen aperture. Situations where you may want to select the aperture include when you're shooting a portrait and want a large aperture (small f/number) to blur out the background, and when you're shooting a landscape and you want a small aperture (large f/number) to ensure the entire scene is in focus.

 In Aperture Priority mode, if there is not enough light to make a proper exposure, the camera displays Lo in place of the shutter speed setting. In the same manner, it will also display Hi if there is too much light.

In my opinion, choosing the aperture to control depth of field is one of the most important parts of photography. This allows you to selectively control which areas of your image are in sharp focus and which areas are allowed to blur and by how much. Controlling depth of field enables you to draw the viewer's eye to a specific part of the image, which can make your images more dynamic and interesting to the viewer.

Shutter Priority

Shutter Priority mode, or S, is another semi-automatic mode. In this mode, you choose the shutter speed and the camera sets the aperture. This mode is good to use when shooting moving subjects or action scenes where you need a fast shutter speed to freeze the motion of your subject and prevent blur.

You can also select a slower shutter speed to *add* motion blur as a creative photographic technique.

 Note *In Shutter Priority mode, if there is not enough light to make a proper exposure, the camera displays Lo in place of the aperture setting. In the same manner, it will also display Hi if there is too much light.*

Manual

When in Manual mode, or M, both the aperture and shutter speed settings are set by you. You can estimate the exposure, use a handheld light meter, or use the D5000's electronic analog exposure display to determine the exposure needed.

Probably the main question that people have about Manual mode is why you would use it when you have these other modes. There are a few reasons why you may want to set the exposure manually:

✦ **To gain complete control over exposure.** Most times, the camera decides the optimal exposure based on technical algorithms and an internal database of image information. Often, what the camera decides is optimal is not necessarily what is optimal in your mind.

You may want to underexpose to make your image dark and foreboding, or you may want to overexpose a bit to make the colors pop (making colors bright and contrasty). If your camera is set to M, you can choose the settings and place your image in whatever tonal range you want without having to adjust the exposure compensation settings.

✦ **When using studio flash.** When using studio strobes or external non-dedicated flash units, the camera's metering system isn't used. When using external strobes, a flash meter or manual calculation is necessary to determine the proper exposure. Using the Manual exposure mode, you can quickly set the aperture and shutter speed to the proper exposure; just be sure not to set the shutter speed above the rated sync speed of 1/200 second.

✦ **When using non-CPU lenses.** When using older non-CPU lenses, the camera must be set to Manual exposure mode or an error displays and the shutter release locks, rendering the camera unable to take a picture.

Metering Modes

The D5000 has three metering modes that you can choose from to help you get the best exposure for your image. You can change the modes by using the metering selector dial directly to the right of the viewfinder.

Metering modes decide how the camera's light sensor collects and processes the information used to determine exposure. Each of these modes is useful for different types of lighting situations.

Matrix

The default metering system that Nikon cameras use is a proprietary system called 3D Color Matrix II, or Matrix metering for short. Matrix metering takes an evaluative reading of the light falling on the entire scene, also taking into account the color information. Then the camera runs the data through some sophisticated algorithms and determines the proper exposure for the scene. When using a Nikkor D- or G-type lens, the camera also takes the focusing distance into consideration.

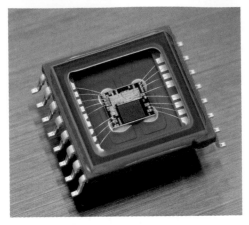

2.1 The D5000's 420-pixel RGB sensor.

 Cross-Reference *For more information on lenses and lens specifications, see Chapter 5.*

The D5000 has a 420-pixel RGB sensor that measures the intensity of the light and the color of a scene. The camera then compares the information to information from 30,000 images stored in its database. Then the D5000 determines the exposure settings based on the findings from the comparison. Simplified, it works like this: You're photographing a portrait outdoors, and the sensor detects that the light in the center of the frame is much dimmer than the edges. The camera takes this information along with the focus distance and compares it to the ones in the database.

The images in the database with similar light and color patterns and subject distance tell the camera that this must be a close-up portrait with flesh tones in the center and sky in the background. From this information, the camera decides to expose primarily for the center of the frame, although the background may be over- or underexposed. The RGB sensor also takes note of the quantity of the colors and uses that information as well.

There are a few different types of Matrix metering that are used by the D5000; which type is employed is based upon the type of lens that is attached to the camera body.

The Matrix metering setting is highly intuitive, and Nikon has been refining it over a number of years, so it works very well for most subjects. I almost always have my camera set to Matrix.

✦ **3D Color Matrix metering II.** As I mentioned earlier, this is the default metering system that the camera employs when a G- or D-type lens is attached to the camera. Most lenses made since the early to mid-90s are these types of lenses. The only difference between the G- and D-type lenses is that on G-type lens, there is no aperture ring. When using this metering method, the camera decides the exposure setting, mostly based on the brightness of the overall scene and the colors of the subject matter; the camera also takes into account the distance from the subject and which focus point is used.

In addition, the camera takes into account the lens focal length to further decide which areas of the image are important to getting the proper exposure. For example, when using a wide-angle lens with a faraway subject and a bright area at the top of the image, the camera sets the exposure so that the sky and clouds don't lose detail.

✦ **Color Matrix metering II.** Most AF lenses made from about 1986 to the early to mid-90s are non-D- and G-type CPU lenses. When this type of Matrix metering is being used, the camera uses only brightness, subject color, and focus information to determine the right exposure.

Note *If a non-CPU lens is attached, the camera's meter defaults to Center-weighted metering.*

Matrix metering is generally suitable for use with most subjects unless you're in a particularly tricky lighting situation. Due to the large amount of image data in the Matrix metering database, the camera can usually make a fairly accurate assessment about what type of image you are shooting and adjust the exposure accordingly. For example, with an image that has a high amount of contrast and brightness across the top of the frame, the camera usually tries to set an exposure so that the highlights retain detail. Paired with Active D-Lighting, your exposures will have good dynamic range throughout the entire image.

Center-weighted

When the camera's metering mode is switched to Center-weighted, the meter takes a light reading of the whole scene, but bases the exposure settings mostly on the light falling on the center of the scene. The camera determines about 75 percent of the exposure from an 8mm circular pattern in the center of the frame, and 25 percent from the edges.

Center-weighted metering is a very useful option. It works great when shooting photos where you know the main subject will be in the middle of the frame. This metering mode is useful when photographing a dark subject against a bright background, or a light subject against a dark background. This mode works especially well for portraits where you want to preserve the background detail while exposing correctly for the subject.

Center-weighted metering can provide you with consistent results without worrying about the fluctuations in exposure settings that can sometimes happen when using Matrix metering.

Spot

In Spot meter mode, the camera does just that: it meters only a spot. This spot is only 3.5mm in diameter and only accounts for 2.5 percent of the entire frame. The spot is linked to the active focus point, which is good, so that you can focus and meter your subject at the same time, instead of metering the subject, pressing AE-L, and then recomposing the photo.

Spot metering is useful when the subject is the only thing in the frame that you want the camera to expose for. For example, when you are photographing a subject on a completely white or black background, you need not be concerned with preserving detail in the background; therefore, exposing just for the subject works out perfectly. One instance where this mode works well is when doing concert photography where the musician or singer is lit by a bright spotlight. You can capture every detail of the subject and just let the shadow areas go black.

Note *When using a non-CPU lens with Spot metering, the center spot is selected by default.*

Autofocus Modes

The Nikon D5000 has three autofocus (AF) modes: Continuous, Single, and Manual. Each mode is useful for different types of shooting conditions, from sports to still-life photographs. The AF modes can be changed in the Information Display Menu or in CSM-2. Some lenses, such as the kit lens, also have a switch to enable you to toggle from AF to Manual focus.

Continuous

When the camera is set to Continuous AF (AF-C), as long as the Shutter Release button is halfway pressed, the camera continues to focus. If the subject moves, the camera activates predictive focus tracking. With predictive focus tracking on, the camera tracks the subject to maintain focus and attempts to predict where the subject will be when the Shutter Release button is pressed completely. When in Continuous AF mode, by default, the camera fires when the Shutter Release button is pressed, whether or not the subject is in focus (this is known as *release priority*). This is the AF mode you want to use when shooting sports or any subject that may be moving erratically.

Single

In Single AF (AF-S) mode, the camera focuses when the Shutter Release button is pressed halfway. When the camera achieves focus, the focus locks. The focus remains locked until you release the shutter or the Shutter

Release button is no longer pressed. By default, the camera does not fire unless focus has been achieved (this is known as *focus priority*). This is the AF mode to use when shooting portraits, landscapes, or other photos where the subject is relatively static.

Using this mode helps to ensure that you to get fewer out-of-focus images.

Auto

When the camera is set to Auto mode (AF-A), it automatically chooses between AF-C and AF-S, depending on the subject. If the camera determines that your subject is not moving, it sets the focus mode to AF-S. If the camera detects a moving subject, it sets the focus mode to AF-C. If the camera determines that the subject is moving, focus tracking is activated.

Manual

When set to Manual mode, the D5000 AF system is off. Focus is achieved by rotating the focus ring of the lens until the subject appears sharp when looking through the viewfinder. The Manual focus setting can be used when shooting still-life photographs or other nonmoving subjects, when you want total control of the focus, or simply when you are using a non-AF lens. Note that the camera shutter will release, regardless of whether or not the scene is in focus.

When using the Manual focus setting, the D5000 offers a bit of assistance in the way of an electronic rangefinder. The electronic rangefinder can be viewed in the viewfinder display where the light meter is normally displayed.

AF Area Modes

The D5000 has inherited the Multi-CAM 1000 AF module from its bigger brother, the D90 (which inherited it in turn from the D200). The Multi-CAM 1000 is a very highly regarded and accurate focusing system. It features 11 focus points: one cross-type sensor, eight vertical sensors, and two horizontal sensors.

The D90 has four AF Area modes to choose from: Single Point AF, Dynamic Area AF, Auto Area AF, and 3D-tracking. AF Area modes can be changed in the Information Display or the CSM.

The D5000 employs 11 separate AF points. The 11 AF points can be used individually in Single Point AF mode, or you can choose one point and have it work in conjunction with the non-active points when in Dynamic Area AF mode.

When set to 3D-tracking, the camera maintains sharp focus on a moving subject as it crosses the frame. With 3D-tracking, the camera recognizes distance, color, and light information and then uses it to track the subject across the frame.

Single Point AF mode

Single Point AF mode is the easiest mode to use when you're shooting slow-moving or completely still subjects. You can press the multi selector up, down, left, or right, to choose one of the AF points. The camera only focuses on the subject if it's in the selected AF area. The selected AF point is displayed in the viewfinder.

Dynamic Area AF mode

Dynamic Area AF mode also allows you to select the AF point manually, but unlike Single Point AF, the remaining unselected points remain active; this way, if the subject happens to move out of the selected focus area, the camera's highly sophisticated autofocus system can track it throughout the frame.

When you set the focus mode to AF-S (discussed earlier in this chapter), the mode operates exactly the same as if you were using Single Point AF. To take advantage of Dynamic Area AF, the camera must be set to AF-C mode.

3D-tracking mode

This mode has all 11 AF points active. You select the primary AF point, but if the subject moves, the camera uses 3D-tracking to automatically select a new primary AF point. The camera performs 3D-tracking by using distance and color information from the area immediately surrounding the focus point. The camera uses this information to determine what the subject is, and if the subject moves, the camera selects a new focus point. This mode works very well for subjects moving unpredictably; however, you need to be sure that the subject and the background aren't similar in color.

When photographing a subject with a color similar to that of the background, the camera may lock focus on the wrong area, so use this mode carefully. I have problems with this mode, particularly when shooting team sports, where the players generally wear the same color uniforms. This is because the AF system can't accurately track the subjects.

Auto Area AF

Auto Area AF is exactly what it sounds like: the camera automatically determines the subject and then chooses one or more AF points to lock focus. When the D5000 is used with Nikkor AF-S D- or G-type lenses, the D5000 MJH is able to recognize human subjects. This means that the camera has a better chance of focusing where you want it than accidentally focusing on the background when shooting a portrait.

Normally, I tend not to use a fully automatic setting such as this, but I've found that it works reasonably well and recommend using it when you're shooting candid photos. When the camera is set to Single AF mode, the active AF points light up in the viewfinder for about one second when the camera attains focus; when in Continuous AF mode, no AF points appear in the viewfinder.

ISO Sensitivity

ISO, which stands for International Organization for Standardization, is the rating for the speed of film, or in digital terms, the sensitivity of the sensor. The ISO numbers are standardized, which allows you to be sure that when you shoot at ISO 100, you get the same exposure no matter what camera you are using.

The ISO for your camera determines how sensitive the image sensor is to the light that is reaching it through the lens opening. Increasing or reducing the ISO affects the exposure by allowing you to use faster shutter speeds or smaller apertures (raising the ISO), or using a slower shutter speed or wider aperture (lowering the ISO).

You can set the ISO on the D5000 by using the Information display. As with other settings for controlling exposure, the ISO can be set in 1/3-, or 1/2-, or 1-stop increments.

The D5000 has an ISO range from 200 to 3200. In addition to these standard ISO settings, the D5000 also offers some settings that extend the available range of the ISO so that you can shoot in very bright or very dark situations. These are labeled as H (high speed) and L (low speed). The H and L options are set in 1/3-stop adjustments. The options are:

✦ **H0.3, H0.7, and H1.0.** These settings are equivalent to approximately ISO 4200, 5500, and 6400, respectively.

✦ **L0.3, L0.7, and L1.0.** These settings are equivalent to approximately ISO 150, 125, and 100, respectively.

The ISO can also be set by going into the shooting menu and choosing the ISO sensitivity settings option.

 Caution *Using the H and L settings does not produce optimal results. Using the L setting can result in images that are low in contrast, and using the H setting can cause your images to have a high amount of noise.*

Auto ISO

The D5000 also offers a feature where the camera adjusts the ISO automatically for you when there isn't enough light to make a proper exposure. Auto ISO is meant to free you up from making decisions about when to raise the ISO. The Auto ISO can be set in the Shooting menu under the ISO sensitivity settings option.

By default, when Auto ISO is on, the camera chooses an ISO setting from 200 up to H1 whenever the shutter speed falls below 1/30 second. Basically what this means is that when Auto ISO is turned on, if you manually change the ISO, the camera cannot be set to a lower ISO than what the Auto ISO was set to in the Shooting menu. So, if you set it to ISO 800, then when you are shooting, Auto ISO does not lower the ISO below 800.

You can also limit how high the ISO can be set so that you can keep control of the noise created when a higher ISO is used (although the amount of overall noise generated by the D5000 is pretty low, even at high ISO settings).

On the opposite end of the spectrum, if you manually set the ISO to 400, the Auto ISO function does not allow the ISO to go lower than ISO 400, no matter how bright the scene is. So when using the Auto ISO feature, be sure to set your ISO to 200 to ensure that you can get the full range of ISO settings.

Using Auto ISO can sometimes yield questionable results because you can't be sure what ISO adjustments the camera will make. So if you're going to use it, be sure to set it to conditions that you deem acceptable to ensure that your images will be neither blurry nor noisy.

In the past, I always eschewed using Auto ISO, but because the high ISO performance on Nikon's newest cameras is so amazing, I have started using it all the time. It especially comes in handy when shooting concerts. This allows me to have a high ISO setting when the lighting is dim, but also reduces the ISO when the lights are turned up on the performer. This setting has actually been quite helpful, allowing me to get many more usable concert photos than I did in the past when I cranked up the ISO and left it set high.

Be sure to set the following options in the Shooting menu/ISO sensitivity settings:

✦ **Maximum Sensitivity.** Choose an ISO setting that allows you to get an acceptable amount of noise in your image. If you're not concerned about noisy images, then you can set it all the way up to H1. If you need your images to have less noise, you can choose a lower ISO;

the choices are 400, 800, 1600, 3200, and H1.

✦ **Minimum Shutter Speed.** This setting determines when the camera adjusts the ISO to a higher level. At the default, the camera bumps up the ISO when the shutter speed falls below 1/30 second. If you're using a longer lens or you're photographing moving subjects, you may need a faster shutter speed. In that case, you can set the minimum shutter speed up to 1/250 second. On the other hand, if you're not concerned about camera shake, or if you're using a tripod, you can set a shutter speed as slow as 1 second.

 Note *The minimum shutter speed is only taken into account when using Programmed Auto or Shutter Priority modes.*

Noise reduction

Since the inception of digital cameras, they've been plagued with what is known as noise. Noise, simply put, is randomly colored dots that appear in your image. This is basically caused by extraneous electrons that are produced when your image is being recorded. When light strikes the image sensor in your D5000, electrons are produced. These electrons create an analog signal that is converted into a digital image by the Analog-to-Digital (A/D) converter in your camera.

There are two specific causes of noise. The first is heat generated or *thermal* noise. While the shutter is open and your camera is recording an image, the sensor starts to generate a small amount of heat. This heat can free electrons from the sensor, which in turn contaminate the electrons that have been created as a result of the light striking the photocells on your sensor. This contamination shows up as noise.

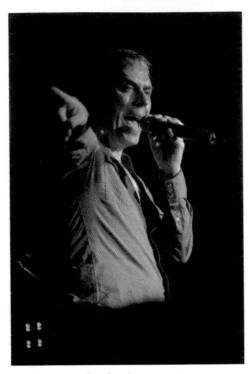

2.2 An example of noise.

The second cause of digital noise is known as *high ISO noise*. In any type of electronic device, there is background electrical noise. For the most part, it's very miniscule and you never notice it. Cranking up the ISO amplifies the signals your sensor is receiving. Unfortunately, as these signals are amplified, so is the background electrical noise. The higher your ISO, the more the background noise is amplified until it shows up as randomly colored specks.

Digital noise is composed of two different elements, *chrominance* and *luminance*. Chrominance refers to the colored specks, and luminance refers mainly to the size and shape of the noise.

Fortunately, with every new camera released, the technology gets better and better, and

the D5000 is no exception. The D5000 has one of the lowest signal-to-noise ratios of any camera on the market; thus, you can shoot at ISO 1600 and not worry about excessive noise. In previous cameras, shooting at ISO 1600 produced a very noisy image that was not suitable for large prints.

Although the D5000 is very low in noise, there is noise there, especially when shooting above ISO 1600 or when using long exposure times. For this reason, most camera manufacturers have built-in noise reduction (NR) features. The D5000 has two types of NR, Long exposure NR and High ISO NR. Each one approaches the noise differently to help reduce it.

Long exposure NR

When this setting is turned on, the camera runs a noise reduction algorithm to any shot taken with a shutter speed longer than 8 seconds. Basically, how this works is that the camera takes another exposure, this time with the shutter closed, and compares the noise from this dark frame image to the original one. The camera then applies the NR. The noise reduction takes about the same amount of time to process as the length of the shutter speed; therefore, expect to double the time it takes to make one exposure. While the camera is applying NR, the LCD panel blinks a message that says "Job nr." No additional images can be taken until this process is finished. If the camera is switched off before the NR is finished, no noise reduction is applied.

You can turn Long exposure NR on or off by accessing it in the Shooting menu.

High ISO NR

When this option is turned on, any image shot at ISO 800 or higher is run through the noise reduction algorithm. This feature works by reducing the coloring in the chrominance of the noise and combining that with a bit of softening of the image to reduce the luminance noise. You can set how aggressively this effect is applied by choosing the High, Normal, or Low settings.

Note When shooting in RAW format, no actual noise reduction is applied to the image.

For the most part, I choose not to use either of these in-camera NR features. In my opinion, even at the lowest setting, the camera is very aggressive in the NR, and for that reason, there is a loss of detail. For most people, this is a minor quibble and not very noticeable, but for me, I'd rather keep all of the available detail in my images and apply noise reduction in post processing. This way, I can decide for myself how much to reduce the chrominance and luminance rather than letting the camera do it. The camera doesn't know whether you're going to print the image at a large size or just display it on screen. I say it's better to be safe than sorry.

Note Noise reduction can be applied in Capture NX2, or by using Adobe Photoshop Camera Raw or some other image-editing software.

White Balance

Light, whether it is sunlight, from a light bulb, fluorescent, or from a flash, all has its own specific color. This color is measured using the Kelvin scale. This measurement is also known as *color temperature*. The white balance allows you to adjust the camera so that your images can look natural no matter what the light source. Because white is the

color that is most dramatically affected by the color temperature of the light source, this is what you base your settings on; hence the term white balance. The white balance can be changed in the Shooting menu or by pressing the WB button on the top of the camera and rotating the main Command dial.

The term color temperature may sound strange to you. "How can a color have a temperature?" you might ask. Once you know about the Kelvin scale, things make a little more sense.

What is Kelvin?

Kelvin is a temperature scale, normally used in the fields of physics and astronomy, where absolute zero (0 K) denotes the absence of all heat energy. The concept is based on a mythical object called a *black body radiator*. Theoretically, as this black body radiator is heated, it starts to glow. As it is heated to a certain temperature, it glows a specific color. It is akin to heating a bar of iron with a torch. As the iron gets hotter, it turns red, then yellow, and then eventually white before it reaches its melting point (although the theoretical black body does not have a melting point).

The concept of Kelvin and color temperature is tricky as it is the opposite of what you likely think of as "warm" and "cool" colors. For example, on the Kelvin scale, red is the lowest temperature, increasing through orange, yellow, white, and to shades of blue, which are the highest temperatures. Humans tend to perceive reds, oranges, and yellows as warmer and white and bluish colors to be cold. However, physically speaking, the opposite is true as defined by the Kelvin scale.

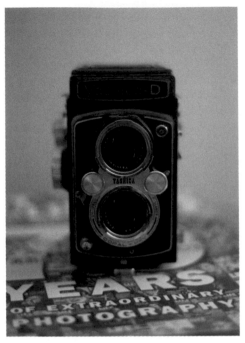

2.3 Auto, 2850 K.

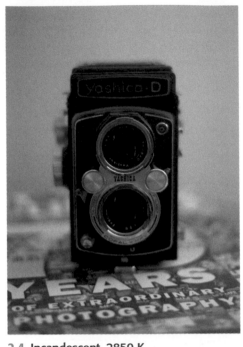

2.4 Incandescent, 2850 K.

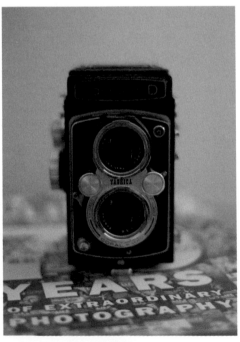

2.5 Fluorescent, 3800 K.

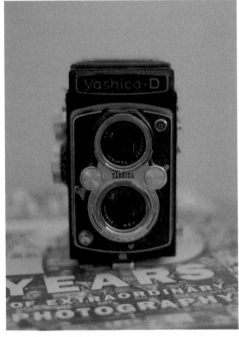

2.6 Flash, 5500 K.

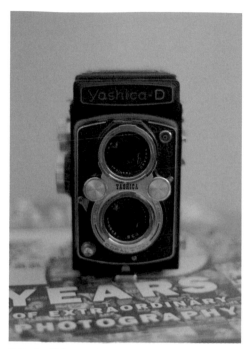

2.7 Daylight, 5500 K.

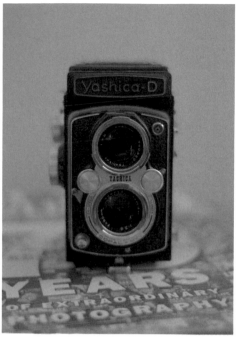

2.8 Cloudy, 6500 K.

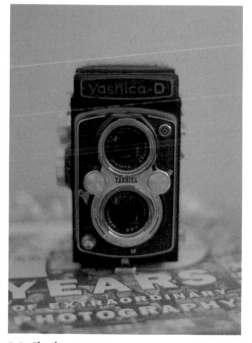

2.9 Shade, 7500 K.

White balance settings

Now that you know a little about the Kelvin scale, you can begin to explore the white balance settings. The reason that white balance is so important is to ensure that your images have a natural look. When dealing with different lighting sources, the color temperature of the source can have a drastic effect on the coloring of the subject.

For example, a standard light bulb casts a very yellow light; if the color temperature of the light bulb is not compensated for by introducing a bluish cast, the subject can look overly yellow and not quite right.

In order to adjust for the colorcast of the light source, the camera introduces a colorcast of the complete opposite color temperature. For example, to combat the green color of a fluorescent lamp, the camera introduces a slight magenta cast to neutralize the green.

The D5000 has eight white balance settings:

 Auto. This setting is best for most circumstances. The camera takes a reading of the ambient light and makes an automatic adjustment. This setting also works well when using a Nikon CLS compatible Speedlight because the color temperature is calculated to match the flash output. I actually recommend using this setting as opposed to the Flash WB setting.

PRE **PRE.** This setting allows you to choose a neutral object to measure for the white balance. It's best to choose an object that is either white or light gray. The PRE setting is best used under difficult lighting situations such as when there are two different light sources lighting the scene (mixed lighting). I usually use this setting when photographing with my studio strobes.

 Incandescent. Use this setting when the lighting is from a standard household light bulb.

 Fluorescent. Use this setting when the lighting is coming from a fluorescent-type lamp. You can also adjust for different types of fluorescent lamps, including high-pressure sodium and mercury vapor lamps. To make this adjustment, go to the Shooting menu and choose

White Balance, then fluorescent. From there, use the multi selector to choose one of the seven types of lamps.

 Flash. Use this setting when using the built-in Speedlight, a hot-shoe Speedlight, or external strobes.

 Daylight. Use this setting outdoors in direct sunlight.

 Cloudy. Use this setting under overcast skies.

 Shade. Use this setting when you are in the shade of a tree or a building, or even under an overhang or a bridge. Any place where the sun is out but is being blocked.

Note *One accessory you can use to set your white balance is a gray card, which is fairly inexpensive. Simply put the gray card in the scene, and balance off of it. Another accessory is the ExpoDisc. This attaches to the front of your lens like a filter; you then point the lens at the light source and set your WB.*

Figures 2.3 to 2.9 show the different results of using the white balance settings.

Picture Controls

All Nikon cameras from the D300 forward use the Picture Control system. This feature allows you to quickly adjust your image settings to your preferences. One great thing about the Picture Control system is that the

Picture Controls are the same for all cameras that use this function. This is great for photographers who shoot more than one camera and batch-process their images. It allows both cameras to record the images the same so that global image correction can be applied without worrying about differences in color, tone, saturation, and sharpening.

Picture Controls can also be saved to the CF card and imported into Nikon's image-editing software, Capture NX2 or View NX. You can then apply the settings to RAW images or even to images taken with other camera models. These Picture Control files can also be saved to a memory card and shared with other Nikon users, either by importing them into Nikon software or loading them directly to another camera.

Original Picture Controls

Right out of the box, the D5000 comes with six Picture Controls installed.

✦ **SD.** This is the Standard setting. This applies slight sharpening and a small boost of contrast and saturation. This is the recommended setting for most shooting situations.

✦ **NL.** This is the Neutral setting. This setting applies a small amount of sharpening and no other modifications to the image. This setting is preferable if you do extensive post-processing to your images.

✦ **VI.** This is also referred to as the Vivid setting. This setting gives your images a fair amount of sharpening, and the contrast and saturation are greatly boosted, resulting in brightly colored images. This setting

is recommended for printing directly from the camera or flash card. Personally, I feel that this mode is a little too saturated and often results in unnatural color tones. This mode is not recommended for portrait situations, as skin tones are not reproduced well.

✦ **PT.** This is the setting for Portraits. This gives you just a small amount of sharpening, which gives the skin a smoother appearance. The colors are muted just a bit to help achieve realistic skin tones.

✦ **LS.** This is the Landscape setting. Obviously, this setting is for shooting landscapes and natural vistas. The saturation of the blues and greens is boosted.

✦ **MC.** This is the Monochrome setting. As the name implies, this option makes the images monochrome. This doesn't simply mean black and white; you can also simulate photo filters and toned images such as sepia, cyanotype, and more.

Custom Picture Controls

All of the original Picture Controls can be customized to fit your personal preferences. You can adjust the settings to your liking, giving the images more sharpening and less contrast or choosing from a myriad of other options.

 Note *Although you can adjust the original Picture Controls, you cannot save over them, and so there is no need to worry about losing them.*

There are a few different customizations to choose from:

✦ **Quick adjust.** This option is not available with the NL setting. This option exaggerates or de-emphasizes the effect of the Picture Control in use. Quick adjust can be set from ±2.

✦ **Sharpness.** This setting controls the apparent sharpness of your images. You can adjust this setting from 0–9, with 9 being the highest level of sharpness. You can also set this to Auto (A) to allow the camera's imaging processor to decide how much sharpening to apply.

✦ **Contrast.** This setting controls the amount of contrast your images are given. In photos of scenes with high contrast (sunny days), you may want adjust the contrast down; in low-contrast scenes, you may want to add some contrast by adjusting the settings up. You can set this from ±3 or to A.

✦ **Brightness.** This setting adds or subtracts from the overall brightness of your image. You can choose 0 (default), +, or −.

✦ **Saturation.** This setting controls how vivid or bright the colors in your images are. You can set this between ±3 or to A. This option is not available in the MC setting.

✦ **Hue.** This setting controls how your colors look. You can choose ±3. Positive numbers make the reds look more orange, the blues look more purple, and the greens look more blue. Choosing a negative number causes the reds to look more purple, the blues to look more green, and the greens to look

more yellow. This setting is not available in the MC Picture Control setting. I highly recommend leaving this in the default setting of 0.

✦ **Filter Effects.** This setting is only available when set to MC. The monochrome filters approximate the types of filters traditionally used with black-and-white film. These filters increase contrast and create special effects. The options are:

• **Yellow.** This adds a low level of contrast. It causes the sky to appear slightly darker than normal and anything yellow to appear lighter.

• **Orange.** This adds a medium amount of contrast. The sky appears darker, giving greater separation between the clouds. Orange objects appear light grey.

• **Red.** This adds a great amount of contrast, drastically darkening the sky while allowing the clouds to remain white. Red objects appear lighter than normal.

• **Green.** This darkens the sky and lightens any green plant life. This color filter can be used for portraits as it softens skin tones.

✦ **Toning.** This setting adds a color tint to your monochrome (black-and-white) images.

• **B&W.** The Black-and-white option simulates the traditional black-and-white film prints done in a darkroom. The camera records the image in black, white, and shades of gray. This mode is suitable for use when the color of the subject is not important. It can be used for

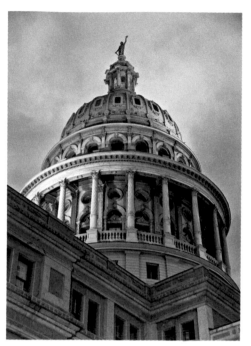

2.10 B&W.

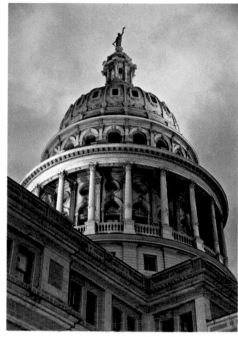

2.11 Sepia.

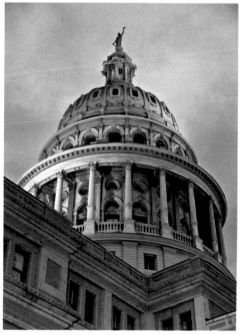

2.12 Cyanotype.

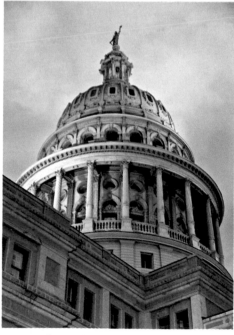

2.13 Color toning green.

artistic purposes or, as with the Sepia mode, to give your image an antique or vintage look.

- **Sepia.** The Sepia color option duplicates a photographic toning process that is done in a traditional darkroom using silver-based black-and-white prints. You may want to use this option when trying to convey a feeling of antiquity or nostalgia to your photograph. This option works well with portraits as well as still life and architecture. You can also adjust the saturation of the toning from 1 to 7, with 4 being the default and the middle ground.

Note *Sepia toning a photographic image requires replacing the silver in the emulsion of the photo paper with a different silver compound, thus changing the color or tone of the photograph. Antique photographs were generally treated to this type of toning; therefore, the sepia color option gives the image an antique look. The images have a reddish-brown look to them.*

- **Cyanotype.** The Cyanotype is another old photographic printing process. The images taken when in this setting are in shades of cyan. Because cyan is considered to be a cool color, this mode is also referred to as cool. This mode can be used to make very interesting and artistic images. You can also adjust the saturation of the toning from 1 to 7, with 4 being the default setting.

Note *Cyanotype is one of the oldest printing processes. When exposed to the light, the chemicals that make up the cyanotype turn a deep-blue color. This method was used to create the first blueprints and was later adapted to photography.*

- ✦ **Color toning.** You can also choose to add colors to your monochrome images. Although this is similar to Sepia and Cyanotype, this type of toning isn't based on traditional photographic processes. This is simply adding a colorcast to a black-and-white image. There are seven different color options you can choose from: red, yellow, green, blue-green, blue, purple-blue, and red-purple. As with Sepia and Cyanotype, you can adjust the saturation of these toning colors.

To customize an original Picture Control:

1. **Go to the Set Picture Control option in the Shooting menu.** Press the multi selector right.

2. **Choose the Picture Control you want to adjust.** For small adjustments, choose the NL or SD option. To make larger changes to color and sharpness, choose the VI mode. To make adjustments to monochrome images, choose MC. Press the multi selector right.

3. **Press the multi selector up or down to highlight the setting you want to adjust (sharpening, contrast, brightness, and so on).** When the setting is highlighted, press the multi selector left or right

to adjust the settings. Repeat this step until you've adjusted the settings to your preferences.

4. **Press the OK button to save the settings.** To return the settings to their defaults (reset), press the Delete button. A confirmation dialog box appears.

5. **Select Yes and press the OK button to reset.** Select No and press the OK button to cancel the reset.

 Note When the original Picture Control settings have been altered, an asterisk is displayed with the Picture Control setting (SD*, VI*, and so on).

To save a custom Picture Control, follow these steps:

1. **Go to the Manage Picture Control option in the shooting menu.** Press the multi selector right.

2. **Press the multi selector up or down to select Save/edit.** Press the multi selector right.

3. **Choose the Picture Control to edit.**

4. **Press the multi selector up or down to highlight the setting you want to adjust (sharpening, contrast, brightness, and so on).** When the setting is highlighted, press the multi selector left or right to adjust the settings. Repeat this step until you've adjusted the settings to your preferences.

5. **Press the OK button to save the settings.** To return the settings to their defaults (reset), press the Delete button. A confirmation dialog box appears.

6. **Select Yes and press the OK button to reset. Select No and press the OK button to cancel the reset.** Once you press the OK button to accept the settings, the camera displays the Save as menu.

7. **Use the multi selector to highlight the Custom Picture Control you want to save to.** You can store up to nine Custom Picture Controls; they are labeled C-1 through C-9. Press the multi selector right.

8. **When the Rename menu appears, press the Zoom in button and press the multi selector left or right to move the cursor to any of the 19 spaces in the Name area of the dialog box.** New Picture Controls are automatically named with the original Picture Control name and a two-digit number (STANDARD _02 or VIVID_03).

9. **Press the multi selector (without pressing the Zoom) to select letters in the keyboard area of the dialog box.** Press the multi selector center button to set the selected letter, and press the Delete button to erase the selected letter in the Name area. Once you have typed in the name you want, press the OK button to save it. The Custom Picture Control is then saved to the Picture Control menu and can be accessed through the Set Picture Control option in the Shooting menu.

Your Custom Picture Controls can be renamed or deleted at any time by using the Manage Picture Control option in the shooting menu. You can also save the Custom Picture Control to your memory card so that you can import the file to Capture NX2 or View NX.

To save a Custom Picture Control to the memory card:

1. **Go to the Manage Picture Control option in the shooting menu.** Press the multi selector right.

2. **Press the multi selector up or down to highlight the Load/save option.** Press the multi selector right.

3. **Press the multi selector up or down to highlight the Copy to card option.** Press the multi selector right.

4. **Press the multi selector up or down to select the Custom Picture Control to copy.** Press the multi selector right.

5. **Select a destination on the memory card to copy the Picture Control file to.** Each CF card is given 99 slots in which to store Picture Control files.

6. **Once you've chosen the destination, press the multi selector right.** The file is then stored to your CF card.

After you've copied your Custom Picture Control file to your card, you can then import the file to the Nikon software by mounting the memory card to your computer by your usual means (card reader or USB camera connection). See the software user's manual for instructions on importing to the specific program.

You can also upload Picture Controls that are saved to a memory card to your camera:

1. **Go to the Manage Picture Control option in the Shooting menu.** Press the multi selector right.

2. **Press the multi selector up or down to highlight the Load/save option.** Press the multi selector right.

3. **Press the multi selector up or down to highlight the Copy to camera option.** Press the multi selector right.

4. **Select the Picture Control to copy.** Press the OK button or multi selector right to confirm.

5. **The camera then displays the Picture Control settings.** Press the OK button. The camera automatically displays the Save as menu.

6. **Select an empty slot to save to (C-1 through C-9).**

7. **Rename the file if necessary.** Press the OK button.

Understanding JPEG Compression

JPEG, which stands for Joint Photographic Experts Group, is a method of compressing photographic files and also the name of the file format that supports this type of compression. The JPEG is the most common type of file used to save images on digital cameras. Due to the small size of the file that is created and the relatively good image quality it produces, JPEG has become the default file format for most digital cameras.

The JPEG compression format came into being because of the immense file sizes that digital images produce. Photographic files contain millions upon millions of separate colors, and each individual color is assigned a number; this causes the files to contain vast amounts of data, therefore making the file size quite large.

In the early days of digital imaging, these huge file sizes made it almost impossible for most people to store any number of images on their computers, which usually had relatively small storage capacities. Less than ten years ago, your standard laptop hard drive was only about 5GB. To efficiently store images, there needed to be some sort of file that could be compressed without losing too much of the image data during reconstruction of the file. Enter the Joint Photographic Experts Group. This group of experts designed what we now affectionately know as the JPEG.

The one problem with JPEG compression is that it is lossy compression, meaning that it loses information. For the most part, this loss of information is imperceptible to the human eye. The real problem with JPEGs comes from what is known as *generation loss*. Every time a JPEG is opened and resaved, a small amount of detail is lost. After multiple openings and savings, the quality of the image starts to deteriorate as less and less information is available. Eventually, the image may start to look pixelated or jagged (this is known as a JPEG artifact). Obviously, this can be a problem, but the JPEG would have to be opened and resaved many hundreds of times before you would notice a drop in image quality as long you save at high quality settings.

Image size

When saving a file as a JPEG, the D5000 allows you to choose an image size. Reducing the image size is like reducing the resolution on your camera: it allows you to fit more images on your card. The size you choose depends on what your output is going to be.

If you know you'll be printing your images at a large size, then you definitely want to record large JPEGs. If you're going to print at a smaller size (8x10 or 5x7), you can get away with recording at the Medium or Small setting. Image size is expressed in pixel dimensions. The Large setting records your images at 4288x2848 pixels; this gives you a file that's equivalent to a 12-megapixel image. The Medium setting gives you an image of 3216x2136 pixels, which is in effect the same as a 6.8-megapixel camera. The Small size setting gives you a dimension of 2144x1424 pixels, which gives you about a 3-megapixel image.

 Note *Image size can only be changed when using the JPEG file format. RAW files are recorded only at the largest size.*

Image quality

For JPEGS, other than the size setting, which changes the pixel dimension, you have the Quality setting which lets you decide how much of a compression ratio to apply to your JPEG image. Your choices are Fine, Normal, and Basic. JPEG Fine files are compressed to approximately 1:4, Normal to about 1:8, and Basic to about 1:16.

The more compression is applied to the JPEG, the smaller the file size. This reduced file size comes at a cost, though; highly compressed images can suffer from JPEG artifacts.

NEF or RAW Flexibility

Nikon's RAW files are referred to as NEF in Nikon literature. NEF stands for Nikon Electronic File. RAW files contain all of the image data acquired by the camera's sensor. When a JPEG is created, the camera applies different settings to the image such as white balance, sharpness, noise reduction, and so on.

When the JPEG is saved, the rest of the unused image data is discarded to help ensure a smaller file size. With a RAW file, this image data is saved so that it can be used more extensively in post processing. In some ways, the RAW file is like a digital negative, in which the RAW files are used in the same way as a traditional photographic negative; that is, you take the RAW information and process it in order to create your final image.

Although some of the same settings are tagged to the RAW file (WB, sharpening, saturation, and so on), these settings aren't fixed and applied as in the JPEG file; as a result, later on, when you import the RAW file into your favorite RAW converter, you can make changes to these settings with no detrimental effects.

Recording your images in RAW format allows you to be more flexible when post processing your images and generally gives you more control over the quality of the images.

The D5000 saves its RAW files as compressed NEFs. Similar to JPEG compression, some of the image data is lost when these types of files are compressed. The complex algorithms they use to create these files actually run two different compression schemes to the same file.

Because our eyes perceive changes in the darker areas of images more than in the lighter areas, the image data for the shadow areas is compressed using a lossless compression, while the mid-tones and lighter areas are compressed using a lossy method.

This compression scheme has very little impact on the image data and allows you be sure that you retain all of your shadow detail. Compressed RAW files allow the file size to be about 30 to 60 percent less than an uncompressed file.

Live View

Live View is one of the newer innovations in dSLR technology and has been finding its way into more dSLR cameras. This feature allows you to use the LCD preview screen as a viewfinder. This feature can be very helpful when you are taking pictures where the camera is at an awkward angle. An example of this would be at a concert, where you could hold the camera over your head and use the screen to frame the shot.

When using Live View, the camera focuses by using contrast detection, which is similar to the way that point-and-shoot digital cameras focus. As you probably are aware, these compact cameras are not very quick to focus. This is why the D5000 focuses much more slowly than it does when focusing in the standard mode.

Live View is accessed simply by pressing the Live View (Lv) button on the back of the camera, just above the multi selector.

Keep these details in mind when you shoot in the Live View mode:

✦ **HDMI.** If the camera is connected to an HDTV, the LCD monitor is switched off and the TV can be used to preview the image.

✦ **Shooting information.** The shooting information, which is normally displayed above the image, can be turned off by pressing the INFO button.

✦ **Monitor brightness.** You can adjust the brightness of the LCD monitor by pressing the Play button and using the multi selector up/down buttons.

✦ **Remote release.** If using an optional remote release cable, you can activate the AF by pressing the button halfway for over a second. If the button is fully depressed without activating the AF, your image may be blurry.

RAW versus JPEG

This issue has caused quite a controversy in the digital imaging world, with some people saying that RAW is the only way to go to have more flexibility in processing images, and others saying that if you get it right in camera, then you don't need to use RAW images. For what it's worth, both factions are right in their own way.

Choosing between RAW and JPEG basically comes down to the final output, or what you're using the images for. Remember that you don't have to choose one file format and stick with it. You can change the settings to suit your needs as you see fit, or you can even choose to record both RAW and JPEG simultaneously.

Here are some reasons to shoot JPEG files:

Small file size. JPEGs are much smaller in size than RAW files; therefore, you can fit many more of them on your CF card, and later, on your hard drive. If space limitations are a problem, shooting JPEG allows you to get more images in less space.

Printing straight from the camera. Some people like to print their images straight from the camera or CF card. RAW files can't be printed without first being converted to JPEGs.

Continuous shooting. JPEG files, being smaller than RAW files, don't fill up the camera's buffer as quickly, allowing you longer bursts without the frame rate slowing down.

Less post processing. If you're confident in your ability to get the image exactly as you want it at capture, then you can save yourself time by not having to process the image in a RAW converter and save straight to JPEG.

Snapshots. JPEG is a good choice if you're just shooting snapshots of family events or if you only plan to post your images on the Internet.

Here are some reasons to shoot RAW files:

16-bit images. When converting the file using a RAW converter such as Adobe Camera RAW (ACR) or Capture NX2, you can save your images with 16-bit color information. (When the information is written to JPEG in camera, the JPEG is saved as an 8-bit file.) This gives you the option of working with more colors in post processing. This can be extremely helpful when trying to save an under- or over-exposed image.

Continued

Continued

White balance. Although the WB that the camera was set to is tagged in the RAW file, it isn't fixed in the image data. Often, the camera can record a WB that isn't quite correct. This isn't always noticeable by looking at the image on the preview. Changing the WB on a JPEG image can cause posterization and usually doesn't yield the best results. Because you have the RAW image data on hand, changing the WB settings doesn't degrade the image at all.

Sharpening and saturation. As with WB, these settings are tagged in the RAW file but not applied to the actual image data. You can add sharpening and saturation (or other options, depending on your software).

Exploring the D5000 Menus

T he first few sections of this book covered how to change the main settings of your D5000. In this chapter, I delve a little more in depth into the menu options. Here you can customize the D5000 options to fit your shooting style, to help refine your workflow, or to make adjustments to refine the camera settings to fit different shooting scenarios.

The D5000 has quite a few customizable features that make taking pictures much easier for you. You can assign a number of buttons to different functions that you use often. Using the My Menu feature, you can create your own personal list of menu options so that you don't have to scroll through all of the menu options for settings that you need to access often.

You can access the menus by pressing the Menu button on the back of the camera. Use the multi selector to scroll through the toolbar on the right side of the LCD. When the desired menu is highlighted in yellow, press the OK button or press the multi selector right to enter the menu. Pressing the Menu button again or tapping the Shutter Release button exits the Menu mode screen and readies the camera for shooting.

> **Note** When using advanced scene modes, not all menu options are available.

Playback Menu

The Playback menu is where you manage the images stored on your flash card. The Playback menu is also where you control how the images are displayed and what image information displays during review.

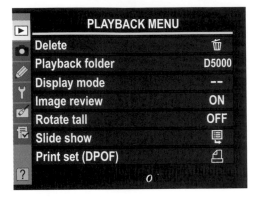

3.1 The Playback menu.

There are seven options available from the Playback menu, which are explained in the following sections. The Playback menu is represented by a Play icon, similar to the one you would find on a DVD player.

Delete

This option allows you to delete selected images from your memory card or to delete all of the images at once.

To delete selected images, choose Delete from the Playback menu and follow these steps:

1. **Press the multi selector right, highlight Selected (default), and press the multi selector right again.** The camera displays an image selection screen. You can now select the image you want to delete.

2. **Press the multi selector left or right to choose the image.** You can also use the Zoom In button to review the image close up before deleting.

3. **Press the Thumbnail/Zoom Out button to set the image for deletion.** More than one image can be

selected. When the image is selected for deletion, it displays a small trash can icon in the right corner.

4. **Press the OK button to erase the selected images.** The camera asks you for confirmation before deleting the images.

5. **Select Yes, and then press the OK button to delete the images.** To cancel the deletion, highlight No (default), and then press the OK button.

You can also choose to delete all images that were taken on a certain date by following these steps:

1. **Choose Select date from the Delete options in the Playback menu, and then press the multi selector right.** A list of dates is shown, along with a thumbnail of one of the images that was taken on that day.

2. **To view all the images taken on that date, press the Thumbnail/ Zoom Out button.** Use the multi selector to browse the images. The Zoom In button can be used to take a closer look at any of the images.

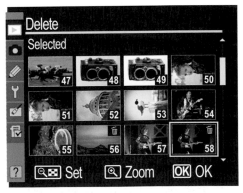

3.2 Selecting images to delete.

3. **Press OK to select the set for deletion.**

4. **Press the multi selector right to set or unset the date.**

5. **Press the OK button to delete the selected images.** A confirmation screen is displayed. Select Yes to delete the images, or No to cancel the action.

To delete all images, select Delete from the Playback menu and follow these steps:

1. **Use the multi selector to highlight All, and then press the OK button.** The camera asks you for confirmation before deleting the images.

2. **Select Yes, and then press the OK button to delete the images.** To cancel deletion, highlight No (default), and then press the OK button.

 Caution *Protected and hidden images aren't deleted when using the Delete All option. Protecting and hiding images is covered later in this chapter.*

Playback folder

The Nikon D5000 automatically creates folders to store your images in. The main folder that the camera creates is called DCIM. Within this folder, the camera creates a subfolder to store the images; the first subfolder the camera creates is titled 100D5000.

After shooting 9,999 images, the camera automatically creates another folder, 101D5000, and so on. Use this menu to choose which folder or folders to display images from. Keep in mind that if you have used the memory card in another camera and have not formatted it, there will be additional folders on the card (ND200, ND50, and so on).

There are two options to choose from:

✦ **Current.** This option displays images only from the folder that the camera is currently saving to. This feature is useful when you have multiple folders from different sessions. Using this setting allows you to preview only the most current images. The current folder can be changed using the Active folder option in the Shooting menu.

✦ **All.** This option plays back images from all folders that are on the CF card, regardless of whether or not they were created by the D5000.

Display mode

There is quite a bit of image information that is available for you to see when you are reviewing images. The Display mode settings allow you to customize the information that is shown when reviewing the images that are stored on your SD card. Enter the Display mode menu by pressing the multi selector right. Then, use the multi selector to highlight the option you want to set.

When the option is highlighted, press the multi selector right or press the OK button to set the display feature. The feature is set when a checkmark appears in the box to the left of the setting. Be sure to scroll up to Done and press OK to set it. If this step is not done, the information does not appear in the display.

The Display mode options are as follows:

✦ **Highlights.** When this option is activated, any highlights that are blown out will blink. If this happens, you may want to apply some exposure compensation or adjust your exposure to be sure to capture highlight detail.

✦ **RGB Histogram.** When this option is turned on, you can view the separate histograms for the Red, Green, and Blue channels, along with a standard luminance histogram.

✦ **Data.** This option allows you to review the shooting data (metering, exposure, lens focal length, and so on).

Generally, the only setting that I use is the RGB Histogram. I can usually tell from the histograms whether the highlights are blown out.

 For more information on exposure compensation and using histograms, see Chapter 4.

Image review

This option allows you to choose whether the image is shown on the LCD immediately after the image is taken. When this option is turned off, the image can be viewed by pressing the Playback button.

Typically, when you take a picture, you want the image to automatically be displayed. This allows you to preview the image to check the exposure, framing, and sharpness.

There are times, however, when you may not want the images to be displayed. For example, when shooting sports at a rapid frame rate, you may not need to check every shot. Turning this option off also conserves battery power because the LCD is actually the biggest drain on your battery.

I often turn off the image review when shooting concerts because when the image is being previewed and I press the multi selector, the information display is being changed instead of moving the focus point. Tapping the Shutter Release button cancels the image review, but because I check my images infrequently when shooting concerts, turning it off is much easier for me in the long run.

Rotate tall

The D5000 has a built-in sensor that can tell whether the camera was rotated while the image was taken. This setting rotates images that are shot in portrait orientation to be displayed upright on the LCD screen. I usually turn this option off because the portrait orientation image appears substantially smaller when displayed upright on the LCD.

The options are as follows:

✦ **On.** The camera automatically rotates the image to be viewed while holding the camera in the standard upright position. When this option is turned on, the camera orientation is recorded for use in image-editing software.

✦ **Off (default).** When the auto-rotating function is turned off, images taken in portrait orientation are displayed on the LCD sideways, in landscape orientation.

Slide show

This option allows you to display a slide show of images from the current active folder. You can use this to review the images that you have shot without having to use the multi selector. This is also a good way to show friends or clients your images.

You can even connect the camera to a standard TV or HDTV to view the slide show on a big screen. You can choose an interval of 2, 3, 5, or 10 seconds.

While the slide show is in progress, you can use the multi selector to skip forward or back (press left or right), and view shooting information or histograms (press up or down). You can also press the Menu button to return to the Playback menu, press the Playback button to end the slide show, or press the Shutter Release button lightly to return to the Shooting mode.

Pressing OK while the slide show is in progress pauses the slide show and offers you the options of restarting the slide show, changing the frame rate, or exiting the slide show. Press the multi selector up and down to make your selection, and then press OK to apply your selection.

Print set (DPOF)

DPOF stands for Digital Print Order Format. This option allows you to select images to be printed directly from the camera. This can be used with PictBridge-compatible printers or DPOF-compatible devices such as a photo kiosk at your local photo printing shop. This is a pretty handy feature if you don't have a printer at home and want to get some prints made quickly, or if you do have a printer and want to print your photos without downloading them to your computer.

To create a print set, follow these steps:

1. **Use the multi selector to choose the Print set (DPOF) option, and then press the multi selector right to enter the menu.**

2. **Use the multi selector to highlight Select/set, and then press the multi selector right to view thumbnails.** Press the Zoom In button to view a larger preview of the selected image.

3. **Press the multi selector right or left to highlight an image to print.** When the desired image is highlighted, press the multi selector up or down to set the image and choose the number of prints you want of that specific image. You can choose from 1 to 99.

    The number of prints and a small printer icon appear on the thumbnail. Continue this procedure until you have selected all of the images that you want to print. Press the multi selector down to reduce the number of prints or to remove it from the print set.

4. **Press the OK button.** A menu appears with three options:

    •   **Done (default).** Press the OK button to save and print the images as they are.

    •   **Data imprint.** Press the multi selector right to set this option. A small checkmark appears in the box next to the menu option. When this option is set, the shutter speed and aperture setting appear on the print.

    •   **Date imprint.** Press the multi selector right to set this option. A small checkmark appears in the box next to the menu option. When this option is set, the date the image was taken appears on the print.

5. **If you choose to set the imprint options, be sure to return to the Done option and press the OK button to complete the print set.**

Note *RAW files can't be added to a DPOF print set. If you shoot in RAW, you can use the NEF (RAW) processing option in the Retouch menu to create a JPEG copy of the image that can be added to the DPOF print set.*

Shooting Menu

The Shooting menu contains most of the controls that deal with your images' settings. This is where you find the most important settings such as ISO, white balance, Active D-Lighting, noise reduction, and others.

A lot of the most commonly changed settings from this menu can also be accessed in the Quick Settings menu, which is covered later in the chapter. The Shooting menu is represented in the Menu tab by a camera icon.

Scene mode

You can use this menu to change the Scene mode only when the camera is set to "SCENE" on the Mode dial. To be perfectly honest, it's much quicker to just rotate the Command dial to change the scene rather than to access it using this menu.

Set Picture Control

This is a menu that you might use quite often. Picture Controls allow you to choose how the images are processed, and they can also be used in Nikon's image-editing software, Nikon View and Nikon Capture NX 2.

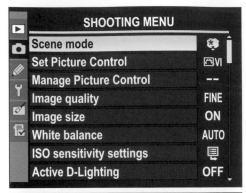

3.3 The Shooting menu is shown here in two sections so that you can see all the available options.

These Picture Controls allow you to get the same results when using different cameras that are compatible with the Nikon Picture Control System.

This option is not available when the camera is set to any of the advanced scene modes or the fully automatic modes.

There are six standard Nikon Picture Controls available in the D5000:

✦ **Standard (SD).** This setting applies slight sharpening and a small boost of contrast and saturation. This is the recommended setting for most shooting situations.

✦ **Neutral (NL).** This setting applies a small amount of sharpening and no other modifications to the image. This setting is preferable if you often do extensive post-processing to your images.

✦ **Vivid (VI).** This setting gives your images a fair amount of sharpening. The contrast and saturation are boosted dramatically, resulting in brightly colored images. This setting is recommended for printing directly from the camera or flash card, as well as for shooting landscapes. Personally, I feel that this mode is a little too saturated and often results in unnatural color tones. This mode is not recommended for portrait situations, as skin tones are not reproduced well.

✦ **Monochrome (MC).** As the name implies, this option makes the images monochrome. This doesn't simply mean black and white — you can also simulate photo filters and toned images such as sepia and cyanotype.

✦ **Portrait (PT).** This setting gives your subject natural color and smooth skin tones.

✦ **Landscape (LS).** This Picture Control boosts the saturation of the greens and the blues for vibrant foliage and skies.

All of these standard Nikon Picture Controls can be adjusted to suit your specific needs or tastes. In the color modes — SD, NL, VI, PT, and LS — you can adjust the sharpening, contrast, brightness, hue, and saturation. In MC mode, you can adjust the filter effects and toning.

After the Nikon Picture Controls are adjusted, you can save them for later use. You can do this in the Manage Picture Control option described in the next section.

 Cross-Reference *For detailed information on customizing and saving Picture Controls, see Chapter 2.*

 Note *When saving to NEF, the Picture Controls are embedded into the metadata. Only Nikon's software can use these settings. However, Adobe products now have a Picture Control simulation plugin that just went live early 2009. This allows ACR, Photoshop and LR to read the Picture Control type and apply a simulated result in the Adobe software.*

Manage Picture Control

This menu is where you can edit, save, and rename your Custom Picture Controls. There are four menu options:

✦ **Save/edit.** In this menu, you choose a Picture Control, make adjustments to it, and then save it. You can rename the Picture Control to help you remember what adjustments were made or to remind you of what the Custom Picture Control is to be used for.

For example, I have one named ultra-VIVID, which has the contrast, sharpening, and saturation boosted as high as they can go. I sometimes use this setting when I want extreme, oversaturated, unrealistic-looking images for abstract shots or light trails.

✦ **Rename.** This menu allows you to rename any of your Custom Picture Controls. You cannot, however, rename the standard Nikon Picture Controls.

✦ **Delete.** This menu gives you the option of erasing any Custom Picture Controls you have saved. This menu only includes controls you have saved or may have downloaded from an outside source. The standard Nikon Picture Controls cannot be deleted.

✦ **Load/save.** This menu allows you to upload Custom Picture Controls to your camera from your memory card, or to delete any Picture Controls saved to your memory; you can also save a Custom Picture Control to your memory card to export to Nikon View or Capture NX, or to another camera that is compatible with Nikon Picture Controls.

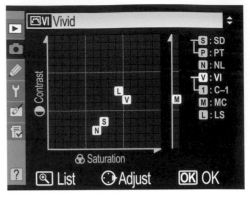

3.4 Picture Control grid.

 For detailed information on creating and managing Picture Controls, see Chapter 2.

The D5000 also allows you to view a grid graph that shows you how the Picture Controls relate to each other in terms of contrast and saturation. Each Picture Control is displayed on the graph represented by a square icon, with the letter of the Picture Control it corresponds to.

Custom Picture Controls are denoted by the number of the custom slot where they have been saved. Standard Picture Controls that have been modified are displayed with an asterisk next to the letter. Picture Controls that have been set with one or more auto settings are displayed in green, with lines extending from the icon to show you that the settings will change, depending on the images.

To view the Picture Control grid, select the Picture Control option from the Shooting menu. Press OK, and the Picture Control list is displayed. Press the Thumbnail/Zoom Out

button to view the grid. Once the Picture Control grid is displayed, you can use the multi selector to scroll though the different Picture Control settings.

Once you have highlighted a setting, you can press the multi selector right to adjust the setting, or press OK to set the Picture Control. Press the Menu button to exit back to the Shooting menu, or tap the Shutter Release button to ready the camera for shooting.

Image quality

This menu option allows you to change the image quality of the file. You can choose from these options:

✦ **NEF (RAW) + JPEG fine.** This option saves two copies of the same image, one in RAW format and one in JPEG with minimal compression.

✦ **NEF (RAW) + JPEG normal.** This option saves two copies of the same image, one in RAW format and one in JPEG with standard compression.

✦ **NEF (RAW) + JPEG basic.** This option saves two copies of the same image, one in RAW format and one in JPEG with high compression.

✦ **NEF (RAW).** This option saves the images in RAW format.

✦ **JPEG fine.** This option saves the images in JPEG format with minimal compression.

✦ **JPEG normal.** This option saves the images in JPEG format with standard compression.

✦ **JPEG basic.** This option saves the images in JPEG format with high compression.

These settings can also be changed in the Quick Settings menu.

 For more detailed information on image quality, compression, and file formats, see Chapter 2.

Image size

This allows you to choose the size of the JPEG files. Change the image size, depending on the intended output of the file or to save space on your memory card.

The choices are as follows:

✦ **Large.** This setting gives you a full-resolution image of 4288x2848 pixels or 12 megapixels.

✦ **Medium.** This setting gives your images a resolution of 3216x2136 pixels or 6.7 megapixels.

✦ **Small.** This setting gives your images a resolution of 2144x1424 pixels or 3 megapixels.

 For more detailed information on image size, see Chapter 2.

The image size can also be changed in the Quick Settings menu.

White balance

You can change the white balance (WB) settings using this menu option. Changing the WB settings through this menu option allows you to fine-tune your settings with more precision and gives you a few more options than you get when using the dedicated WB button located on the top of the camera.

You can select a WB setting from the standard settings (auto, incandescent, fluorescent, direct sunlight, flash, cloudy, or shade) or you can choose to preset the white balance.

 For detailed information on white balance settings and color temperature, see Chapter 2.

Using standard WB settings

To select one of the standard settings, choose the White balance option from the Shooting menu, then use the multi selector button to highlight the preferred setting, and then press the multi selector right or center. This brings up a new screen that gives you the option to fine-tune the standard setting. Displayed on this screen is a grid that allows you to adjust the color tint of the selected WB setting.

The horizontal axis of the grid allows you to adjust the color from amber to blue, making the image warmer or cooler, while the vertical axis of the grid allows you to change the tint by adding a magenta or green cast to the image.

Using the multi selector, you can choose a setting from 1 to 6 in either direction; additionally, you can add points along the horizontal and vertical axes simultaneously. For example, you can add 4 points of amber to give it a warmer tone and also add 2 points of green, shifting the amber tone more towards yellow.

Choosing the Fluorescent setting brings up some additional menu options; you can choose between seven different non-incandescent lighting types. This is handy if you know what specific type of fixture is being used. For example, I was shooting a night football game recently. I had the camera set to Auto WB, but I was getting very different colors from shot to shot, and none of them were looking right.

Because I wasn't shooting RAW, I needed to get more consistent shots. I knew that most outdoor sporting arenas use mercury vapor

lights to light the field at night. I selected the Fluorescent WB setting from the Shooting menu and chose the #7 option, High temp. Mercury vapor.

I took a few shots and noticed I was still getting a sickly greenish cast, and so I went back to the fine-tuning option and added 2 points of magenta to cancel out the green colorcast. This gave me an accurate and consistent color.

There are seven different settings:

✦ **Sodium-vapor lamps.** These are the types of lights often found in streetlights and parking lots. They emit a distinct, deep-yellow color.

✦ **Warm-white fluorescent.** These types of lamps give a white light with a bit of an amber cast to add some warmth to the scene. These lights burn at around 3000 K, similar to an incandescent light bulb.

✦ **White fluorescent.** These lights cast a very neutral white light at around 5200 K.

✦ **Cool-white fluorescent.** As the name suggests, this type of lamp is a bit cooler than a white fluorescent lamp and has a color temperature of 4200 K.

✦ **Day white fluorescent.** This lamp approximates sunlight at about 5500 K.

✦ **Daylight fluorescent.** This type of lamp gives you about the same color as daylight. This lamp burns at about 6300 K.

✦ **High temp. mercury-vapor.** These lights vary in temperature, depending on the manufacturer, and usually run between 4200 K and 5200 K.

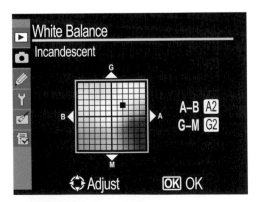

3.5 The White balance fine-tuning grid.

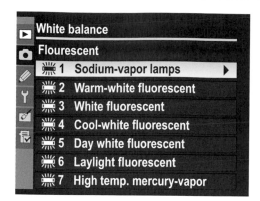

3.6 Fluorescent options menu.

 Sunlight and daylight are quite different color temperatures. Sunlight is light directly from the sun and is about 5500 K. Daylight is the combination of sunlight and skylight and has a color temperature of about 6300 K.

Preset white balance

Preset white balance allows you to make and store up to five custom white balance settings. You can use this option when shooting in mixed lighting, for example, in a room with an incandescent light bulb and sunlight coming in through the window, or when the camera's auto white balance isn't quite getting the correct color.

You can set a custom white balance in two different ways: direct measurement, which occurs when you take a reading from a neutral-colored object (a gray card works best for this) under the light source; or copy the white balance setting from an existing photograph, which allows you to choose a WB setting directly from an image that is stored on your memory card.

Direct measurement

To take a direct measurement for white balance, follow these steps:

1. **Place a neutral object (preferably a gray card) under the light source you want to balance for.**

2. **Select White balance from the Shooting menu.** Use the multi selector to scroll down to Preset manual and press OK. This brings up the White balance preset manual screen.

3. **Select Measure from the menu and press OK.** A dialog box is displayed, asking you to confirm that you want to overwrite the existing preset. Select Yes and press OK.

4. **Looking through the viewfinder, frame the reference object.** Press the Shutter Release button as if you were taking a photo.

5. **If the camera was successful in recording the white balance, "GD" flashes in the viewfinder control panel and a "data acquired" message is displayed in the information settings on the LCD panel.** If the scene is too dark or too bright, the camera may not be able to set the WB; in this case, "No GD" flashes in the viewfinder control panel and a message is displayed on the LCD warning you that the WB was unable to be set.

   You may need to change your settings to adjust the exposure settings on your camera. If the result was unsuccessful, repeat steps 2 to 5 until you obtain results that are acceptable to you.

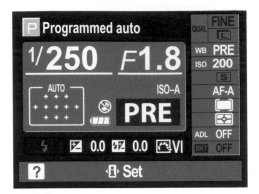

3.7 The shooting information when presetting WB.

> **Tip** *When presetting a custom WB, it's usually best to switch the camera to Manual focus, because the AF system has a hard time focusing on an object with little contrast, such as a gray card. You don't need to be in focus to set the WB.*

Copy white balance from an existing photograph

As I mentioned before, you can also copy the white balance setting from any photo saved on the memory card that's inserted into your camera. You can do this if you're shooting in a similar lighting situation or if you simply like the effect.

> **Tip** *If you have particular white balance settings that you like, you may consider saving the images on a memory card. This way, you can always have your favorite WB presets saved so that you don't accidentally erase them from the camera.*

1. **Press the menu button.** Use the multi selector to choose White balance from the Shooting menu.

2. **Select Preset manual from the White balance menu.** Press the multi selector right, or press OK to view the preset choices.

3. **Use the multi selector to highlight Use photo.** You have two options: This image, which is the current image being used for WB reference (either selected from the camera or custom shot); or Select image.

4. **Use the multi selector to highlight Select image.** Press OK, and the folders on the SD card are displayed. Highlight the appropriate folder and press OK.

5. **The LCD displays thumbnails of the images saved to your CF card.** This is similar to the Delete and DPOF thumbnail display. Use the multi selector to scroll through the images. You can zoom in on the highlighted image by pressing the Zoom In button.

6. **Once the desired image is highlighted, press OK.** Select This image and press OK to save the setting, or choose Select image to choose a different photo.

ISO sensitivity settings

This menu option allows you to set the ISO sensitivity. This is also where you set the parameters for the Auto-ISO feature.

> **Cross-Reference** *For more information on ISO settings and Auto ISO, see Chapter 2.*

Active D-Lighting

Active D-Lighting is a setting that is designed to help ensure that you retain highlight detail when shooting in a high-contrast situation, such as shooting a picture in direct, bright sunlight, which can cause dark shadows and bright highlight areas.

Active D-Lighting basically tells your camera to underexpose the image a bit; this underexposure helps to keep the highlights from becoming blown out and losing detail. The D5000 also uses a subtle adjustment to avoid losing any detail in the shadow area that the underexposure may cause.

Using Active D-Lighting changes all of the Picture Control brightness and contrast settings to Auto; adjusting the brightness and contrast is how Active D-Lighting keeps detail in the shadow areas.

Active D-Lighting has six settings, which are pretty self-explanatory: Auto, Extra high, High, Normal, Low, and Off.

From my experiences of using Active D-Lighting on the D300, D90, and D5000, I find that it works, but it is sometimes very subtle in the changes that it makes. If you're going to use this feature for general shooting, I recommend setting Active D-Lighting to Auto and forgetting it. I prefer to shoot in RAW, and although the settings are saved to the metadata for use with Nikon software, I prefer to do the adjustment myself in Adobe Photoshop, and so I turn this feature off.

When using Active D-Lighting, some extra time has to be taken to process the images, and so your buffer will fill up more quickly when shooting continuously; as a result, expect shorter burst rates.

Auto distortion control

This is a handy feature that corrects the common distortion that is found in most lenses. Wide-angle lenses suffer from what is known as *barrel distortion,* in which the images are bowed outwards (similar to a barrel), and telephoto lenses have the opposite problem in which the images are pinched inward slightly. When this option is turned on, the camera automatically corrects for this distortion as the image is being saved to the memory card. This feature can only be used when using Nikkor type-D and -G lenses. Note that fisheye lenses and Perspective Control lenses are not affected by this feature.

I recommend only using this feature when you are shooting subjects that have many straight lines, where distortion can be very apparent. As with Active D-Lighting, the extra processing time can cause the buffer to fill up quickly, and so you may notice shorter burst rates.

Color space

Color space simply describes the range of colors, also known as the *gamut,* that a device can reproduce. You have two choices of color spaces with the D5000: sRGB and Adobe RGB. The color space you choose depends on what the final output of your images will be.

✦ **sRGB.** This is a narrow color space, meaning that it deals with fewer colors and also less-saturated colors than the larger Adobe RGB color space. The sRGB color space is designed to mimic the colors that can be reproduced on most low-end monitors and is more saturated than the Adobe RGB color space.

✦ **Adobe RGB.** This color space has a much broader color spectrum than is available with sRGB. The Adobe gamut was designed for dealing with the color spectrum that can be reproduced with most high-end printing equipment.

This leads to the question of which color space you should use. As I mentioned earlier, the color space you use depends on what the final output of your images is going to be. If you take pictures, download them straight to your computer, and typically only view them on your monitor or upload them for viewing on the Web, then sRGB will be fine. The sRGB color space is also useful when printing directly from the camera or memory card with no post-processing.

If you are going to have your photos printed professionally or you intend to do a bit of post-processing to your images, using the Adobe RGB color space is recommended. This allows you to have subtler control over the colors than is possible using a narrower color space like sRGB.

For the most part, I capture my images using the Adobe RGB color space. I then do my post-processing and make a decision on the output. Anything that I know I will be posting to the Web I convert to sRGB; anything destined for my printer is saved as Adobe RGB. I usually end up with two identical images saved with two different color spaces. Because most Web browsers don't recognize the Adobe RGB color space, any images saved as Adobe RGB and posted on the Internet usually appear dull.

Long exp. NR

This menu option allows you to turn on noise reduction (NR) for exposures of eight seconds or longer. When this option is on, after taking a long-exposure photo, the camera runs a dark frame noise-reduction algorithm, which involves taking a second "dark" exposure at the same shutter speed, analyzing the noise, and reducing it.

High ISO NR

This allows you to choose how much noise reduction (NR) is applied to images that are taken at ISO 800 or higher. There are four settings:

✦ **High.** This setting applies a fairly aggressive NR. A fair amount of image detail can be lost when this setting is applied.

✦ **Normal.** This is the default setting. Some image detail may be lost when using this setting.

✦ **Low.** A small amount of NR is applied when this option is selected. Most of the image detail is preserved when using this setting.

✦ **Off.** When this setting is chosen, no NR is applied to images taken between ISO 100 (L 0.1) and ISO 3200; however, a very small amount of NR is applied to images shot at H 0.3 and above.

Active folder

As I discussed earlier, the D5000 automatically creates folders in which to store your images. The camera creates a folder named DCIM, and then stores the images in subfolders starting with folder 100NCD5000; when the folder gets 9,999 images in it, the camera automatically starts a new folder. You can choose to rename this folder or change the folder that the camera is saving to. You can name this folder whatever you like. You can use this option to separate different subjects into different folders.

When I shoot SCCA sports car races, there are different groups of cars. I use a different folder for each group to make it easier to sort through the images later. If there are five groups, I start out naming my first folder GRP1, then GRP2 for the second group's folder, and so on.

If you are on a road trip, you could save your images from each destination to separate folders. These are just a couple of different examples of how this feature can be used.

When selecting the active folder, you can choose a new folder or you can select a folder that has already been created. When you format your CF card, all preexisting folders are deleted and the camera creates a folder with whatever number the active folder is set to. For example, if you set it to a folder named ABC01, when the card is formatted, the camera will create folder 100ABC01.

To change the Active folder, follow these steps:

1. **Go to the Shooting menu.** Using the multi selector, choose Active folder, and then press the multi selector center to view options.

2. **Choose the Select folder option (default) to start a new folder.** Press the multi selector right. Press the multi selector up and down to select from the list of folders. Of course, if you haven't created any new folders, you will only have the NCD5000 folder to choose from.

3. **Press the OK button or the multi selector center to save changes.**

To create a new folder, follow these steps:

1. **Go to the Shooting menu.** Using the multi selector, choose New folder and then press the OK button to view options.

2. **Select the New folder option.** Press OK or press the multi selector right. This brings up a text entry menu. You have five spaces in which you can input numbers or letters. Enter a name for your new folder and press OK to save folder. The folder is now Active.

You can also rename preexisting folders by selecting the Rename option, selecting a folder to rename, and applying a new name using the text entry menu. To delete a folder, it must be empty. Select Delete from the menu, and all empty folders are deleted.

Movie settings

This menu option is where you adjust the resolution and aspect ratio of the movies that your camera records. You can turn off the sound recording option here, as well. All of the options record at 24 frames per second (fps) to ensure high-quality video that doesn't appear jerky.

Under the Quality sub-heading, there are three options:

✦ **1280x720 (16:9).** This is the HD setting. The camera records high-definition video using an aspect ratio of 16:9; this is the same aspect ratio in which most major films are shot. The file size of videos shot at this resolution can get pretty big pretty quickly. Using this resolution, you are limited to shooting clips that run no longer than five minutes. This is the type of video you want to shoot if you're planning on showing your movies on an HD display.

✦ **640x420 (3:2).** This is the default setting. Videos shot using this setting have a standard aspect ratio of

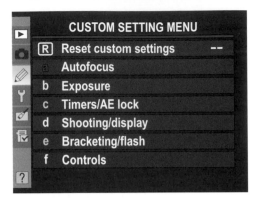

CUSTOM SETTING MENU

▣	Ⓡ Reset custom settings	--
○	ⓐ Autofocus	
🖉	b Exposure	
Y	c Timers/AE lock	
☑	d Shooting/display	
☷	e Bracketing/flash	
?	f Controls	

3.8 The Custom Setting menu.

3:2, which is the same aspect ratio that your still photos have. This setting is good for videos that will be published to the Web on sites such as YouTube.com. There is no time limit on the length of the clips you can record (as long as you have space on your card).

✦ **320x216 (3:2).** This is the setting that records at the lowest resolution, and so the file sizes are smaller. This setting also shoots video with an aspect ratio of 3:2. You can use this setting to film videos that you can easily send as an e-mail attachment due to the smaller file size.

Custom Setting Menu

The Custom Setting menu (CSM) is where you really start getting into customizing your D5000 to shoot to your personal preferences. Basically, this is where you make the camera yours. There are dozens of options that you can turn off or on to make shooting easier for you. The CSM is probably the most powerful menu in the camera.

The CSM is set up with six sets of sub-menus to make it easier for you to navigate through the menus so that you can find what you need and change it quickly. These menus are broken into different types of camera functions that are fairly self-explanatory.

Note *When using advanced scene modes, not all options may be available.*

Reset custom settings

Quite simply, you use this option to restore the camera default settings for all of the CSM options.

CSM a - Autofocus

The CSM sub-menu a controls how the camera performs its autofocus (AF) functions. Because focus is a very critical operation, this is a very important menu. There are four choices to choose from.

a1 – AF-area mode

This is where you set the mode that controls how the focus active point is selected; there are four different options:

✦ **Single point.** Using the multi selector, you choose which focus point is active.

✦ **Dynamic area.** When this option is selected, use the multi selector to choose the active focus point. If the subject leaves the focus point, the camera uses information from the surrounding focus points to maintain focus on the subject.

✦ **Auto-area.** When this option is selected, the camera automatically chooses the focus point.

✦ **3D-tracking (11 points).** With this option activated, the camera tracks moving subjects across the frame.

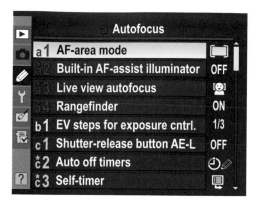

3.9 CSM a and b.

 For more detailed information on AF area modes, see Chapter 2.

a2 – Built-in AF-assist illuminator

The AF-assist illuminator lights up when there isn't enough light for the camera to focus properly. In certain instances, you may want to turn this option off, such as when shooting faraway subjects in dim settings (concerts or plays). When set to On, the AF-assist illuminator lights up in a low-light situation only when in AF-S mode and Auto-area AF is chosen. When in Single point mode or Dynamic area AF is chosen, the center AF point must be active.

When set to Off, the AF-assist illuminator does not light at all, even in dim lighting.

a3 – Live View autofocus

CSM a3 allows you to choose how your AF functions when using the Live View mode. There are four different options that you can choose:

✦ **Face priority.** When using this mode, the camera's autofocus module can detect and focus on faces in the composition. This mode is best used when photographing single portraits or groups of people. When using this feature, allow the camera to detect the face or faces before half-pressing the Shutter Release button to focus. When the AF system detects a face, a yellow box is displayed on the subject's face.

✦ **Wide area.** This gives you an AF area that is wider than the standard area. This makes it easier for the AF system to find an area of contrast to focus on. The focus area can be moved around anywhere in the frame using the multi selector. Use this AF mode for most standard photography.

✦ **Normal area.** This is similar to Wide area AF, except that the area is smaller. Use this option when you have a particular feature that you want to focus on. This is a good mode to use when doing macro or close-up photography where focusing on a specific spot is important.

✦ **Subject tracking.** This AF mode allows the camera to track a subject as it moves across the frame. To activate tracking, you must press the multi selector up. While attempting to find a subject, the AF area appears as a white box and blinks. Once the AF finds a subject, the focus area turns yellow and moves across the frame, following the subject.

Half-pressing the Shutter Release button initiates focusing and locks the AF area in place. To continue tracking the subject, let go of the Shutter Release button. When focus is achieved, the AF area box turns green.

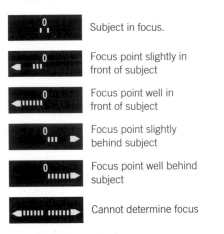

Subject in focus.

Focus point slightly in front of subject

Focus point well in front of subject

Focus point slightly behind subject

Focus point well behind subject

Cannot determine focus

3.10 The Rangefinder.

a4 – Rangefinder

The Rangefinder option helps you determine whether the camera is in focus when using your camera in MF mode or when using a non AF-S lens equipped with a CPU. The rangefinder appears where the electronic exposure meter is displayed when the camera or lens is switched to MF (or a non-AF-S lens is attached). The rangefinder also displays whether the subject is in front of or behind the focus point.

Caution

The Rangefinder option is not available when in Manual exposure. For this reason, the rangefinder does not work when using non-CPU lenses because these lenses require you to shoot in Manual exposure mode to release the shutter. You can, however, momentarily switch the Mode dial to A, S, or P, check the rangefinder, and then switch back to M to shoot.

CSM b – Exposure

This menu is where you change the settings that control exposure and metering. These settings allow you to change the adjustment increments for exposure, ISO, and exposure compensation. Setting the increments to

1/3 stops allows you to fine-tune the settings with more accuracy than setting them to 1/2 stops.

b1 – EV steps for exposure cntrl.

This determines how the shutter speed, aperture, exposure compensation, flash exposure compensation, and auto bracketing are set. The choices here are 1/3 or 1/2 step. Choosing a smaller increment gives a much less drastic change in exposure and allows you to get a more exact exposure in critical situations. I recommend keeping this set to 1/3 step for finer control of your exposure settings.

CSM c – Timers/AE lock

This small sub-menu controls the D5000's various timers, as well as the Auto-exposure lock setting. There are four options to choose from:

c1 – Shutter-release button AE-L

Set to default (Off), the camera only locks exposure when the AE-L/AF-L button is pressed. When set to On, the auto-exposure settings are locked when the camera's Shutter Release button is half-pressed.

c Timers/AE lock	
c1 Shutter-release button AE-L	OFF
c2 Auto off timers	
c3 Self-timer	
c4 Remote on duration	15m
d1 Beep	OFF
d2 Viewfinder grid display	ON
d3 ISO display	OFF
d4 File number sequence	ON

3.11 CSM c menu options.

c2 – Auto off timers

This menu option is used to determine how long the camera's exposure meter and LCD monitor are active before turning off when no other actions are being performed. There are four different options:

✦ **Short.** When this option is selected, the menus and playback turn off after 8 seconds, the image review after 4 seconds, and the meter after 4 seconds.

✦ **Normal.** When this option is selected, the menus and playback turn off after 12 seconds, the image review after 4 seconds, and the meter after 8 seconds.

✦ **Long.** When this option is selected, the menus and playback turn off after 20 seconds, the image review after 20 seconds, and the meter after 60 seconds.

✦ **Custom.** You can use this option to customize the auto off timer for each operation, Playback/menus, Image review, and Auto meter-off. The options for each are as follows:

 • Playback/menus: 8 sec., 12 sec., 20 sec., 1 min., or 10 min.

 • Image review: 4 sec., 8 sec., 20 sec., 1 min., or 10 min.

 • Auto meter-off: 4 sec., 8 sec., 20 sec., 1 min., or 30 min.

c3 – Self-timer

This setting puts a delay on when the shutter is released after the Shutter Release button is pressed when using the Self-timer release mode. This is handy when you want to do a self-portrait and you need some time to get yourself into the frame.

You can also use the self-timer to reduce camera shake caused by pressing the Shutter Release button on long exposures. You can set the delay at 2, 5, 10, or 20 seconds. Additionally, you can set the self-timer for one to nine shots; this causes the camera to fire a continuous series of shots at the Continuous setting.

For some people, especially those interested in HDR imaging, there's a trick you can do to allow the camera to fire off an auto-bracketing burst with one press of the Shutter Release button. This allows you to be sure that you get no camera movements between shots (if you use a tripod), and so your images will be in perfect registration. Follow these steps:

1. **Using the Quick Settings menu, turn on Auto bracketing.** Choose whatever exposure increment you like; I prefer 1-stop intervals.

2. **Go to CSM c3 Self-timer.** Set the delay time; 5 seconds should be enough to allow the camera and tripod to stabilize. Next, set the number of shots to 3.

3. **Using the Quick Settings menu, set the release mode to self-timer.**

4. **Press the Shutter Release button.** After the self-timer delay, the camera will perform auto-bracketing with one push of the Shutter Release button.

c4 – Remote on duration

This setting controls how long the camera waits for a signal from the optional ML-L3 infrared remote control before the camera exits the remote release mode and returns to the default release mode (Single frame). The choices are 1, 5, 10, or 15 minutes.

CSM d – Shooting/ display

CSM sub-menu d is where you make changes to some of the minor shooting and display details. There are seven options to choose from:

d1 – Beep

When this option is on, the camera emits a beep when the self-timer is counting down or when the AF locks in Single focus mode. You can choose High, Low, or Off. For most photographers, this option is absolutely the first thing that is turned off when the camera is taken out of the box. Although the beep can be kind of useful when in self-timer mode, it's a pretty annoying option, especially if you are photographing in a relatively quiet area.

d2 – Viewfinder grid display

This handy option displays a grid in the viewfinder to assist you with composition of the photograph.

3.12 CSM d.

d3 – ISO display

When this option is turned on, the viewfinder display shows the ISO sensitivity settings where the remaining frame count is seen by default.

d4 – File number sequence

The D5000 names files by sequentially numbering them. This option controls how the sequence is handled. When this option is set to Off, the file numbers reset to 0001 when a new folder is created, a new memory card is inserted, or the existing memory card is formatted. When this option is set to On, the camera continues to count up from the last number until the file number reaches 9,999. The camera then returns to 0001 and counts up from there. When this option is set to Reset, the camera starts at 0001 when the current folder is empty. If the current folder contains images, the camera starts at one number higher than the last image in the folder.

d5 – Exposure delay mode

When this setting is turned on, the shutter is released 1 second after the reflex mirror is raised. This allows the camera to stop vibrating from the "mirror slap" before the exposure is made. This mode is generally used when using a tripod and shooting long exposures or extreme close-up macro photography where the slightest movement can cause the image to blur.

d6 – Date imprint

Turning this option on imprints your images with the date and/or time that they were shot. You can choose to imprint only the date, the time and date, or the date counter, which displays the number of days that have elapsed between the date that the picture was taken and a selected date.

Caution *Once the date is imprinted, it cannot be removed.*

d7 – Live View display options

This menu allows you to control what information, indicators, and guides are displayed on the LCD panel when using the Live View mode. There are four separate options:

✦ **Show indicators.** When this option is selected, all of the different shooting options are displayed on the LCD panel when Live View is activated. The indicators include ISO, release mode, AF mode, metering mode, and more.

✦ **Hide indicators.** When this option is selected, none of the settings and indicators is displayed. This gives you a clear view of what you're shooting; I prefer this setting for its simplicity.

✦ **Framing grid.** Selecting this option displays a grid across the screen to aid in compositions and to help keep the horizons straight. I'm a big fan of framing grids because it always reminds me to make sure everything is straight.

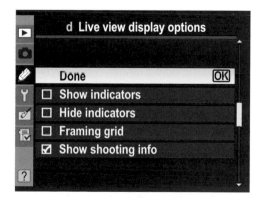

3.13 Live View display options.

✦ **Show shooting info.** When this option is selected, all of the shooting information is displayed on the LCD similar to the Shooting info display. The actual Live View feed is displayed smaller in the upper-left corner.

CSM e – Bracketing/flash

This sub-menu is where you set the controls for the built-in Speedlight and the options for auto bracketing.

e1 – Flash cntrl for built-in flash

This sub-menu has other sub-menus nested within it. Essentially, this option controls how your built-in flash operates. The sub-menus are as follows:

✦ **TTL.** This is the fully automatic flash mode. Minor adjustments can be made using FEC (Flash Exposure Compensation).

✦ **Manual.** You choose the power output in this mode. You can choose from Full power all the way down to 1/128 power.

 Cross-Reference *For more information on flash photography with Nikon Speedlights, see Chapter 6 or pick up a copy of the Nikon Creative Lighting System Digital Field Guide, by J. Dennis Thomas (Wiley, 2006).*

e2 – Auto bracketing set

This option allows you to choose how the camera brackets when Auto-bracketing is turned on. You can choose Auto exposure bracketing, WB bracketing, or a series of images using Active D-lighting. WB bracketing is not available when the image quality is set to record RAW images.

CSM f – Controls

This sub-menu allows you to customize some of the functions of the different buttons and dials of your D5000. There are ten options to choose from:

f1 – Assign self-timer/Fn button

This button chooses what functions the Function (Fn) button performs when pressed. The function assigned to the button makes it easy to change a setting quickly and can speed up your shooting process.

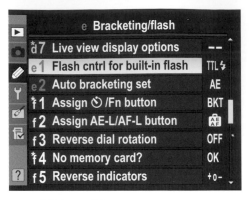

	e Bracketing/flash	
d7	Live view display options	--
e1	Flash cntrl for built-in flash	TTL⚡
e2	Auto bracketing set	AE
♻1	Assign ⏱ /Fn button	BKT
f2	Assign AE-L/AF-L button	🅰
f3	Reverse dial rotation	OFF
♻4	No memory card?	OK
f5	Reverse indicators	+0-

3.14 CSM e and f.

✦ **Self-timer.** When this option is set, pressing the button activates the self-timer delay. Press the button again to turn off the self-timer.

✦ **Release mode.** This option allows you to quickly change the release mode by pressing the Fn button and rotating the Command dial.

✦ **Image quality/size.** Pressing the Fn button and rotating the Command dial allows you to change the size and compression quality of your images.

✦ **ISO sensitivity.** Pressing the Fn button and rotating the Command dial allows you to change the ISO setting.

✦ **White balance.** Pressing the Fn button and rotating the Command dial allows you to adjust the white balance settings.

✦ **Active D-Lighting.** Pressing the Fn button and rotating the Command dial allows you to choose the Active D-Lighting settings.

Note *ISO sensitivity, White balance, and Auto bracketing options are only available when the camera is set to P, S, A, or M exposure modes.*

✦ **+ NEF (RAW).** Pressing the Fn button when this option is set causes the camera to record both a JPEG and a NEF file on the next frame taken after the Fn button is pressed. To cancel without recording a NEF, press the button again or turn off the camera. This option can come in handy sometimes if you run into a tricky lighting situation or when photographing a scene with an odd white balance.

✦ **Auto bracketing.** Pressing the Fn button and rotating the Command dial allows you to turn on the Auto bracketing function and to choose the increments when the Auto bracketing feature is set to Auto exposure or White balance. When auto bracketing is set to ADL, you can turn it on or off.

f2 – Assign AE-L/AF-L button

This option allows you to customize the function of the AE-L/AF-L button. There are five options:

✦ **AE/AF lock.** This locks the exposure and the focus as long as the button is pressed and held.

Releasing the button resets the meter and allows the AF to function normally.

✦ **AE lock only.** This locks the exposure as long as the button is pressed and held.

✦ **AF lock only.** This locks the AF on your subject, allowing you to recompose the shot while maintaining focus on your subject.

✦ **AE lock (hold).** This locks the exposure when the button is pressed. To unlock the exposure, press the button a second time or turn the camera off. This option is useful when shooting video to keep the exposure from changing and causing your video to dim and brighten intermittently.

✦ **AF-ON.** This allows you to activate the camera's AF system without pressing the Shutter Release button.

f3 – Reverse dial rotation

This option causes the settings to be controlled in reverse of what is normal. For example, by default, when in Aperture Priority, rotating the Command dial right makes your aperture smaller. Reversing the dial rotation gives you a larger aperture when rotating the dial to the right.

f4 – No memory card?

This setting controls whether the shutter will release when no memory card is present in the camera. When set to Enable release, the shutter fires and an image is displayed in the monitor; the image is temporarily saved but will be lost when you turn off the camera. When set to Release locked, the shutter does not fire. If you happen to be using Camera Control Pro 2 shooting, tethered directly to your computer, the camera

shutter will release no matter what this option is set to.

f5 – Reverse indicators

This option allows you to reverse the indicators on the electronic light meter displayed in the viewfinder and on the LCD control panel. For some people, the default setting showing the overexposure on the left and the underexposure on the right is counterintuitive. Reversing these makes more sense to some people (including me). This option also reverses the display for the Auto Bracketing feature.

Setup Menu

This menu contains a smattering of options, most of which aren't changed very frequently. Some of these settings include the time and date and the video mode. A couple of other options are Clean image sensor and GPS, which you may want to access from time to time. There are 16 different options.

Format memory card

This option allows you to completely erase everything on your memory card. Formatting your memory card erases all of the data on the card. It's a good idea to format your card every time you download the images to your computer (just be sure that all of the files are successfully transferred before formatting).

Formatting the card helps protect against corrupt data. Simply deleting the images leaves the data on the card and allows it to be overwritten; sometimes this older data can corrupt the new data as it is being written. Formatting the card gives your camera a blank slate on which to write.

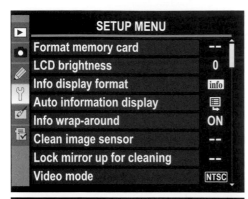

3.15 The Setup menu shown in two frames.

LCD brightness

This menu sets the brightness of your LCD screen. You may want to make it brighter when viewing images in bright sunlight, or make it dimmer when viewing images indoors or to save battery power. You can adjust the LCD ±3 levels.

The menu shows a graph with ten bars ranging from black to gray to white. The optimal setting is where you can see a distinct change in color tone in each of the ten bars. If the last two bars on the right blend together, your LCD is too bright; if the last two bars on the left side blend together, your LCD is too dark.

Info display format

This menu option allows you to set the different display options for the LCD shooting information. You can choose between displaying the shooting information in the Classic format or the Graphic format in three different colors. You can also select an image off of your memory card to display as wallpaper behind the shooting information.

Additionally, you can choose for the camera to display the shooting information differently, depending on whether you're using the DVP modes or the P, S, A, or M modes.

Auto information display

Setting this option to On brings up the Shooting Display Information when the Shutter Release button is half-pressed and released. The settings are applied individually for P, S, A, and M modes and the advanced scene modes.

Info wrap-around

This option allows you to continue scrolling through the menu options in the Quick Settings Menu when pressing the multi selector in one direction by allowing the cursor to "wrap around" through to the other side of the frame. When this option is turned off, the selection cursor stops at the edge of the frame and you have to press the multi selector in the opposite direction to scroll back through the options.

Clean image sensor

This is a great feature that was released with the D300 and added to the D5000 as well. The camera uses ultrasonic vibration to knock any dust off the filter in front of the

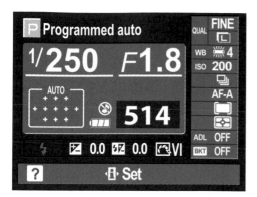

3.16 Classic shooting information.

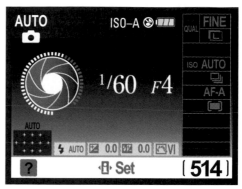

3.17 Graphic shooting information.

sensor. This helps keep some of the dust off of your sensor but is not going to keep it absolutely dust-free forever. You may have to have the sensor professionally cleaned periodically.

You can choose Clean now, which cleans the image sensor immediately, or you have four separate options for cleaning, which you access in the Clean at startup/shutdown option. These options include the following:

✦ **Clean at startup.** The camera goes through the cleaning process immediately upon turning the camera on. This may delay your startup time a little.

✦ **Clean at shutdown.** The camera goes through the cleaning process immediately upon turning the camera off.

✦ **Clean at startup and shutdown.** The camera cleans the image sensor when the camera is turned on and also when it is powered down.

✦ **Off.** The camera doesn't clean the sensor at any time.

Lock mirror up for cleaning

This option locks up the mirror to allow access to the image sensor for inspection or for additional cleaning. The sensor is also powered down to reduce any static charge that may attract dust. Because it's a fairly simple process, some people prefer to clean their own sensor; however, I recommend taking your camera to an authorized Nikon service center for any sensor cleaning.

Any damage caused to the sensor by improper cleaning will not be covered by the warranty and can lead to a very expensive repair bill.

Video mode

There are two options in this menu: NTSC and PAL. Without getting into too many specifics, these are standards relating to the resolution of televisions. All of North America, including Canada and Mexico, uses the NTSC standard, while most of Europe and Asia use the PAL standard. Check your television owner's manual for the specific setting if you plan to view your images on a TV directly from the camera.

HDMI

The D5000 has an HDMI (High-Definition Multimedia Interface) output that allows you to connect your camera to a high-definition TV to review your images. There are five settings: 480p, 576p, 720p, 1080i, and Auto. The Auto feature automatically selects the appropriate setting for your TV.

Before plugging your camera into an HDTV, I recommend reading your TV's owner's manual for specific settings. When the camera is attached to an HDMI device, the LCD monitor on the camera is automatically disabled.

Time zone and date

This is where you set the camera's internal clock. You also select a time zone, choose the date display options, and turn the daylight-saving time options on or off.

Language

This is where you set the language that the menus and dialog boxes display.

Image comment

You can use this feature to attach a comment to the images taken by your D5000. You can enter the text using the Input comment menu. The comments can be viewed in Nikon's Capture NX 2 or View NX software or they can be viewed in the photo information on the camera.

Setting the Attach comment option applies the comment to all images taken until this setting is disabled. Some comments you may want to attach are copyright information or your name, or even the location where the photos were taken.

Auto image rotation

This option tells the camera to record the orientation of the camera when the photo is shot (portrait or landscape). This allows both the camera and image-editing software to show the photo in the proper orientation so that you don't have to take the time in post-processing to rotate images shot in portrait orientation.

Image Dust Off ref photo

This option allows you to take a dust reference photo that shows any dust or debris that may be stuck to your sensor. Capture NX 2 then uses the image to automatically retouch any subsequent photos where the specks appear.

To use this feature, either select "Start" or "Clean sensor and then start." Next, you are instructed by a dialog box to take a photo of a bright, featureless, white object that is about 10cm from the lens. The camera automatically sets the focus to infinity. A Dust Off reference photo can only be taken when using a CPU lens. It's recommended to use at least a 50mm lens, and when using a zoom lens, you should zoom all the way in to the longest focal length.

GPS

This menu is used to adjust the settings of an optional GPS unit, which can be used to record longitude and latitude to the image's Exif data. The GPS is connected to the camera's accessory terminal. There are two options:

✦ **Auto meter off.** This option allows you to control whether the exposure meter turns off when the optional GP-1 is connected. The GPS unit is synced with the exposure meters so that if the exposure meter turns off, the GPS unit's connection is severed. It may take several minutes for the GP-1 to regain contact with the GPS satellites. Choosing the Enable options allows your meters to turn off using the parameters set in CSM c2. Choosing Disable allows the meters to stay on, keeping the connection with the GPS unit active.

✦ **Position.** This option displays the geographical location of your GPS reading.

Eye-Fi Upload

This option allows you to enable wireless transfer of images when using an Eye-Fi SD memory card.

Caution | *This Eye-Fi upload option only appears if an Eye-Fi card is inserted into the D5000. You will not see this option otherwise.*

Firmware version

This menu option displays which firmware version your camera is currently operating under. Firmware is a computer program that is embedded in the camera that tells it how to function. Camera manufacturers routinely update the firmware to correct for any bugs or to make improvements on the camera's functions.

Nikon posts firmware updates on its Web site at www.nikonusa.com.

Retouch Menu

The Retouch menu allows you to make changes and corrections to your images with the use of imaging-editing software. As

a matter of fact, you don't even need to download your images. You can make all of the changes in-camera using the LCD preview (or hooked up to a TV, if you prefer).

The options include D-Lighting, Red-eye correction, Trim, Monochrome, Filter effects, Color balance, and Image overlay.

Cross-Reference | *The Retouch menu is discussed at length in Chapter 8.*

My Menu

This is a great menu option that was introduced with the D300. It is much better than the Recent Settings menu in the D200 (you can also choose to replace the My Menu tab with the Recent Settings tab). The My Menu option allows you to create your own customized menu by choosing the options you want.

You can also set the different menu options to whatever order you want. This allows you to have all of the settings you change the most right at your fingertips without having to go searching through all the menus and sub-menus.

For example, I have the My Menu option set to display all of the menu options I frequently use, including Set Picture Control, Image review, AF area mode, and Active D-Lighting, among others. This saves me an untold amount of time because I don't have to go through a lot of different menus to find what I'm looking for.

To set up your custom My Menu, follow these steps:

1. **Select My Menu, and press the OK button.**

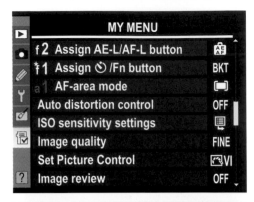

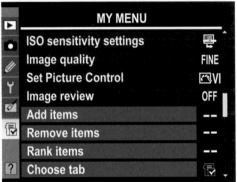

3.18 This figure shows the My Menu options that I have set on my camera.

2. **Select Add items, and press the OK button.**

3. **Use the multi selector to navigate through the menus to add specific menu options, and press the OK button.**

4. **Use the multi selector to position where you want the menu item to appear, and press the OK button to save the order.**

5. **Repeat steps 2 to 4 until you have added all of the menu items you want.**

To reorder the items in My Menu, follow these steps:

1. **Select My Menu and press the OK button.**

2. **Select Rank items and press the OK button.** This brings up a list of all of the menu options that you have saved to My Menu.

3. **Use the multi selector to highlight the menu option you want to move, and press the OK button.**

4. **Using the multi selector, move the yellow line to where you want to move the selected item.** Press the OK button to set. Repeat this step until you have moved all of the menu options that you want.

5. **Press the menu button or tap the Shutter Release button to exit.**

To delete options from My Menu, simply press the Delete button when the option is highlighted. The camera asks for confirmation that you indeed want to delete the setting. Press the Delete button again to confirm, or press the Menu button to exit without deleting the menu option.

As I mentioned earlier, you can replace the My Menu option with the Recent settings option. The Recent settings menu stores the last 20 settings you have adjusted. To switch from My Menu to Recent settings, follow these steps:

1. **Select My Menu from the Menu tabs.** Press the OK button to view My Menu.

2. **Use the multi selector to scroll down to the Choose tab menu option.** Press the OK button.

3. **Select Recent settings and press the OK button or press the multi selector right to change the setting.**

4. **Press the Menu button or tap the Shutter Release button to exit.**

Quick Settings Display

Although this is not a true menu, it gives you access to several of the most commonly changed menu items. To access the Quick Settings Display, press the info button. This displays the shooting information screen on the rear LCD.

While the shooting information is displayed, press the info button again. This grays out the shooting information and highlights the settings shown at the bottom of the shooting information screen. Use the multi selector to highlight the setting you want to change, and then press the OK button. This takes you straight to the specific menu option. The Quick Settings Display options are:

✦ Flash mode.

✦ Exposure compensation.

✦ Flash exposure compensation (FEC).

✦ Set Picture Control.

✦ Image size/quality.

✦ White balance.

✦ ISO sensitivity.

✦ Release mode.

✦ Focus mode.

✦ AF area mode.

✦ Metering.

✦ Active D-Lighting.

✦ Bracketing.

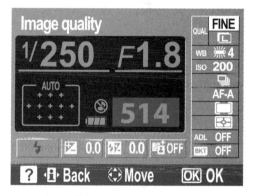

3.19 The Quick Settings Display.

Essential Photography Concepts

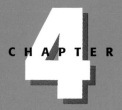
Photography, whether traditional film photography or working with a digital SLR, is built on concepts that are the foundation for every photo you take. This chapter gives you essential coverage of those items, including information on exposure, the effects the aperture has on depth of field, and some tips and hints on composition techniques.

Understanding Exposure

An exposure is the resulting creation of three elements that are all interrelated. Each depends on the others to create a good exposure. If one of the elements changes, the others must increase or decrease proportionally. Here are the elements you need to consider:

✦ **Shutter speed.** The shutter speed determines the length of time the sensor is exposed to light.

✦ **ISO sensitivity.** The ISO setting you choose controls your camera's sensitivity to light.

✦ **Aperture/f-stop.** How much light reaches the sensor of your camera is controlled by the aperture, or f-stop. Each camera has an adjustable opening on the lens. As you change the aperture (the opening), you allow more or less light to reach the sensor.

Shutter speed

Shutter speed is the amount of time that light entering from the lens is allowed to expose the image sensor. Shutter speeds are indicated in fractions of a second; common shutter speeds (in 1-stop increments) include the following: 1, 1/2, 1/4, 1/8, 1/15, 1/30, 1/60, 1/125, 1/250, 1/500, 1/1000, and so on. Slow shutter speeds mean the shutter is open longer, such as for 1/2 second or 1 second. Fast shutter speeds mean the shutter is only open for a very short time, such as 1/1000 second or 1/1500 second.

Increasing or decreasing shutter speed by one setting doubles or halves the exposure, respectively. When the shutter speed changes, the amount of light entering the camera changes, and so it stands to reason that if you increase or decrease the time that the light is reaching the sensor, you also have to make an adjustment to other settings to ensure that you still have the proper exposure. This is done in one of two ways: you can either adjust the aperture to increase or decrease the amount of light reaching the sensor, or you can adjust the ISO sensitivity.

The D5000 allows you to adjust the shutter speed in 1/3-stops for fine-tuning the exposure (1, 1/1.3, 1/1.6, 1/2, 1/2.5, 1/3, 1/4, and so on). It may seem like math (okay, technically it does involve math), but it is relatively easy to figure out.

For example, if you take a picture with a 1/2-second shutter speed and it turns out too dark, logically you want to keep the shutter open longer to let in more light. To do this, you need to adjust the shutter speed to 1 second, the next full stop, which lets in twice as much light.

The shutter speed can also affect the sharpness of your images. When using a longer focal-length lens, a faster shutter speed is required to counteract camera shake, which can cause your image to be blurry. Longer lenses not only magnify your subject but also magnify movement such as camera shake.

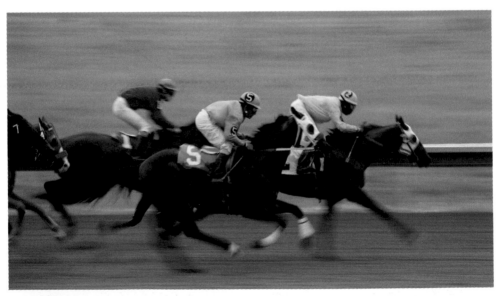

4.1 In this image, a relatively slow shutter speed of 1/50 second was used to create a motion blur. Panning was also employed to keep the subject of the image mostly in sharp focus.

A good rule to follow when using a longer lens is to use a shutter speed that is the reciprocal of the focal length of the lens. For example, when using a focal length of 200mm, the slowest speed you should use is 1/200 second, although if you're using a VR lens, you can shoot with an even slower shutter speed.

When taking photographs in low light, a slow shutter speed is often required, which can also cause blur from camera shake or fast-moving subjects.

 Cross-Reference *For more information on lenses, see Chapter 5.*

The shutter speed can also be used to show motion. Panning (moving the camera horizontally with a moving subject) while using a slower shutter speed can cause the background to blur while keeping the subject in focus. This is an effective way to portray motion in a still image, as shown in figure 4.1. Conversely, using a fast shutter speed can freeze action, such as the splash of water from a surfer, which can also give the illusion of motion in a still photograph.

ISO

The ISO (International Organization for Standardization) setting is how your camera determines how sensitive it is to light. The higher the ISO number is, the less light you need to take a photograph, meaning the sensor is more sensitive to light.

For example, you might choose an ISO of 200 on a bright, sunny day when you are photographing outside because you have plenty of light. However, on a dark, cloudy day, you want to consider an ISO of 400 or higher to make sure your camera captures all the available light. This allows you to use a faster shutter speed should it be appropriate to the subject you are photographing.

You can also use a higher ISO if you need to use a small aperture to achieve greater depth of field.

It is helpful to know that each ISO setting is twice as sensitive to light as the previous setting. For example, at ISO 400, your camera is twice as sensitive to light as it is at ISO 200. This means it needs only half the light at ISO 400 that it needs at ISO 200 to achieve the same exposure.

Additionally, when in Auto ISO mode, the D5000 adjusts the ISO in 1/3-stop increments (100, 125, 160, 200, and so on), which enables the camera to fine-tune the ISO to reduce the noise that is inherent in higher ISO settings.

Aperture

To control the amount of light the lens lets into the camera, the lens has a diaphragm inside of it that operates more or less like the iris in the human eye. The size of the opening can be made larger or smaller. Aperture is expressed as f-stop numbers, such as f/2.8, f/5.6, f/4, and f/8. Here are a couple of important things to know about aperture:

✦ **Smaller f/numbers equal wider apertures.** A small f-stop number, such as f/2.8, opens the lens so that more light reaches the sensor. If you have a wide aperture (opening), the amount of time the shutter needs to stay open to let light into the camera decreases.

✦ **Larger f/numbers equal narrower apertures.** A large f-stop, such as f/11, closes the lens so that less light reaches the sensor. If you have a narrow aperture, the amount of time the shutter needs to stay open to let light into the camera increases.

Deciding what aperture to use depends on what kind of photo you are going to take. If you need a fast shutter speed to freeze action, and you don't want to raise the ISO, you can use a wide aperture to let more available light into the sensor. Conversely, if the scene is very bright, you may want to use a small aperture to avoid overexposure.

The aperture also has an impact on the depth of field in your image. Depth of field is covered later in this chapter.

Fine-tuning Exposure

Your camera's meter may not always be completely accurate. There can be a lot of variables in different types of scenes, and large bright or dark areas can trick the meter into thinking a scene is brighter or darker than it really is, causing the image to be over- or underexposed.

The D5000 allows you to use exposure compensation so that you can fine-tune the amount of exposure to vary from what is set by the camera's exposure meter. You can also use bracketing, which gives you different exposures so that you can pick the image with the right exposure. The most accurate way to determine whether you need to adjust the exposure is to use the histogram. All of this is covered in the next few sections.

Exposure compensation is adjusted by pressing the Exposure Compensation button, just behind the Shutter Release button on the right side, and rotating the Command dial to the left for more exposure (+EV) or to the right for less exposure (-EV). Depending on your settings, the exposure compensation is adjusted in 1/3 or 1/2 stops of light. You can change this setting in the Custom Settings menus (CSM b1).

Exposure compensation can be adjusted up to +5EV and down to -5EV, which is a large range of 10 stops. To remind you that exposure compensation has been set, the exposure compensation indicator appears in the viewfinder display. It also appears on the rear LCD when the shooting information is being displayed.

 Caution *Be sure to reset the exposure compensation to 0 after you're done to avoid unwanted over- or underexposure.*

Histograms

The easiest way to determine if you need to adjust exposure compensation is to simply preview your image. If it looks too dark, add some exposure compensation; if it's too bright, adjust the exposure compensation down. This, however, is not the most accurate method of determining how much exposure compensation to use.

To accurately determine how much to add or subtract, look at the *histogram*. A histogram is a visual representation of the tonal values in your image. Think of it as a graph that charts the lights, darks, and mid-tones in your picture.

The histogram charts a tonal range of about 5 stops, which is about the limit of what the D5000's sensor can record. This range is broken down into 256 separate brightness levels from 0 (absolute black) to 255 (absolute white), with 128 coming in at middle or 18-percent gray.

Ideally, you want to expose your subject so that it falls approximately in the middle of the tonal range, which is why your camera's meter exposes for 18-percent gray. If your histogram graph has most of the information bunched up on the left side, then your image is probably underexposed; if it's bunched up on the right side, then your image is probably overexposed.

With most average subjects that aren't bright white or extremely dark, you want to try to get your histogram to look sort of like a Bell curve, with most of the tones in the middle range tapering off as they get to the dark and light ends of the graph. But this is only for most average types of images, and let's face it: most photos we take aren't of scenes with average lighting.

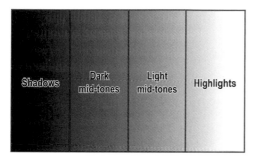

4.2 Representation of the tonal range of a histogram.

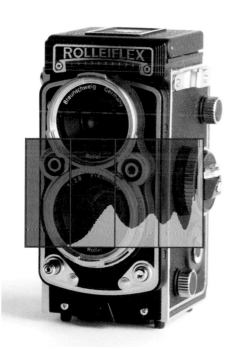

4.3 Example of a histogram from an overexposed image (no highlight detail). Notice the spikes at the far right of the graph.

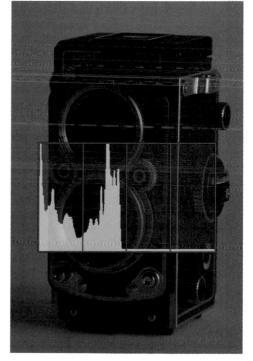

4.4 Example of a histogram from an underexposed image (no shadow detail). Notice the spikes at the far left of the graph.

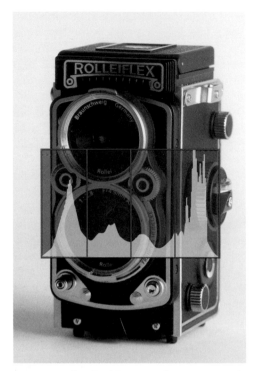

4.5 Example of a histogram from a properly exposed image. Notice that the graph does not spike against the edge on the left or the right, but tapers off.

As with almost everything in photography, there are exceptions to the rule. If you take a photo of a dark subject on a dark background (a *low-key* image), then naturally your histogram will have most of the tones bunched up on the left side of the graph. Conversely, when taking a photograph of a light subject on a light background (a *high-key* image) the histogram will have most of the tones bunched up to the right.

The most important thing to remember is that there is no such thing as a perfect histogram. A histogram is just a factual representation of the tones in the image.

The other important thing to remember is that although it's okay for the graph to be near one side or the other, you usually don't want your histogram to have spikes bumping up against the edge of the graph; this indicates that your image has blown-out highlights (completely white, with no detail) or blocked-up shadow areas (completely black, with no detail).

Now that you know a little bit about histograms, you can use them to adjust exposure compensation. Here is a good order of operations to follow when using the histogram as a tool to evaluate your photos:

1. **After taking your picture, review its histogram on the LCD.** To view the histogram in the image preview, press the Playback button to view the image. Press the multi selector to the right, and the histogram appears directly to the right of the image preview.

2. **Look at the histogram.** An example of an ideal histogram can be seen in figure 4.5.

3. **Adjust the exposure compensation.** To move the tones to the right to capture more highlight detail, add a little exposure compensation by pressing the Exposure Compensation button and rotating the Command dial to the right. To move the tones to the left, press the Exposure Compensation button and rotate the Command dial to the left.

4. **Retake the photograph if necessary.** After taking another picture, review the histogram again. If needed, adjust the exposure compensation more until you achieve the desired exposure.

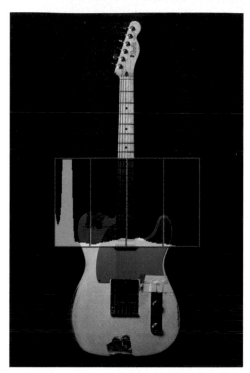

4.6 Example of a histogram from a low-key image. Notice that although the graph is mostly on the left, there is some shadow detail in the image.

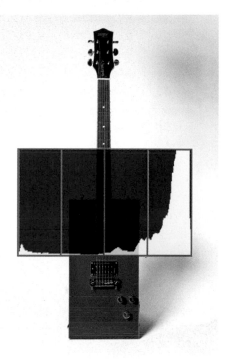

4.7 Example of a histogram from a high-key image. Notice that although the graph is mostly on the right, there is highlight detail in the image.

Bracketing

Another way to ensure that you get the proper exposure is to *bracket* your exposures. Bracketing is a photographic technique in which you vary the exposure of your subject over three or more frames. By doing this, you can be sure to get the proper exposure in difficult lighting situations where your camera's meter can be fooled. Bracketing is usually done with at least one exposure under and one exposure over the metered exposure.

You can bracket your images manually or you can choose to use the D5000's auto bracketing function.

To use the auto bracketing function, you must access the bracketing feature in the Quick Settings menu or set the Function (Fn) button for Auto bracketing. To do this, follow these steps:

1. **Press the Menu button.**

2. **Use the multi selector to enter the Custom Settings menu (CSM).** Scroll down to CSM e/Controls. Press the multi selector right.

3. **Scroll down to CSM f1, Assign Fn button.** Press the multi selector right to choose the Fn button options.

4. **Use the multi selector to choose Auto bracketing.** Press the multi selector right.

5. **Choose Auto bracketing from the Assign Fn button menu.**

6. **Press the OK button.** Pressing the Fn button now accesses Auto bracketing in the Quick Settings menu.

7. **Rotate the Command dial while pressing the button to set the Auto bracketing increments.** You can choose 0.3, 0.7, 1.0, 1.3, 1.7, or 2.0 stop differences between the images.

 You must go back into the Auto bracketing menu and change the setting to Off to disable auto bracketing; otherwise, the camera will continue to bracket all of your images whether you want it to or not.

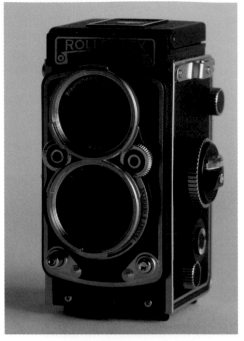

4.9 An image bracketed at 0 EV.

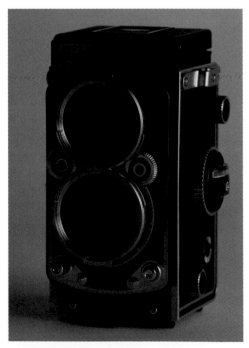

4.8 An image bracketed at -1 EV.

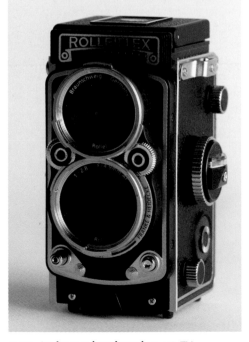

4.10 An image bracketed at +1 EV.

In addition to helping ensure that you got the correct exposure, you can also use different elements from the exposures and combine them using image-editing software to give you a final image that has a wider tonal range than is possible for your image sensor to capture (HDR).

Understanding Depth of Field

Depth of field is the distance range in a photograph in which all included portions of an image are at least acceptably sharp. It is heavily affected by aperture, but how far your camera is from the subject can also have an effect.

If you focus your lens on a certain point, everything that lies on the horizontal plane of that same distance is also in focus. This means that everything in front of the point and everything behind it is technically not in focus. Because our eyes aren't acute enough to discern the minor blur that occurs directly in front of and directly behind the point of focus, it still appears sharp to us. This is known as the zone of acceptable sharpness, which we call depth of field.

✦ **Shallow depth of field.** This results in an image where the subject is in sharp focus, but the background has a soft blur. You often see it used in portraits. Using a wide aperture, such as f/2.8, results in a subject that is sharp with a softer background. Using a shallow depth of field is a great way to get rid of distracting elements in the background of an image.

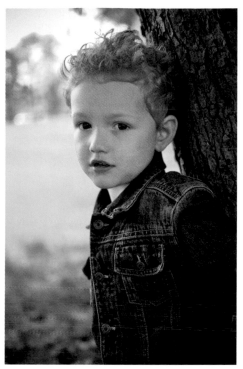

4.11 An image with a shallow depth of field has only the main subject in focus.

✦ **Deep depth of field.** This results in an image that is reasonably sharp from the foreground to the background. Using a narrow aperture, such as f/11, is an ideal way to keep photographs of landscapes or groups in focus throughout.

A factor to consider when working with depth of field is your distance from the subject. The farther you are from the subject you are focusing on, the greater the depth of field in your photograph.

For example, if you stand in your front yard to take a photo of a tree a block away, it has a deep depth of field with the tree, background, and foreground all in relatively sharp focus. If you stand in the same spot

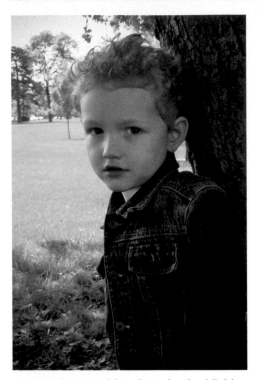

4.12 An image with a deep depth of field has most of the image in focus.

Photography, like any artistic discipline, has general rules. Actually, although they are called rules, they are really nothing more than guidelines. Some photographers — notably Ansel Adams, who was quoted as saying, "The so-called rules of photographic composition are, in my opinion, invalid, irrelevant, and immaterial" — claim to have eschewed the rules of composition. However, when you look at Adams's photographs, they follow the rules perfectly in most cases.

Another famous photographer, Edward Weston, said, "Consulting the rules of composition before taking a photograph is like consulting the laws of gravity before going for a walk." Again, as with Adams, when you look at Weston's photographs, they tend to follow these very rules.

This isn't to say that you need to follow all of the rules every time you take a photograph. As I said, these are really just general guidelines that, when followed, can make your images more powerful and interesting.

and take a picture of your dog standing just several feet away, your dog is in focus, but that tree a block away is just a blur of color.

> **Tip** *Remember, to get a deep depth of field, use a higher aperture number; to get a shallow depth of field, use a smaller aperture number.*

In fact, when you're starting out in photography, you should pay attention to the rules of composition. Eventually, you become accustomed to following these guidelines, and they become second nature. At that point, you no longer need to consult the rules of composition; you just inherently follow them.

Rules of Composition

Whether you are well versed in the rules of composition or you are coming in cold, this section is intended as both a refresher course and a general outline of some of the most commonly used rules of composition.

Keep it simple

Simplicity is arguably the most important rule in creating a good image. In most cases, you want to be sure the viewer can identify what the intended subject of your photograph is. When you have too many competing elements in your image, it can be hard for the viewer to decide what to focus on.

One of the most commonly used techniques for achieving simplicity in images is to frame a single subject against a plain backdrop. Another popular technique is using a shallow depth of field to isolate the subject from a background that may be busy. By causing the background to go out of focus, the subject stands out better.

Sometimes changing your perspective to the subject is all you need to do to remove a distracting element from your image. A good tip is to try walking around and shooting the same subject from different angles.

Simplicity in an image can speak volumes. Try to concentrate on removing any unnecessary elements to achieve simplicity.

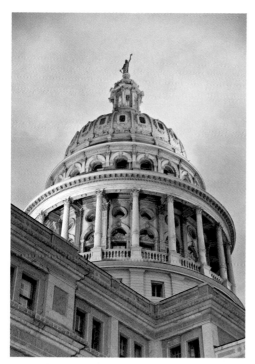

4.13 There's no question as to what the subject is in this photograph.

Rule of Thirds

Often times, beginning photographers are likely to take the main subject of the photograph and stick it right in the middle of the frame. This seems to make sense, and it can often work pretty well for snapshots.

However, your goal is to create more interesting and dynamic images, and so it often works better to put the main subject of the image a little off-center. But placing the subject off-center in a random position also rarely works to make a good composition. Fortunately, we have what is known as the *Rule of Thirds.*

The Rule of Thirds is a compositional guideline that has been in use for hundreds of years, and famous artists throughout the centuries have followed it. With the Rule of Thirds, you divide the image into nine equal parts using two equally spaced horizontal and vertical lines, like a tic-tac-toe pattern. You want to center the main subject of the image at an intersection, as was illustrated in figure 4.15. The subject doesn't necessarily have to be right on the intersection of the line, but merely close enough to it to take advantage of the Rule of Thirds.

Another way to use the Rule of Thirds is to place the subject in the center of the frame, but at the top or bottom third of the frame, as illustrated in figure 4.16.

This part of the rule is especially useful when photographing landscapes. You can place the horizon on or near the top or bottom line, but you almost never want to place it in the middle.

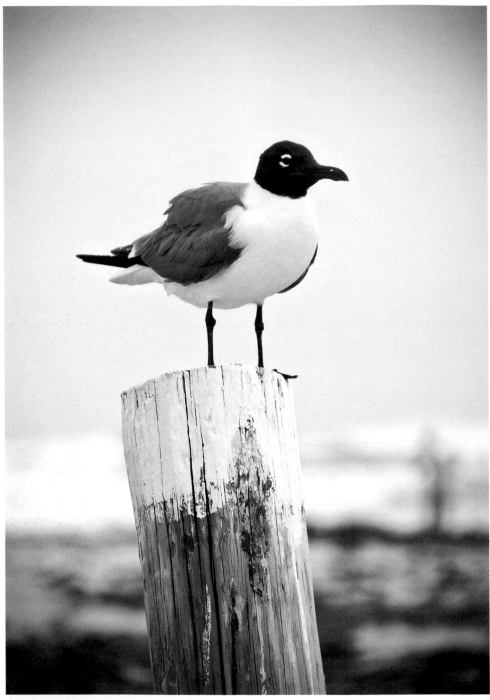

4.14 Getting down and shooting this seagull from a lower angle allowed me to place the sky behind him. Shooting the bird from up high would have placed the distracting elements of the beach behind the main subject of the photo.

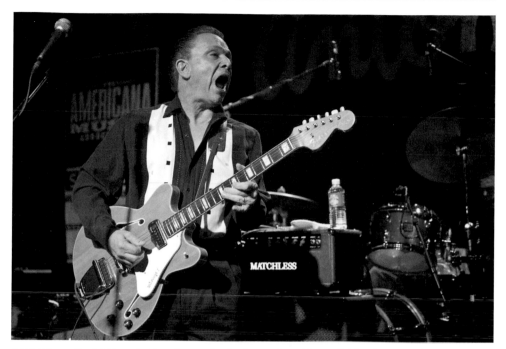

4.15 The guitarist Jimmie Vaughan, who is the main subject of this photograph, is placed to the left of the frame according to the Rule of Thirds.

Notice in figure 4.17 that the mountain range is covering the bottom third of the entire frame. Of course, there are always exceptions, and so if you think that the subject might look better in the middle, by all means give it a shot.

It never hurts to experiment, and it's better to have tried a shot and failed than not to have tried it at all.

When using the Rule of Thirds with a moving subject, you want to be sure to keep most of the frame in front of the subject to present the illusion that the subject has someplace to go within the frame. You can see the difference the framing makes in figures 4.18 and 4.19.

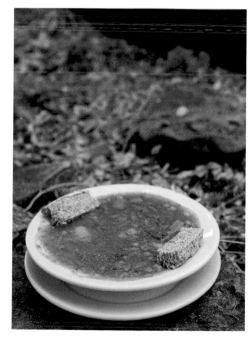

4.16 In this image, the subject is in the center of the frame, but in the bottom third.

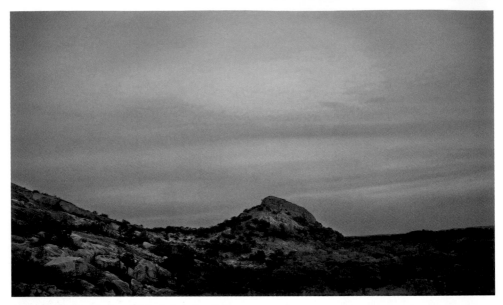

4.17 Using the Rule of Thirds in a landscape.

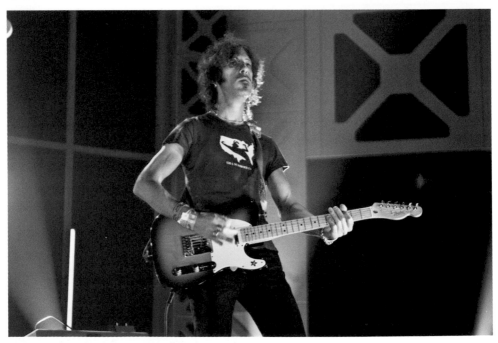

4.18 Placing the guitarist directly in the middle of the frame results in a nice picture.

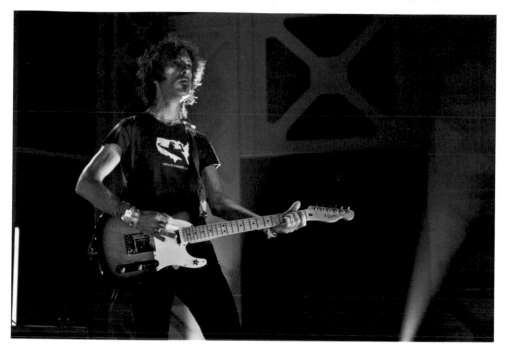

4.19 Recomposing to place the guitarist toward the left part of the frame results in a more dramatic image.

Leading lines and S-curves

Another good way to add drama to an image is to use a *leading line* to draw the viewer's eye through the picture. A leading line is an element in a composition that leads the eye toward the subject. A leading line can be a lot of different things: a road, a sidewalk, railroad tracks, buildings, or columns, to name a few.

In general, you want your leading line to go in a specific direction. Most commonly, a leading line leads the eye from one corner of the picture to another. A good rule to follow is to have your line go from the bottom-left corner toward the top right.

You can also use leading lines that go from the bottom of the image to the top, and vice versa. Often, leading lines heading in this direction lead to a vanishing point. A vanishing point is the point at which parallel lines appear to converge and disappear. Figure 4.20 shows a leading line ending in a vanishing point.

Depending on the subject matter, a variety of directions for leading lines can work equally well.

Another nice way to use a leading line is with an *S-curve.* An S-curve is exactly what it sounds like: It resembles the letter S. The S-curve draws the viewer's eye up from the bottom of the image, through the middle, over to the corner, and back to the other side again.

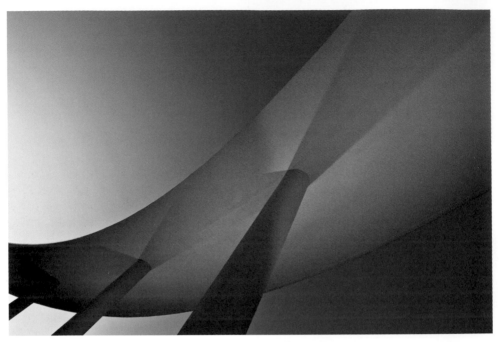

4.20 A leading line draws the viewer's eye through the image.

Helpful hints

Along with the major rules of composition, there are all sorts of other useful guidelines. Here are just a few that I've found most helpful:

✦ **Frame the subject.** Use elements of the foreground to make a frame around the subject to keep the viewer's eye from wandering.

✦ **Avoid having the subject looking directly out of the side of the frame he or she is closest to.** Having the subject looking out of the photograph can be distracting to the viewer. For example, if your subject is on the left side of the composition, having him or her face the right is better, and vice versa.

✦ **Avoid mergers.** A *merger* occurs when an element from the background appears to be a part of the subject, like the snapshot of granny at the park that looks like she has a tree growing out of the top of her head.

✦ **Try not to cut through the joint of a limb.** When composing or cropping your picture, it's best not to end the frame on a joint, such as an elbow or a knee. This can be unsettling to the viewer.

✦ **Avoid having bright spots or unnecessary details near the edge.** Having anything bright or detailed near the edge of the frame draws the viewer's eye away from the subject and out of the image.

✦ **Avoid placing the horizon or strong horizontal or vertical lines in the center of the composition.** This cuts the image in half and makes it hard for the viewer to decide which half of the image is important.

✦ **Separate the subject from the background.** Make sure the background doesn't have colors or textures similar to the subject. If necessary, try shooting from different angles, or use a shallow depth of field to achieve separation.

✦ **Fill the frame.** Try to make the subject the most dominant part of the image. Avoid having a lot of empty space around the subject unless it's essential to making the photograph work.

✦ **Use odd numbers.** When photographing multiple subjects, odd numbers seem to work best.

These are just a few of the hundreds of guidelines that exist. Remember, these are not inflexible rules, just simple pointers that can help you create interesting and amazing images.

Selecting and Using Lenses

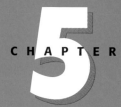

The lens that you put on your camera is almost as important as the camera body. Some may argue that the lens is more important than the actual camera. There are many different types of lenses, from ultrawide-angle lenses to super-telephoto lenses. The lens that you use depends on the subject you're photographing, as well as how you want the subject to appear in your images. The different types of lenses all have an impact on the way the subject looks to the viewer.

Although your D5000 may have come with a kit lens — the 18-55mm f/3.5-5.6G VR — one advantage to owning a digital SLR camera is the ability to change out lenses to fit the specific photographic style or scene that you want to capture. After a while, you may find that the kit lens doesn't meet your needs and you want to upgrade. Nikon dSLR owners have quite a few lenses from which to choose, all of which benefit from Nikon's expertise in the field of lens manufacturing.

One of the great things about photography is that through your lens choice, you can show things in a way that the human eye can't perceive. The human eye is basically a fixed focal-length lens. We can only see a certain set angular distance. This is called our *field of view* (or angle of view). Our eyes have about the same field of view as a 35mm lens on a DX-format Nikon dSLR camera (such as the D5000). Changing the focal length of your lens, whether by switching lenses or zooming, changes the field of view, allowing the camera to "see" more or less of the scene that you're photographing. Changing the focal length of the lens allows you to change the perspective of your images. In the following sections, I discuss the different types of lenses and how they can influence the subjects that you're photographing.

In This Chapter

Kit Lenses

Understanding zoom lenses

Understanding prime lenses

Wide-angle and ultrawide-angle lenses

Standard or midrange zoom lenses

Telephoto lenses

Special-purpose lenses

Using Vibration reduction lenses

Third-party lenses

If you've decided to upgrade your kit lens — or you just want to add to your lens collection — there are literally hundreds of options to choose from. You have a lot to consider when purchasing a lens, whether it's a zoom or prime lens, a wide-angle or telephoto lens, or any of the numerous other options. The goal of this chapter is to give you a head start on knowing what kind of lens you want before you actually start looking.

Kit Lenses

The Nikon D5000 comes paired with Nikon's 18-55mm f/3.5-5.6G VR AF-S DX lens that was first offered coupled with the D60. This lens covers the most commonly used focal lengths for everyday photography. The 18mm setting covers the wide-angle range, and zooming all the way out to 55mm gives you a moderate telephoto setting, allowing you to get close-up photos of subjects that may not be very close. Nikon also offers a D5000 kit with two lenses, the 18-55mm and a 55-200mm f/4-5.6 AF-S DX VR. The 55-200mm lens allows you a good medium-to-long telephoto range to really pull those far-off subjects closer.

This kit lens offers Nikon's Vibration Reduction (VR) feature. This feature allows you to hand-hold the camera at slower shutter speeds without worrying about image blur that can be caused by camera shake.

This lens has received many good reviews. The optics give you sharp images with good contrast when stopped down a bit. However, when shooting wide open, the images can appear a little soft around the corners.

Although Nikon offers many very high-quality professional lenses, the D5000 kit lenses are very good performers for their

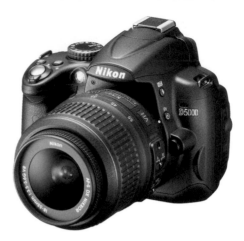

Image courtesy of Nikon, Inc.
5.1 The D5000 with the 18-55mm kit lens.

price range and they offer some advantages when paired with the D5000 that even some of Nikon's more-expensive lenses don't. These advantages include the following:

✦ **Low cost.** The 18-55mm VR lens costs less than $200, while the 55-200mm VR lens comes in at around $250. The 18-200mm VR lens retails for around $750. Buying both the 18-55mm and 55-200mm VR lenses can save you around $300!

✦ **Superior image quality.** These lenses offer very high quality for the price. They offer aspherical lens elements, which help to eliminate distortion, and Nikon's Super Integrated Coating on the lens helps to ensure accurate color and reduce lens flare. These lenses have been praised by professional and amateur reviewers alike. They are uncommonly sharp for a lens in this price range.

✦ **Compact size.** Being designed specifically for dSLR cameras, these lenses are small in size and super-light. They are great lenses for everyday use or long trips where you don't want a lot of gear weighing you down.

✦ **VR.** Vibration Reduction is a very handy feature, especially when working in low-light situations or when using a long focal length. It can allow you to handhold your camera at slower shutter speeds than you can with standard lenses.

Deciphering Nikon's lens codes

When shopping for lenses, you may notice all sorts of letter designations in the lens name. For example, the kit lens is the AF-S DX Nikkor 18-105mm f/3.5-5.6G ED VR. So, what do all those letters mean? Here's a simple list to help you decipher them:

✦ **AI/AIS.** These are auto-indexing lenses that automatically adjust the aperture diaphragm down when the Shutter Release button is pressed. All lenses, including AF lenses, made after 1977 are auto-indexing, but when referring to AI lenses, most people generally mean the older MF lenses.

✦ **E.** These lenses were Nikon's budget series lenses, made to go with the lower-end film cameras, such as the EM, FG, and FG-20. Although these lenses are compact and are often constructed with plastic parts, some of them, especially the 50mm f/1.8, are of quite good quality. These lenses are also manual focus only.

✦ **D.** Lenses with this designation convey distance information to the camera to aid in metering for exposure and flash.

✦ **G.** These are newer lenses that lack a manually adjustable aperture ring. You must set the aperture on the camera body.

✦ **AF, AF-D, AF-I, and AF-S.** All these lens codes denote that the lens is an autofocus (AF) lens. The AF-D represents a distance encoder for distance information, the AF-I indicates an internal focusing motor type, and the AF-S indicates an internal Silent Wave Motor.

✦ **AI-P.** This designates a Manual focus lens that has a CPU chip.

✦ **DX.** This lets you know the lens was optimized for use with Nikon's DX-format sensor.

✦ **VR.** This code denotes that the lens is equipped with Nikon's Vibration Reduction image stabilization system.

✦ **ED.** This indicates that some of the glass in the lens is Nikon's Extra-Low Dispersion glass, which means the lens is less prone to lens flare and chromatic aberrations.

✦ **Micro-Nikkor.** Even though they're labeled as micro, these are Nikon's macro lenses.

✦ **IF.** IF stands for Internal Focus. The focusing mechanism is inside the lens, so the front of the lens doesn't rotate when focusing. This feature is useful when you don't want the front of the lens element to move — for example, when you use a polarizing filter. The internal focus mechanism also allows for faster focusing.

✦ **DC.** DC stands for Defocus Control. Nikon only offers a couple of lenses with this designation. These lenses make the out-of-focus areas in the image appear softer by using special lens elements to add spherical aberration. The parts of the image that are in focus aren't affected. Currently, the only Nikon lenses with this feature are the 135mm and the 105mm f/2. Both of these are considered portrait lenses.

✦ **N.** On some of Nikon's newest professional lenses, you may see a large, golden N. This means that the lens has Nikon's Nano Crystal Coating, which is designed to reduce flare and ghosting.

Nikon lens compatibility

One thing you need to remember before purchasing a lens for your D5000 is that only Nikon AF-S (or the third-party equivalent) lenses autofocus with the D5000. Until recently, all Nikon AF lenses were focused by a screw-type motor in the camera body. Most high-level cameras have this focus motor, but some models leave it out to make the cameras more compact; the D5000 is one such model.

AF-S lenses are focused by an internal mechanism in the lens, which uses ultrasonic vibrations to drive the focus motor. This eliminates the need for an external motor to move the lens elements and also makes for very quiet and fast autofocus. Previous to the AF-S lens, Nikon offered AF-I lenses that worked on the same principle. These lenses also autofocus with the D5000.

Although AF-S lenses such as the kit lens are the only lenses that offer full AF functionality, almost any Nikon lens made since 1977 can mount to the camera and offers some, but not all, available features.

Any AF-D or AF-G lens allows all functions (except AF, of course). Any lens that doesn't have a CPU (non-CPU) does not autofocus, nor does the exposure meter work. Metering has to be done by using an external light meter or estimation and you have to shoot in Manual exposure mode. All non-CPU lenses are manual focus lenses, but some manual focus lenses have a CPU; these lenses are known as AI-P. With AI-P lenses, all features are available, except AF and 3D Color Matrix metering.

Understanding Zoom Lenses

A zoom lens, such as the AF-S Nikkor 14-24mm, is a lens that has multiple optical elements that move within the lens body; this allows the lens to change focal length, and therefore field of view, which is how much of the scene you can see at any given focal length.

One of the main advantages of the zoom lens is its versatility. You can attach one lens to your camera and use it in a wide variety of situations. Gone is the need for constantly changing out lenses, which reduces the exposure of your camera's image sensor to dust and debris.

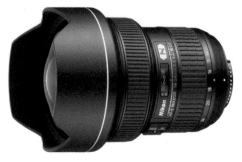

5.2 The AF-S Nikkor 14-24mm f/2.8.

There are a few things to consider when buying zoom lenses (or upgrading from one you already have).

Variable aperture

One of the major issues when buying a consumer-level lens such as the 18-55mm VR lens is that it has a variable aperture, which means that as you zoom in on something, the aperture of the lens gets smaller, allowing less light to reach the sensor, and causing the need for a slower shutter speed or higher ISO setting. In daylight or brightly lit situations, this may not be a factor, but when shooting in low light, this can be a drawback. Although the VR feature helps when shooting relatively still subjects, moving subjects in low light are blurred.

If you do a lot of low-light shooting of moving subjects, such as concert photography, you may want to look into getting a zoom lens with a wider aperture such as f/2.8. These are fast aperture pro lenses and usually cost quite a bit more than your standard consumer zoom lens. The lens I use most when photographing action in low light is the Nikkor 28-70mm f/2.8; this lens allows me to use an ISO of about 800 (keeping the noise levels low) and relatively fast shutter speeds to freeze the motion of the subject. To keep the same shutter speed while using the 18-55mm VR, you would need to boost your ISO up to 3200, which can add quite a bit of noise to your image. What it boils down to is how much action shooting you may do in low light.

Depth of field

Another consideration when buying a zoom lens is depth of field. For example, the 18-55mm lens gives you more depth of field at all focal lengths than a lens with a wider aperture. If you are shooting landscapes, this may not be a problem, but if you are getting into portrait photography, you may want a shallower depth of field; therefore, a lens with a wider aperture is probably what you want.

Quality

In order to make consumer lenses like the 18-55mm VR and the 55-200mm VR affordable, Nikon makes them mostly out of a composite plastic. Although the build quality is pretty good, the higher-end lenses have metal lens mounts and some have metal alloy lens bodies. This makes them a lot more durable in the long run, especially if you are rough on your gear like I sometimes am. Conversely, the plastic bodies of the consumer lenses are much smaller and lighter than their pro-level counterparts. This is a great feature when traveling or if you want to pack light. If I'm going on a trip, more often than not, I'll just grab my D60 kit and go. It's more compact and much lighter than my other cameras and lenses and I appreciate the small size.

The range of the zoom lens has vastly improved over the years. Nikon makes an 18-200mm zoom lens, which is an amazing range that almost makes it unnecessary to ever take your lens off. Of course, a zoom range like this comes with a few drawbacks. For example, the lens has a maximum aperture of f/3.5 at the 18mm setting (which is not bad) but a maximum of f/5.6 at the 200mm setting (which is relatively slow). Nikon makes up for the slow aperture by adding Vibration Reduction, which allows you to handhold the camera at much slower shutter speeds.

Understanding Prime Lenses

Before zoom lenses were available, the only option a photographer had was using a prime lens, which is also called a fixed-focal-length lens. Because each lens is fixed at a certain focal length, when the photographer wants to change the angle of view, he has to either physically move farther away from or closer to the subject, or swap out the lens with one that has a focal length more suited to the range.

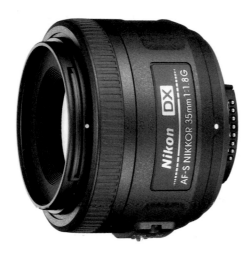

Image courtesy of Nikon, Inc.
5.3 The Nikkor 35mm f/1.8G AF-S fixed-focal-length prime lens.

The most important features of the prime lens are that they offer a faster maximum aperture, they are generally far lighter, and they cost much less. The standard prime lenses aren't very long, so the maximum aperture can be faster than with zoom lenses. Prime lenses in standard focal lengths also require fewer lens elements and moving parts, so the weight can be kept down considerably; and because there are

fewer elements, the overall cost of production is less; therefore, you pay less.

One might say, "Well, if I can buy one zoom lens that encompasses the same range as four or five prime lenses, then why bother with prime lenses?" While this may sound logical, there are a lot of reasons why you might choose a prime lens over a zoom lens.

In the past, prime lenses were far superior to zoom lenses. While this is no longer the case, prime lenses can still offer some advantages over zoom lenses. For example, prime lenses don't require as many lens elements (pieces of glass) as zoom lenses do, and this means that prime lenses are almost always sharper than zoom lenses. The differences in optical quality are not as noticeable as they were in the past, but with digital camera resolutions getting higher, the differences are definitely becoming more noticeable.

As discussed earlier in the chapter, the Nikon D5000 can only autofocus when an AF-S lens is attached to the camera. At this time, Nikon only offers a limited number of AF-S prime lenses and most of them tend to be somewhat expensive and have longer focal lengths. Currently, the AF-S prime lens lineup consists of the 35mm f/1.8, 50mm f/1.4, 60mm f/2.8 macro, and 105mm f/2.8 VR macro. For telephoto primes, you have the 200mm, 300mm, 400mm, 500mm, and 600mm telephoto lenses.

Wide-angle and Ultrawide-angle Lenses

Wide-angle lenses, as the name implies, provide a very wide angle of view of the scene you're photographing. Wide-angle lenses are great for photographing a variety of subjects, but they're really excellent for subjects such as landscapes and group portraits where you need to capture a wide area of view.

The focal-length range of wide-angle lenses starts out at about 10mm (ultrawide) and extends to about 24mm (wide angle). Most wide-angle lenses on the market today are zoom lenses, although there are quite a few prime lenses available. Wide-angle lenses are generally *rectilinear,* meaning that there are lens elements built into the lens to correct the distortion that's common with wide-angle lenses; this way, the lines near the edges of the frame appear straight. Fisheye lenses, which are also a type of wide-angle lens, are *curvilinear;* the lens elements aren't corrected, resulting in severe optical distortion. I discuss fisheye lenses later in this chapter.

In recent years, lens technology has grown by leaps and bounds, making high-quality ultrawide-angle lenses affordable. In the past, ultrawide-angle lenses were rare, prohibitively expensive, and out of reach for most amateur photographers. These days, it's very easy to find a relatively inexpensive ultrawide-angle lens. Most wide-angle zoom lenses run the gamut from ultrawide to wide angle. Some of the ones that work with the D5000 include the following:

✦ **Nikkor 10-24mm f/3.5-4.5.** This is Nikon's newest ultrawide DX zoom. The 10-24mm was specifically designed for DX cameras. This lens gives you a very wide field of view, and it's small and well built with little distortion. The AF-S motor allows it to focus perfectly with the D5000.

✦ **Sigma 10-20mm f/5-5.6.** When it comes to third-party lenses, I prefer Sigma lenses. They have superior build quality and their Hyper-Sonic Motor (HSM), which is similar to Nikon's Silent Wave AF-S motor, allows this lens to autofocus with the D5000. This lens is a little less sharp than the Nikon and it has a reduced range on the long end, but it's much cheaper. You may not even miss the longer range at all, as it's most likely covered by one of your other lenses such as the 18-55mm kit lens. It's also slower than most other manufacturers' offerings, but sometimes you must make concessions with your lens choices.

Sigma also offers a 12-24mm lens. It's built like a tank and has an HSM motor. The Sigma is also useable with Nikon FX cameras, which may be something to consider if you're planning to upgrade to FX sometime in the future.

When to use a wide-angle lens

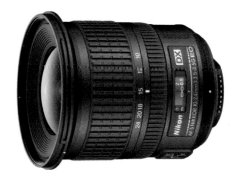

Image courtesy of Nikon, Inc.
5.4 Nikkor 10-24mm f/3.5-4.5.

You can use wide-angle lenses for a broad variety of subjects, and they're great for creating dynamic images with interesting results.

Once you get used to "seeing" the world through a wide-angle lens, you may find that your images start to be more creative, and you may look at your subjects differently. There are many different considerations to think about when you use a wide-angle lens. Here are a few examples:

✦ **More depth of field.** Wide-angle lenses allow you to get more of the scene in focus than you can when you're using a midrange or tele-photo lens at the same aperture and distance from the subject.

✦ **Wider field of view.** Wide-angle lenses allow you to fit more of your subject into your images. The shorter the focal length, the more you can fit in. This can be especially beneficial when you're shooting landscape photos where you want to fit an immense scene into your photo or when you're shooting a large group of people.

✦ **Perspective distortion.** Using wide-angle lenses causes things that are closer to the lens to look disproportionately larger than things that are farther away. You can use perspective distortion to your advantage to emphasize objects in the foreground if you want the subject to stand out in the frame.

✦ **Handholding.** At shorter focal lengths, it's possible to hold the camera steadier than you can at longer focal lengths. At 14mm, it's entirely possible to handhold your camera at 1/15 second without worrying about camera shake.

✦ **Environmental portraits.** Although using a wide-angle lens isn't the best choice for standard close-up portraits, wide-angle lenses work great for environmental portraits where you want to show a person in his or her surroundings.

Wide-angle lenses can also help pull you into a subject. With most wide-angle lenses, you can focus very close. This helps you get right up close and personal with the subject while creating the perspective distortion that wide-angle lenses are known for. Don't be afraid to get close to your subject to make a more dynamic image. The worst wide-angle images are the ones that have a tiny subject in the middle of an empty area.

Understanding limitations

Wide-angle lenses are very distinctive when it comes to the way they portray your images, and they also have some limitations that you may not find in lenses with longer focal lengths. There are also some pitfalls that you need to be aware of when using wide-angle lenses:

✦ **Soft corners.** The most common problem that wide-angle lenses, especially zooms, have is that they soften the images in the corners. This is most prevalent at wide apertures, such as f/2.8 and f/4, and the corners usually sharpen up by f/8 (depending on the lens). This problem is greatest in lower-priced lenses.

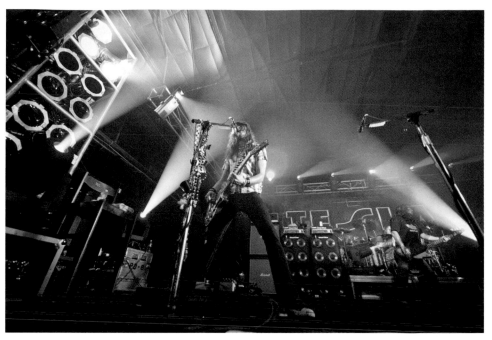

5.5 A shot taken with a wide-angle lens.

✦ **Vignetting**. This is the darkening of the corners in the image. This occurs because the light that's needed to capture such a wide angle of view must come from an oblique angle. When the light comes in at such an angle, the aperture is effectively smaller. The aperture opening no longer appears as a circle but is shaped like a cat's eye. Stopping down the aperture reduces this effect, and reducing the aperture by three stops usually eliminates any vignetting.

✦ **Perspective distortion.** Perspective distortion is a double-edged sword: It can make your images look very interesting or make them look terrible. One of the reasons that a wide-angle lens isn't recommended for close-up portraits is that it distorts the face, making the nose look too big and the ears too small. This can make for a very unflattering portrait.

✦ **Barrel distortion.** Wide-angle lenses, even rectilinear lenses, are often plagued with this specific type of distortion, which causes straight lines outside the image center to appear to bend outward (similar to a barrel). This can be unwanted when doing architectural photography. Fortunately, Adobe Photoshop and other image-editing software allow you to fix this problem relatively easily.

DX Crop Factor

Crop factor is a ratio that describes the size of a camera's imaging area as compared to another format; in the case of SLR cameras, the reference format is 35mm film.

SLR camera lenses were designed around the 35mm film format. Photographers use lenses of a certain focal length to provide a specific field of view. The field of view, also called the angle of view, is the amount of the scene that's captured in an image. This is usually described in degrees. For example, when you use a 16mm lens on a 35mm camera, it captures almost 180 degrees of the scene horizontally, which is quite a bit. Conversely, when you use a 300mm focal length, the field of view is reduced to a mere 6.5 degrees horizontally, which is a very small part of the scene. The field of view is consistent from camera to camera because all SLRs use 35mm film, which has an image area of 24mmx36mm.

With the advent of digital SLRs, because the sensors are more expensive to manufacture, the sensor was made smaller than a frame of 35mm film to keep costs down. This sensor size was called APS-C or, in Nikon terms, the DX-format. The lenses that are used with DX-format dSLRs have the same focal length they've always had, but because the sensor doesn't have the same amount of area as the film, the field of view is effectively decreased. This causes the lens to provide the field of view of a longer focal lens when compared to 35mm film images.

Fortunately, the DX sensors are a uniform size, thereby supplying consumers with a standard to determine how much the field of view is reduced on a DX-format dSLR with any lens. The digital sensors in Nikon DX cameras have a 1.5x crop factor, which means that to determine the equivalent focal length of a 35mm or FX camera, you simply have to multiply the focal length of the lens by 1.5. Therefore, a 28mm lens provides an angle of coverage similar to a 42mm lens, a 50mm is equivalent to a 75mm, and so on.

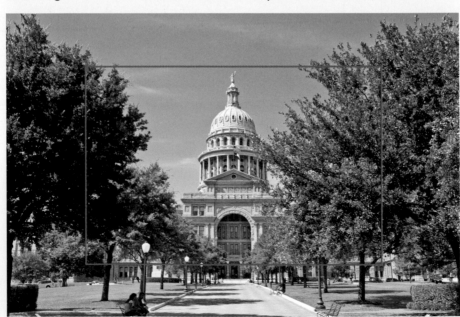

This image was shot with a 28mm lens on a D700 FX camera. Inside the red square is the amount of the scene that would be captured with the same lens on a DX camera like the D5000.

Early on, when dSLRs were first introduced, all lenses were based on 35mm film. The crop factor effectively reduced the coverage of these lenses, causing ultrawide-angle lenses to act like wide-angle lenses, wide-angle lenses to perform like normal lenses, normal lenses to provide the same coverage as short telephotos, and so on. Nikon created specific lenses for dSLRs with digital sensors. These lenses are known as DX-format lenses. The focal length of these lenses was shortened to fill the gap to allow true super-wide-angle lenses. These DX-format lenses were also redesigned to cast a smaller image inside the camera so that the lenses could actually be made smaller and use less glass than conventional lenses. The byproduct of designing a lens to project an image circle to a smaller sensor is that these same lenses can't effectively be used with FX-format and can't be used at all with 35mm film cameras (without severe vignetting) because the image won't completely fill an area the size of the film sensor. FX cameras can use the DX, but the image is cropped in the camera, resulting in an image with a much lower resolution.

There is an upside to this crop factor. Lenses with longer focal lengths now provide a bit of extra reach. A lens set at 200mm now provides the same amount of coverage as a 300mm lens, which can offer a great advantage for sports and wildlife photography or when you simply can't get close enough to your subject.

Standard or Midrange Zoom Lenses

Standard, or midrange, zoom lenses fall in the middle of the focal-length scale. Zoom lenses of this type usually start at a moderately wide angle of around 16–18mm and zoom in to a short telephoto range. These lenses work great for most general photography applications and can be used successfully for everything from architectural to portrait photography. Basically, this type of lens covers the most useful focal lengths and will probably spend the most time on your camera. The 18-55mm kit lens falls into this range.

Here are some of the options for midrange lenses:

✦ **Nikkor 17-55mm f/2.8.** This is Nikon's top-of-the-line standard DX zoom lens. It's a professional lens that has a fast aperture of f/2.8 over the whole zoom range and is extremely sharp at all focal lengths and apertures. The build quality on this lens is excellent, as most of Nikon's pro lenses are. The 17-55mm has Nikon's super-quiet and fast-focusing Silent Wave Motor as well as ED glass elements to reduce chromatic aberration. This lens is top-notch all around and is worth every penny of the price tag.

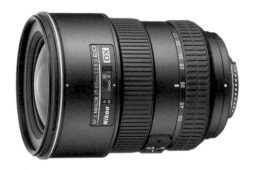

Image courtesy of Nikon, Inc.

5.6 Nikkor 17-55mm f/2.8.

✦ **Sigma 17-35mm f/2.8-4.** This lens is a low-cost alternative to the Nikon 17-55mm that has a variable aperture of f/2.8 on the wide end and f/4 on the long end. You can get this lens for about one-quarter of the cost of the Nikon 17-55mm and it's much smaller and lighter. It's got Sigma's HSM, and so it can autofocus with the D5000. It's a great walking-around lens for standard shots. This lens also works with FX cameras for future compatibility.

There are a few prime lenses that fit into this category: the 28mm, 30mm, and 35mm. These lenses are considered "normal" lenses for DX cameras, in that they approximate the normal field of view of the human eye. They are great all-around lenses. They come with apertures of f/2.8 or faster and can be found for less than $400, with the exception of the rare Nikon 28mm f/1.4, which can run up to $5,000 in new condition (if you can find it). Unfortunately, with the exception of the Nikon 35mm f/1.8, these lenses need to be focused manually with the D5000, although Sigma offers a highly regarded 30mm f/1.4 with an HSM motor at a reasonable price.

Telephoto Lenses

Telephoto lenses have very long focal lengths and are used to get closer to distant subjects. They provide a very narrow field of view and are handy when you're trying to focus on the details of a subject. Telephoto lenses have a much shallower depth of field than wide-angle and midrange lenses, and you can use them effectively to blur out background details to isolate a subject.

Telephoto lenses are commonly used for sports and wildlife photography. The shallow depth of field also makes them one of the top choices for photographing portraits.

As with wide-angle lenses, telephoto lenses also have their quirks, such as perspective distortion. As you may have guessed, telephoto perspective distortion is the opposite

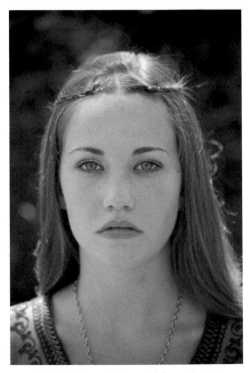

5.7 Portrait shot with a telephoto lens.

of the wide-angle variety. Because everything in the photo is so far away with a telephoto lens, the lens tends to compress the image. Compression causes the background to look too close to the foreground. Of course, you can use this effect creatively. For example, compression can flatten out the features of a model, resulting in a pleasing effect. Compression is another reason why photographers often use a telephoto lens for portrait photography.

A standard telephoto zoom lens usually has a range of about 70–200mm. If you want to zoom in close to a subject that's very far away, you may need an even longer lens. These super-telephoto lenses can act like telescopes, really bringing the subject in close. They range from about 300mm up to about 800mm. Almost all super-telephoto lenses are prime lenses, and they're very heavy, bulky, and expensive. Some of these lenses are a little slower than your normal high-end telephoto zoom lens — such as the 70-200mm f/2.8G — and often have a maximum aperture of f/4 or smaller.

There are quite a few telephoto prime lenses available. Most of them, especially the longer ones (105mm and longer), are pretty expensive, although you can sometimes find some older Nikon primes that are discontinued or used — and at decent prices. One of these lenses is the 300mm f/4. A couple of relatively inexpensive telephoto primes are in the shorter range of 50–85mm. The 50mm is considered a normal lens for FX format, but the DX format makes this lens a 75mm equivalent, landing it squarely in the short telephoto range for use with the D5000.

Nikon has recently released an AF-S version of the 50mm f/1.4. This is a G lens with the Silent Wave Motor. It's fast focusing and sharp.

Super-Zooms

Most lens manufacturers, Nikon included, offer what's commonly termed a *super-zoom,* or sometimes called a *hyper-zoom.* Super-zooms are lenses that encompass a very wide focal length, from wide angle to telephoto. The most popular of the super-zooms is the Nikon 18-200mm f/3.5-5.6 VR, shown here.

These lenses allow you to have a huge focal-length range that you can use in a wide variety of shooting situations without having to switch out lenses. This can come in handy if, for example, you are photographing a landscape scene by using a wide-angle setting, and lo and behold, Bigfoot appears on the horizon. You can quickly zoom in with the super-telephoto setting and get a good close-up shot without having to fumble around in your camera bag to grab a telephoto and switch out lenses, possibly causing you to miss the shot of a lifetime.

Of course, there's no free lunch, and these super-zooms come with a price (figuratively and literally). In order to achieve the great ranges in focal length, some concessions must be made with regard to image quality. These lenses are usually less sharp than lenses with a shorter zoom range and are more often plagued with optical distortions and chromatic aberration. Super-zooms often show pronounced barrel distortion at the wide end and can have moderate to severe pincushion distortion at the long end of the range. Luckily, these types of distortions can be fixed in Adobe Photoshop or other image-editing software.

Continued

Continued

Another caveat to using these lenses is that they generally have appreciably smaller maximum apertures than zoom lenses with shorter ranges. This can be a problem, especially because larger apertures are generally needed at the long end to keep a high enough shutter speed to avoid blurring from camera shake when handholding. Of course, some manufacturers include some sort of Vibration Reduction feature to help control this problem.

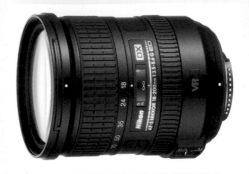

Some popular super-zooms include the Nikon 18-200mm f/3.5-5.6 VR (mentioned earlier), the Sigma 18-200mm f/3.5-6.3 with Optical Stabilization, and the Tamron 18-200mm f/3.5-5.6. There are also a few super-zoom super-telephoto lenses, including the Nikon 80-400mm and the Sigma 50-500mm.

Here are some of the most common telephoto lenses:

✦ **Nikkor 70-200mm f/2.8 VR.** This is Nikon's top-of-the-line standard telephoto lens. The VR makes this lens useful when photographing far-off subjects handheld. This is a great lens for sports, portraits, and wildlife photography.

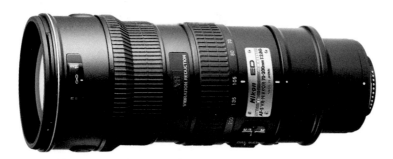

Image courtesy of Nikon, Inc.
5.8 Nikkor 70-200mm f/2.8 VR.

Zoom Lenses versus Prime Lenses

This debate has been a hot topic for many years. More recently, in the past eight years or so, lens technology has grown by leaps and bounds, and zoom lenses are just about as sharp as primes or, in the case of the Nikkor 14-24mm f/2.8, even sharper than most primes. Some photographers prefer primes, and some prefer zooms. It's largely a personal choice, and there are some things to consider.

One of the main advantages of the zoom lens is its versatility. You can attach one lens to your camera and use it in a wide variety of situations. Gone is the need for constantly changing out lenses, which is a very good feature because every time you take the lens off your camera, the sensor is vulnerable to dust and debris.

Although today's zoom lenses can be just as sharp as a prime lens, you do have to pay for this quality. A $150 zoom lens isn't going to give you nearly the same quality as a $1,500 zoom lens. These days, you can easily find a fast zoom lens — one with an aperture of at least f/2.8. Because you can easily change the ISO on a digital camera and the noise created from using a high ISO is decreasing, a fast zoom lens isn't a complete necessity. I prefer a zoom lens with a wider aperture — not so much for the speed of the lens but for the option of being able to achieve a shallower depth of field, which is very important in shooting portraits.

Prime lenses still offer some advantages over zoom lenses. For example, prime lenses don't require as many lens elements as zoom lenses do, and this means prime lenses are sometimes sharper than zoom lenses. The differences in optical quality aren't as noticeable as they were in the past, but with digital camera resolutions getting higher, the differences are definitely becoming more noticeable.

The most important features of the prime lenses are that they can have a faster maximum aperture, they are far lighter, and they cost much less. The standard prime lenses aren't very long, so the maximum aperture can be faster than with zoom lenses. Standard primes also require fewer lens elements and moving parts, so the weight can be kept down considerably. And because there are fewer elements, the overall cost of production is less; therefore, you pay less.

✦ **Nikkor 55-200mm f/4-5.6 VR.** This is one of Nikon's most affordable lenses and is actually a pretty strong performer for its price range. The 55-200mm VR is quite sharp and only has mild barrel distortion issues.

✦ **Nikkor 80-200mm f/2.8D.** This is a great, affordable alternative to the 70-200mm VR lens. This lens is sharp and has a fast, constant f/2.8 aperture.

✦ **Nikkor 80-400mm f/4.5-5.6 VR.** This is a high-power, VR image stabilization zoom lens that gives you quite a bit of reach. Its very versatile zoom range makes it especially useful for wildlife photography where the subject is very far away. As with most lenses with a very broad focal-length range, you make concessions with fast apertures and a moderately lower image quality when compared to the 70-200mm or 80-200mm f/2.8 lenses.

Special-Purpose Lenses

Nikon has a few options when it comes to lenses that are designed specifically to handle a certain task. Nikon's special-purpose lenses are the Perspective Control (PC) and Micro-Nikkor (macro) lenses. It even has a lens that combines both of these features! These lenses, especially the PC lenses, aren't typically designed for everyday use and are pretty specific in their applications.

Micro-Nikkor lenses

A macro lens is a special-purpose lens used in macro and close-up photography. It allows you to have a closer focusing distance than regular lenses, which in turn allows you to get more magnification of your subject, revealing small details that would otherwise be lost. True macro lenses offer a magnification ratio of 1:1; that is, the image projected onto the sensor through the lens is the exact same size as the actual object being photographed. Some lower-priced "macro" lenses offer a 1:2 or even a 1:4 magnification ratio, which is one-half to one-quarter of the size of the original object. Although lens manufacturers refer to these lenses as macro, strictly speaking, they are not.

One major concern with a macro lens is the depth of field. When focusing at such a close distance, the depth of field becomes very shallow; it's often advisable to use a small aperture to maximize your depth of field and ensure everything is in focus. Of course, as with any downside, there's an upside: you can also use the shallow depth of field creatively. For example, you can use it to isolate a detail in a subject.

Macro lenses come in a variety of different focal lengths, and the most common is 60mm. Some macro lenses have substantially longer focal lengths, which allow more distance between the lens and the subject. This comes in handy when the subject needs to be lit with an additional light source. A lens that's very close to the subject while focusing can get in the way of the light source, casting a shadow.

When buying a macro lens, you should consider a few things: How often are you going to use the lens? Can you use it for other purposes? Do you need AF? Because newer dedicated macro lenses can be pricey, you may want to consider some cheaper alternatives.

The first thing you should know is that it's not absolutely necessary to have an AF lens. When shooting very close up, the depth of focus is very small, so all you need to do is move slightly closer or farther away to achieve focus. This makes an AF lens a bit unnecessary. You can find plenty of older Nikon manual focus (MF) macro lenses that are very inexpensive, and the lens quality and sharpness are still superb.

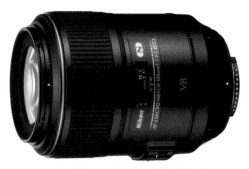

5.9 Nikon 105mm f/2.8G VR macro lens.

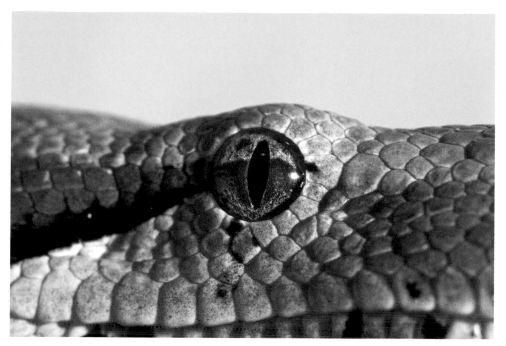

5.10 A shot taken with a macro lens.

Note *Some other manufacturers also make good-quality MF macro lenses. I have a 50mm f/4 Macro-Takumar made for early Pentax screw-mount camera bodies. I bought this lens for next to nothing, and I found an inexpensive adapter that allows it to fit the Nikon F-mount. The great thing about this lens is that it's super-sharp and allows me to focus close enough to get a 4:1 magnification ratio, which is 4x life size.*

Nikon currently offers three different focal-length macro lenses under the Micro-Nikkor designation:

✦ **Nikkor 60mm f/2.8.** Nikon offers two versions of this lens — one with a standard AF drive and one with an AF-S version with the Silent Wave Motor. The AF-S version also has the new Nano Crystal Coat lens coating to help eliminate ghosting and flare.

✦ **Nikkor 105mm f/2.8 VR.** This is a great lens that not only allows you to focus extremely close but also enables you to back off and still get a good close-up shot. This lens is equipped with VR. This can be invaluable with macro photography because it allows you to handhold at slower shutter speeds — a necessity when stopping down to maintain a good depth of field. This lens can also double as a very impressive portrait lens. This is currently the favored lens in my arsenal.

Fisheye lenses

Fisheye lenses are ultrawide-angle lenses that aren't corrected for distortion like standard rectilinear wide-angle lenses. These lenses are known as *curvilinear,* meaning that straight lines in your image, especially near the edge of the frame, are curved. Fisheye lenses have extreme barrel distortion, but that's what makes them fisheye lenses.

Fisheye lenses cover a full 180-degree area, allowing you to see everything that's immediately to the left and right of you in the frame. Special care has to be taken so that you don't get your feet in the frame, as so often happens when you're using a lens with a field of view this extreme.

Fisheye lenses aren't made for everyday shooting, but with their extreme perspective distortion, you can achieve interesting, and sometimes wacky, results. You can also "de-fish" or correct for the extreme fisheye by using image-editing software, such as Adobe Photoshop, Nikon's Capture NX or NX2, and

DxO Optics. The end result of correcting your image is that you get a reduced field of view. This is akin to using a rectilinear wide-angle lens.

Using Vibration Reduction Lenses

Nikon has an impressive list of lenses that offer Vibration Reduction (VR). This technology is used to combat image blur caused by camera shake, especially when you're hand-holding the camera at long focal lengths. The VR function works by detecting the motion of the lens and shifting the internal lens elements. This allows you to shoot up to 3 stops slower than you would normally.

If you're an experienced photographer, you probably know this rule of thumb: To get a reasonably sharp photo when handholding the camera, you should use a shutter speed that corresponds to the reciprocal of the lens' focal length. In simpler terms, when

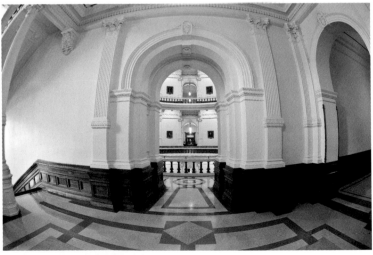

5.11 An image taken with a Nikon 10.5mm fisheye lens.

shooting at a 200mm zoom setting, your shutter speed should be at least 1/200 second. When shooting with a wider setting, such as 28mm, you can safely handhold at around 1/30 second. Of course, this is just a guideline; some people are naturally steadier than others and can get sharp shots at slower speeds. With the VR enabled, you should be able to get a reasonably sharp image at a 200mm setting with a shutter speed of around 1/30 second.

Although the VR feature is good for providing some extra latitude when you're shooting with low light, it's not made to replace a fast shutter speed. To get a good, sharp photo when shooting action, you need to have a fast shutter speed to freeze the action. No matter how good the VR is, nothing can freeze a moving subject but a fast shutter speed.

Another thing to consider with the VR feature is that the lens's motion sensor may overcompensate when you're panning, causing the image to actually be blurrier. So, in situations where you need to pan with the subject, you may need to switch off the VR. The VR function also slows down the AF a bit, so when catching the action is very important, you may want to keep this in mind. However, Nikon's newest lenses have been updated with VR II, which Nikon claims can tell the difference between panning motion and regular side-to-side camera movement.

While VR is a great advancement in lens technology, few things can replace a good exposure and a solid monopod or tripod for a sharp image.

Third-party Lenses

Nikon is by no means the only manufacturer of lenses that fit the D5000. There are quite a few different companies that make lenses that work flawlessly with Nikon cameras. In the past, third-party lenses had a bad reputation of being, at best, cheap knock-offs of the original manufacturers' lenses. This is not the case anymore, as a lot of third-party lens manufacturers have stepped up to the plate and started releasing lenses that rival some of the originals (usually at half the price).

Although you can't beat Nikon's professional lenses, there are many excellent third-party lens choices available to you. The three most prominent third-party lens manufacturers are Sigma, Tokina, and Tamron. Each of these companies makes lenses that cover the entire zoom range.

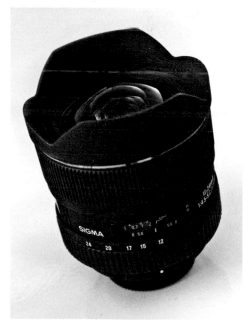

5.12 Sigma 12-24mm f/4-5.6.

Working with Light

The most important factor in photography is light; without it, your camera is rendered useless. You need light to make the exposure that results in an image. Whether the light is recorded to silver halide emulsion on a piece of film or to the CMOS sensor on your D5000, you can't make a photograph without it.

Not only is light necessary to make an exposure, but it also has different qualities that can impact the outcome of your image. Light can be soft and diffuse, or it can be hard and directional. Light can also have an impact on the color of your images; different light sources emit light at different temperatures, which changes the colorcast of the image.

When there is not enough light to capture the image you're after, or when the available light isn't suitable for your needs, you can employ alternative sources of light, such as flash, to achieve the effect you're after.

The ability to control light is a crucial step toward being able to make images that look exactly how you want them to. In this chapter, I explain some of the different types of light and how to modify them to suit your needs.

Natural Light

Though it is by far the easiest type of light to find, natural light is sometimes the most difficult to work with. Because it comes from the sun, it is often unpredictable, and can change from minute to minute. I often hear people say, "Wow, it's such a nice, sunny day; what a perfect day to take pictures," but unfortunately, this is not often the case. A bright day when the sun is high in the sky presents many obstacles. First, you have serious contrast issues on a sun-drenched day. Oftentimes, the digital sensor doesn't have the latitude to capture the whole scene effectively. For example, it is nearly impossible to capture detail in the shadows of your subject while keeping the highlights from blowing out or going completely white.

Fortunately, if you want to use natural light, it isn't necessary to stand in direct sunlight at noon. You can get desirable lighting effects when working with natural light in many ways. Here are a few examples:

✦ **Use fill flash.** You can use the flash as a secondary light source (not as your main light) to fill in the shadows and reduce contrast.

✦ **Try window lighting.** Believe it or not, one of the best ways to use natural light is to go indoors. Seating your model next to a window provides a beautiful, soft light that is very flattering. A lot of professional food photographers use window light. It can be used to light almost any subject softly and evenly.

✦ **Find some shade.** The shade of a tree or the overhang of an awning or porch can block the bright sunlight while still giving you plenty of diffuse light with which to light your subject.

✦ **Take advantage of the clouds.** A cloudy day softens the light, allowing you to take portraits outside without worrying about harsh shadows and too much contrast. Even if it's only partly cloudy, you can wait for a cloud to pass over the sun before taking your shot.

✦ **Use a modifier.** Use a reflector to reduce the shadows, or a diffusion panel to block the direct sun from your subject.

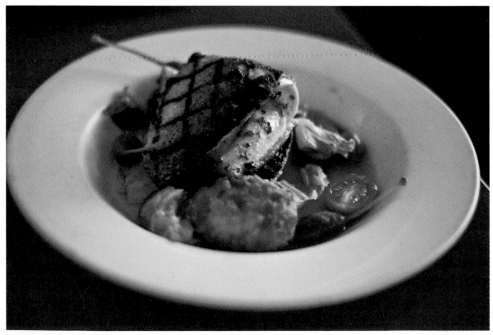

6.1 A food shot using natural light from a window.

D5000 Flash Basics

A major advantage of the Nikon D5000 is the fact that it has a built-in flash for quick use in low-light situations. Even better is the fact that Nikon has additional flashes called Speedlights, which are much more powerful and versatile than the smaller built-in flash.

Nikon Speedlights are dedicated flash units, meaning they are built specifically for use with the Nikon camera system and offer much more functionality than a non-dedicated flash. A non-dedicated flash is a flash made by a third-party manufacturer; these flashes usually don't offer fully automated flash features. There are, however, some non-Nikon flashes that use Nikon's i-TTL flash metering system. The i-TTL system allows the flash to operate automatically, usually resulting in a perfect exposure without your having to do any calculations.

Achieving proper exposures

If you are new to using an external Speedlight flash, exposure can seem confusing when you first attempt to use it. There are a lot of settings you need to know, and there are different formulas you can use to get the right exposure. Once you understand the numbers and where to plug them in, using the Speedlight becomes quite easy.

If you are using your Speedlight in the i-TTL mode, the calculations you would otherwise do manually are done for you, but it's always good to know how to achieve the same results if you don't have the technology to rely on, and to understand how to work with the numbers. When you know these calculations, you can use any flash and get excellent results.

Three main components go into making a properly exposed flash photograph: Guide Number (GN), aperture, and distance. If one of these elements is changed, another one must be changed proportionally to keep the exposure consistent. The following sections cover each element one by one, as well as how to put them together.

Guide Number

The first component in the equation for determining proper flash exposure is the GN, which is a numeric value that represents the amount of light emitted by the flash. You can find the GN for your specific Speedlight in the owner's manual. The GN changes with the ISO sensitivity to which your camera is set; for example, the GN for a Speedlight at ISO 400 is greater than the GN for the same Speedlight when it's set to ISO 100 (because of the increased sensitivity of the sensor). The GN also differs depending on the zoom setting of the Speedlight. The owner's manual has a table that breaks down the GNs according to the flash output setting and the zoom range selected on the Speedlight.

Tip   *If you plan to do a lot of manual flash exposures, I suggest making a copy of the GN table from the owner's manual and keeping it in your camera bag with the flash.*

Note   *If you have access to a flash meter, you can determine the GN of your Speedlight at any setting by placing the meter 10 feet away and firing the flash. Next, take the aperture reading from the flash meter and multiply by ten. This is the correct GN for your flash. Remember that this calculation assumes you are at ISO 100.*

Aperture

The second component in the flash exposure equation is the aperture setting. As you already know, the wider the aperture is, the more light falls on the sensor. Using a wider aperture allows you to use a lower power setting (such as 1/4 when in Manual mode) on your flash, or if you're using the automatic i-TTL mode, the camera fires the flash using less power.

Distance

The third component in the flash exposure equation is the distance from the light source to the subject. The closer the light is to your subject, the more light falls on it. Conversely, the farther away the light source is, the less illumination your subject receives. This is important because if you set your Speedlight to a certain output, you can still achieve a proper exposure by moving the Speedlight closer or farther away as needed.

Guide Number/Distance = Aperture

Here's where the GN, aperture, and distance all come together. The basic formula allows you to take the GN and divide it by the distance to determine the aperture at which you need to shoot. You can change this equation to find out what you want to know specifically:

✦ **GN / D = A.** If you know the GN of the flash and the distance of the flash from the subject, you can determine the aperture to use to achieve the proper exposure.

✦ **A / GN = D.** If you know the aperture you want to use and the GN of the flash, you can determine the distance to place your flash from the subject.

✦ **A × D = GN.** If you already have the right exposure, you can take your aperture setting and multiply it by the distance of the flash from the subject to determine the approximate GN of the flash.

Flash exposure modes

Flashes have different modes that determine how they receive the information on how to set the exposure. Be aware that, depending on the Speedlight or flash you are using, some flash modes may not be available.

i-TTL

The D5000 determines the proper flash exposure automatically by using Nikon's proprietary i-TTL system. The camera gets most of the metering information from monitor preflashes emitted from the Speedlight. These preflashes are emitted almost simultaneously with the main flash, and so it almost appears as if the flash has only fired once. The camera also uses data from the lens, such as distance information and f-stop values, to help determine the proper flash exposure.

Additionally, two separate types of i-TTL flash metering are available for the D5000: Standard i-TTL flash and i-TTL Balanced Fill-Flash (BL). With Standard i-TTL flash mode, the camera determines the exposure for the subject only, and does not take the background lighting into account. With i-TTL BL flash mode, the camera attempts to balance the light from the flash with the ambient light to produce a more natural-looking image.

When using the D5000's built-in flash, the default mode is the i-TTL BL flash mode. To switch the flash to Standard i-TTL flash mode, the camera must be switched to Spot metering.

The Standard i-TTL and i-TTL BL flash modes are available with Nikon's current Speedlight lineup, including the SB-900, SB-800, SB-600, SB-400, and the R1C1 Macro flash kit.

Manual

When you set your Speedlight (either the built-in or accessory flash) to full Manual mode, you must adjust the settings yourself. The best way to figure out the settings is by using a handheld flash meter or by using the GN / D = A formula I discussed previously.

Auto

With Speedlights that offer the Auto mode (sometimes referred to as Non-TTL Auto Flash), such as the SB-900 and SB-800, you decide the exposure setting. These flashes usually have a sensor on the front of them that detects the light reflected back from the subject. When the flash determines that enough light has been produced to make the exposure, it automatically stops the flash tube from emitting any more light.

When using this mode, you need to be aware of the limitations of the flash you are using. If the flash doesn't have a high GN or the subject is too far away, you may need to open the aperture. Conversely, if the flash is too powerful or the subject is very close, you may need to stop the aperture down a bit.

 Caution *When using Auto mode with a non-Nikon flash, be sure not to set the D5000's shutter speed above the rated sync speed, which is 1/200 second. If you do, you will have an incompletely exposed image.*

Auto Aperture

Some flashes, such as the SB-900 and SB-800, also offer what is called an Auto Aperture flash mode. In this mode, you decide what aperture is best suited for the subject you are photographing, and the flash determines how much light to add to the exposure.

Guide Number distance priority

In the Guide Number distance priority mode, available with the SB-800 and SB-900, the flash controls the output according to aperture and subject distance. You manually enter the distance and f-stop value into the flash unit, and then select the f-stop with the camera. The flash output remains the same if you change the aperture. You can use this mode when you know the distance from the camera to the subject.

 Caution *Changing the aperture or the distance to the subject after entering the setting on the flash can cause improper exposures.*

Repeating flash

When in Repeating flash mode, the flash fires repeatedly like a strobe light during a single exposure. You must manually determine the proper flash output you need to light your subject using the formula to get the correct aperture (GN / D = A), and then you must decide the frequency (Hz) and the number of times you want the flash to fire. The slower the shutter speed, the more flashes you are able to capture. For this reason, I recommend only using this mode in low-light situations because the ambient light tends to overexpose the image. Use this mode to create a multiple exposure-type image.

To determine the correct shutter speed, use this simple formula: shutter speed = number of flashes per frame / Hz. For example, if you want the flash to fire ten times with a frequency of 40 Hz (40 times per second), divide 10 by 40, which gives you .25 or 1/4 second.

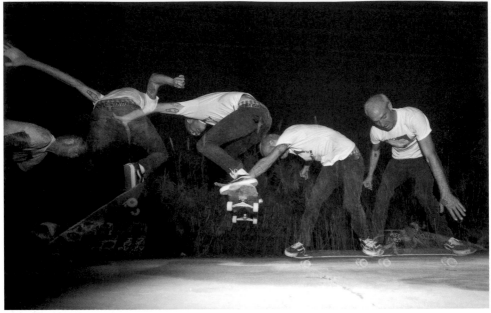

6.2 This image was shot using repeating flash.

Flash sync modes

Flash sync modes control how the flash operates in conjunction with your D5000. These modes work with both the built-in Speedlight and accessory Speedlights, such as the SB-900, SB-800, SB-600, and so on. These modes allow you to choose when the flash fires, either at the beginning of the exposure or at the end, and they also allow you to keep the shutter open for longer periods, enabling you to capture more ambient light in low-light situations.

Sync speed

Before getting into the different sync modes, you need to understand *sync speed*. The sync speed is the fastest shutter speed that can be used while achieving a full flash exposure. This means that if you set your shutter speed at a speed faster than the rated sync speed of the camera, then you don't get a full exposure and end up with a partially underexposed image. With the D5000, you can't actually set the shutter speed above the rated sync speed of 1/200 second when using a dedicated flash because the camera won't let you; as a result, there's no need to worry about having partially black images when using a Speedlight. But if you're using a studio strobe or a third-party flash, this is a concern you should consider.

Limited sync speeds exist because of the way shutters in modern cameras work. As you already know, the shutter controls the amount of time the light is allowed to reach the imaging sensor. All dSLR cameras have what is called a *focal plane shutter.* This term stems from the fact that the shutter is located directly in front of the focal plane, which is essentially on the sensor. The focal plane shutter has two shutter curtains that travel vertically in front of the sensor to control the time the light can enter through the lens. At slower shutter speeds, the front curtain covering the sensor moves away, exposing the sensor to light for a set amount of time. When the exposure has been made, the second curtain then moves in to block the light, thus ending the exposure.

To achieve a faster shutter speed, the second curtain of the shutter starts closing before the first curtain has exposed the sensor completely. This means the sensor is actually exposed by a slit that travels the length of the sensor. This allows your camera to have extremely fast shutter speeds, but limits the flash sync speed because the entire sensor must be exposed to the flash at once to achieve a full exposure.

Front-curtain sync

Front-curtain sync is the default sync mode for your camera, whether you are using the built-in flash, one of Nikon's dedicated Speedlights, or a third-party accessory flash. With Front-curtain sync, the flash is fired as

soon as the shutter's front curtain has fully opened. This mode works well with most general flash applications.

One thing worth mentioning about Front-curtain sync is that although it works well when you're using relatively fast shutter speeds, when the shutter is slowed down (also known as *dragging the shutter* when doing flash photography), especially when you're photographing moving subjects, your images have an unnatural-looking blur in front of them. This is caused by ambient light recording the moving subject.

When doing flash photography at slow speeds, your camera is actually recording two exposures: the flash exposure and the ambient light. When you're using a fast shutter speed, the ambient light usually isn't bright enough to have an effect on the image. When you slow down the shutter speed substantially, it allows the ambient light to be recorded to the sensor, causing what is known as *ghosting*. Ghosting is a

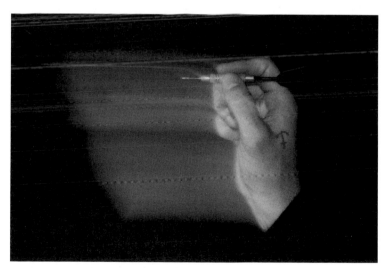

6.3 A shot using Front-curtain sync with a shutter speed of 1 second. Notice that the flash freezes the hand during the beginning of the exposure and the trail caused by the ambient exposure appears in the front, causing the hand to look like it's moving backward.

partial exposure that is usually transparent-looking on the image.

Ghosting causes a trail to appear in front of the subject because the flash freezes the initial movement of the subject. Because the subject is still moving, the ambient light records it as a blur that appears in front of the subject, creating the illusion that it's moving backward. To counteract this problem, you can use a Rear-curtain sync setting, which I explain later in this section.

Red-eye reduction

We've all seen red-eye in a picture at one time or another — that unholy red glare emanating from the subject's eyes that is caused by light reflecting off the retina. Fortunately, the D5000 offers a Red-Eye Reduction flash mode. When this mode is

activated, the camera fires some preflashes (when using an accessory Speedlight) or turns on the AF-assist illuminator (when using the built-in flash), which cause the pupils of the subject's eyes to contract. This stops the light from the flash from reflecting off of the retina and reduces or eliminates the red-eye effect. This mode is useful when taking portraits or snapshots of people or pets when there is little light available.

Slow sync

Sometimes when using a flash at night, especially when the background is very dark, the subject is lit but appears to be in a black hole. Slow sync mode helps take care of this problem. In Slow sync mode, the camera allows you to set a longer shutter speed (up to 30 seconds) to capture the ambient light of the background. Your subject and the

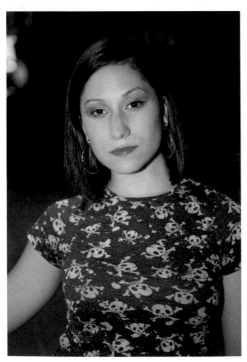

6.4 A picture taken with a standard flash at night. Notice the dark background and the bright subject.

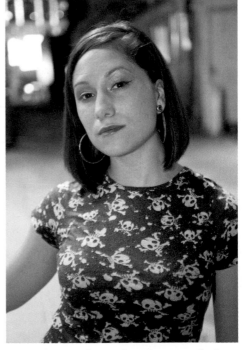

6.5 A picture taken using Slow sync flash mode. Notice how the subject and background are more evenly exposed.

background are lit, so you can achieve a more natural-looking photograph.

Caution *When using Slow sync mode, be sure the subject stays still for the whole exposure to avoid ghosting. Ghosting is a blurring of the image caused by motion during long exposures. Of course, you can use ghosting creatively.*

Note *Slow sync mode can be used in conjunction with Red-Eye Reduction mode for night portraits.*

Rear-curtain sync

When using Rear-curtain sync, the camera fires the flash just before the rear curtain of the shutter starts moving. This mode is useful when taking flash photographs of moving subjects. Rear-curtain sync allows you to more accurately portray the motion of the subject by causing a motion blur trail behind the subject rather than in front of it, as is the case with Front-curtain sync. Rear-curtain sync is used in conjunction with Slow sync.

Flash Exposure Compensation

When you're photographing subjects using flash, whether you're using an external Speedlight or your D5000's built-in flash, there may be times when the flash causes your principal subject to appear too light or too dark. This usually occurs in difficult lighting situations, especially when you're using TTL metering, and your camera's meter can get fooled into thinking the subject needs more or less light than it actually does. This can happen when the background is very bright or very dark, or when the subject is off in the distance or very small in the frame.

Flash Exposure Compensation (FEC) allows you to manually adjust the flash output while still retaining TTL readings so that your flash exposure is at least in the appropriate range. With the D5000, you can vary the output of your built-in flash's TTL setting (or

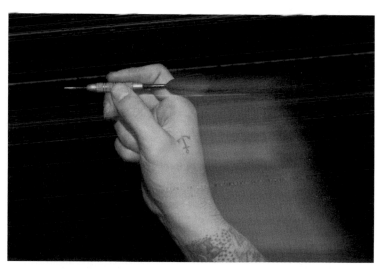

6.6 A picture taken using Rear-curtain sync flash.

your own manual setting) from -3 Exposure Value (EV) to +1 EV. This means that if your flash exposure is too bright, you can adjust it down to 3 full stops under the original setting. Or, if the image seems underexposed or too dark, you can adjust it to be brighter by 1 full stop. Additionally, the D5000 allows you to fine-tune how much exposure compensation is applied by letting you set the FEC incrementally in either 1/3, 1/2, or 1 stop of light.

Fill flash

Fill flash is a handy flash technique that allows you to use your Speedlight as a secondary light source to fill in the shadows rather than as the main light source; hence the term *fill flash*. Fill flash is used mainly in outdoor photography when the sun is very bright, creating deep shadows and bright highlights that result in an image with very high contrast and a wide tonal range. Using fill flash allows you to reduce the contrast of the image by filling in the dark shadows, thus allowing you to see more detail in the image.

You also may want to use fill flash when your subject is backlit (lit from behind). When the subject is backlit, the camera's meter automatically tries to expose for the bright part of the image that is behind your subject. This results in a properly exposed background while your subject is underexposed and dark. However, if you use the spot meter to obtain the proper exposure on your subject, the background will be overexposed and blown out. The ideal solution is to use fill flash to provide an amount of light on your subject that is equal to the ambient light of the background. This brings sufficient detail to both the subject and the background, resulting in a properly and evenly exposed image.

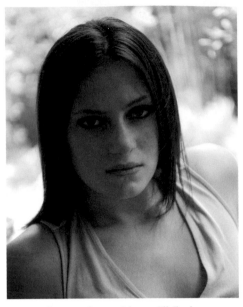

6.7 A picture taken without fill flash.

All of Nikon's dSLR cameras offer i-TTL BL (Nikon calls this Balanced Fill-Flash) or, in layman's terms, automatic fill flash, with both the built-in flash and the detachable Speedlights, the SB-900, SB-800, SB-600, and SB-400. When using a Speedlight, the camera automatically sets the flash to apply fill flash (as long as you're not in Spot metering mode). This is a very handy feature because it allows you to concentrate on composition and not worry about your flash settings. If you decide that you don't want to use the i-TTL BL option, you can set the camera's metering mode to Spot metering, or if you are using an SB-900, SB-800, or SB-600, simply press the Speedlight's Mode button.

Of course, if you don't own an additional i-TTL dedicated Speedlight or you'd rather control your flash manually, you can still use fill flash. It's actually a pretty simple process that can vastly improve your images when you use it in the right situations.

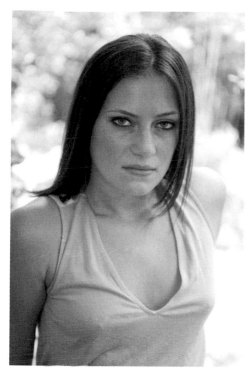

6.8 A picture taken with fill flash.

To execute a manual fill flash, follow these steps:

1. **Use the camera's light meter to determine the proper exposure for the background or ambient light.** A typical exposure for a sunny day is 1/250 second at f/16 with an ISO of 200. Be sure not to set the shutter speed higher than the rated sync speed of 1/200 second.

2. **Determine the flash exposure.** Using the GN / D = A formula, find the setting that you need to properly expose the subject with the flash.

3. **Use FEC to reduce the flash output.** Setting the Flash Exposure Compensation down 1/3 to 2/3 stops allows the flash exposure to be less noticeable while filling in

the shadows or lighting your backlit subject. This makes your images look more natural, as if a flash didn't light them, which is the ultimate goal when attempting fill flash.

Note *The actual amount of FEC needed varies with the intensity of the ambient light source. Use your LCD to preview the image and adjust the amount of FEC as needed.*

Bounce flash

One of the easiest ways to improve your flash pictures, especially snapshots, is to use bounce flash. Bounce flash is a technique in which the light from the flash unit is bounced off of the ceiling or off of a wall onto the subject to diffuse the light, resulting in a more evenly lit image. To do this, your flash must have a head that swivels and tilts. Most flashes made within the last ten years have this feature, but some may not.

When you attempt to use bounce flash, you want to get as much light from the flash onto your subject as you can. To do this, you need to first look at the placement of the subject and adjust the angle of the flash head appropriately. Consider the height of the ceiling or distance from the surface you intend to bounce the light from to the subject.

Unfortunately, not all ceilings are useful for bouncing flash. For example, the ceiling in my studio is corrugated metal with iron crossbeams. If I attempted to bounce flash from a ceiling like that, it would make little or no difference to the image because the light wouldn't reflect evenly and would scatter in all different directions. In a situation where the ceiling is not usable, you can position the subject next to a wall and swivel the flash head in the direction of the wall

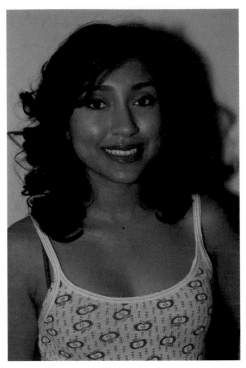

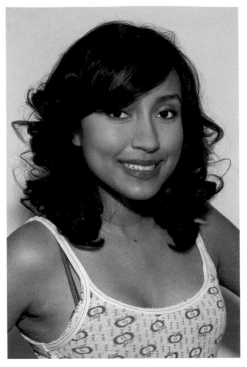

6.9 A picture taken with straight flash.

6.10 A picture taken with bounce flash.

and bounce it from there. To bounce the flash at the correct angle, remember that the angle of incidence equals the angle of reflection.

You want to aim the flash head at such an angle that the flash isn't going to bounce in behind the subject so it is poorly lit. You want to be sure that the light is bounced so that it falls onto your subject. When the subject is very close to you, you need to have your flash head positioned at a more obtuse angle than when the subject is farther away. I recommend positioning the subject at least 10 feet away and setting the angle of the flash head at 45 degrees for a typical-height ceiling of about 8 to 10 feet.

An important pitfall to be aware of when bouncing flash is that the reflected light

picks up and transmits the color of the surface from which it is bounced. This means that if you bounce light off a red surface, your subject will have a reddish tint to it.

The best approach is to avoid bouncing light off of surfaces that are brightly colored, and stick with bouncing light from a neutral-colored surface. White surfaces tend to work the best because they reflect more light and don't add any color. Neutral gray surfaces also work well, although you can lose a little light due to lessened reflectivity and the darker color.

Unfortunately, you can't use bounce flash with the D5000's built-in flash; you need an external Speedlight such as an SB-900, SB-800, SB-600, or SB-400.

Nikon Creative Lighting System Basics

Nikon introduced the Creative Lighting System (CLS) in 2004. In simple terms, it is a system designed to enable you to take Nikon Speedlights off of the camera and attach them to stands. This allows you to position the Speedlights wherever you want and control the direction of light to make the subject appear exactly how you want.

The Nikon CLS enables you to achieve creative lighting scenarios similar to what you would achieve with expensive and much larger studio strobes. You can do it wirelessly with the benefit of full i-TTL metering. To take advantage of the Nikon CLS, you need the D5000 and at least one SB-900, SB-800, or SB-600 Speedlight. With the CLS, there is no more struggling with huge power packs and heavy strobe heads on heavy-duty stands, with cables and wires running all over the place.

The Nikon CLS is not a lighting system in and of itself, but is comprised of many different pieces that you can add to your system as you see fit (or your budget allows). The first and foremost piece of the equation is your camera.

Understanding the Creative Lighting System

The Nikon CLS is basically a communication system that allows the camera, the commander, and the remote units to share information regarding exposure.

A *commander,* which is also called a master, is the flash that controls external Speedlights. Remote units are the external flash units

the commander controls remotely. Communications between the commander and the remotes are accomplished by using pulse modulation. *Pulse modulation* is a term that means the commanding Speedlight fires rapid bursts of light in a specific order. The pulses of light are used to convey information to the remote groups, which interpret the bursts of light as coded information.

Firing the commander tells the other Speedlights in the system when and at what power to fire. The D5000's built-in flash can act as a commander. Using an SB-800 or SB-900 Speedlight or an SU-800 Commander as a master allows you to control three separate groups of remote flashes and gives you an extended range. Using the built-in Speedlight as a commander, you can only control two groups of external Speedlights and have a limited range on how far the camera can be from the remote flashes.

This is how CLS works in a nutshell:

1. **The commander unit sends out a series of monitor preflashes to the remote groups to signal them to fire a series of monitor preflashes to determine the exposure level.** The camera's i-TTL metering sensor reads the preflashes from all of the remote groups and also takes a reading of the ambient light.

2. **The camera tells the commander unit the proper exposure readings for each group of remote Speedlights.** Just before the shutter is released, the commander, using pulse modulation, relays the information to each group of remote Speedlights.

3. **The remotes fire at the output specified by the camera's i-TTL meter, and the shutter closes.**

All these calculations happen in a fraction of a second as soon as you press the Shutter Release button. It almost appears to the naked eye as if the flash just fires once. There is almost no waiting for the camera and the Speedlights to do the calculations.

Given the ease of use and the portability of the Nikon CLS, I highly recommend purchasing at least one (if not two) SB-900, SB-800, or SB-600 Speedlights to add to your setup. With this system, you can produce almost any type of lighting pattern you want. It can definitely get you on the road to creating more professional-looking images.

 Cross-Reference *For a definitive and in-depth look into the Nikon CLS, read the Nikon Creative Lighting System Digital Field Guide, by J. Dennis Thomas (Wiley, 2006).*

Speedlights

Speedlights are Nikon's line of flashes. They are amazing accessories to add to your kit, and you can control most of them wirelessly. Currently, Nikon offers four shoe-mounted flashes — the SB-900, SB-800, SB-600, and SB-400 — along with two macro lighting ring flash setups — the R1 or R1C1 that include two SB-R200 Speedlights. The R1C1 kit also includes the SU-800 Wireless Commander unit. This is not meant to be a definitive guide to the Nikon Speedlight system, but a quick overview of some of the flashes Nikon has to offer, as well as their major features.

 Note *The SB-400 cannot be used as a wireless remote.*

SB-900 Speedlight

The SB-900 Speedlight is Nikon's newest and most powerful Speedlight. This flash takes all the features of Nikon's previous

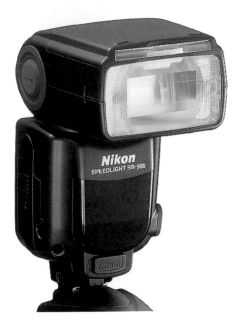

Image courtesy of Nikon Inc.

6.11 The SB-900.

flagship flash, the SB-800, and expands on them, adding more power, a greater range, and a more intuitive user interface. You can use the SB-900 as an on-camera flash, a commander flash that can control up to three groups of external Speedlights on four channels, another SB-900, SB-800, or an SU-800 Wireless Commander. The SB-900 automatically detects whether it's attached to an FX- or DX-format camera, ensuring that you get maximum efficiency.

Another new feature the SB-900 offers is a choice of three different lighting distribution options: Standard for normal photos, Center-weighted for portrait photography, and Even for evenly illuminating large groups or interior shots.

The SB-900 can also automatically identify the supplied color filters to ensure proper white balance when using the filters.

Flash Diffusers

One of the best things you can buy for your flash is a flash diffuser. This is possibly the most important accessory you can get after batteries. Flash diffusers, quite simply, diffuse the light coming from the flash. As you're probably aware, when using flash, the light can be harsh and unnatural. For this reason, photographers often use techniques such as bounce flash to improve the quality of light in their images.

The SB-900 has a wider range of coverage than the SB-800, covering from 17–200mm in FX mode or 12–200mm in DX mode. With the built-in wide-angle flash diffuser, you can get coverage from 12–17mm in FX mode or 8–11mm in DX mode.

The SB-900 has a GN of 183 at ISO 200 and the 200mm zoom setting, and can be used to light subjects as far as 70 feet away.

SB-800 Speedlight

The SB-800 can be used not only as a flash but also as a commander to control up to three groups of external Speedlights on four channels. You can also set the SB-800 to work as a remote flash for off-camera applications. The SB-800 has a built-in AF-assist illuminator to assist in achieving focus in low light. The SB-800 has a powerful GN of 184 at ISO 200 and can be used to photograph subjects as far as 66 feet away.

The SB-800 offers a wide variety of flash modes:

✦ i-TTL and i-TTL Balanced Fill-Flash (i-TTL BL)

✦ Auto Aperture Flash

✦ Non-TTL Auto Flash

✦ Distance Priority Manual Flash

✦ Manual Flash

✦ Repeating Flash

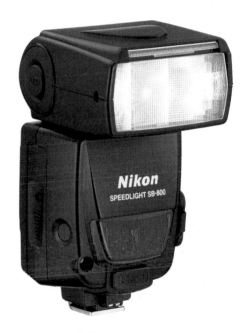

Image courtesy of Nikon Inc.
6.12 The SB-800.

SB-600 Speedlight

The SB-600 Speedlight is the SB-800's little brother. Although this flash has fewer features than its bigger sibling, it has everything you need. You can use it on the camera, as well as off-camera by setting it as a remote. Like the SB-900 and SB-800, the SB-600 also has a built-in AF-assist illuminator. The SB-600 cannot, however, be used as a commander to control off-camera flash units. The SB-600 has an impressive GN of 138 at

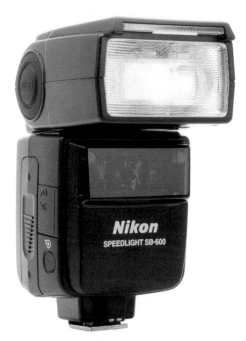

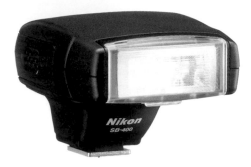

Image courtesy of Nikon Inc.
6.14 The SB-400.

Image courtesy of Nikon Inc.
6.13 The SB-600.

ISO 200, which, although it gives about 1 stop less light than the SB-800, is more than enough for most subjects.

The SB-600 only has the three most important flash modes:

✦ i-TTL

✦ i-TTL BL

✦ Manual

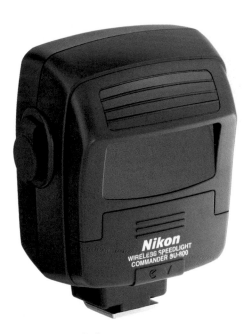

Image courtesy of Nikon Inc.
6.15 The SU-800.

SB-400 Speedlight

The SB-400 is Nikon's entry-level Speedlight. It can only be used in the i-TTL/i-TTL BL mode. One nice feature is the horizontally tilting flash head that allows you to use bounce flash. Unfortunately, this only works when the camera is in the horizontal position, unless you bounce off a wall when holding the camera vertically. For such a small flash, the SB-400 has a decent GN of 98 at ISO 200.

 Caution *The SB-400 does not work wirelessly with the Nikon CLS. It only works when connected to the camera's hot shoe or an off-camera hot-shoe cord.*

SU-800 Wireless Speedlight commander

The SU-800 is a wireless Speedlight commander that uses infrared technology to communicate wirelessly with off-camera Speedlights. It can control up to three groups of Speedlights on four different channels.

Using the Built-in Speedlight

The D5000's built-in Speedlight is a handy little flash that's great for taking casual snapshots. Although it lacks the versatility of the bigger external flashes, the built-in Speedlight is always there when you need it and requires no extra batteries because the camera's battery powers it. Activate it by pressing the flash pop-up button on the top left of the camera (as you would hold it for shooting) near the built-in Speedlight.

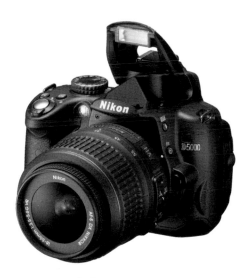

Image courtesy of Nikon Inc.
6.16 The D5000 with built-in flash.

The built-in Speedlight is set to i-TTL mode by default (i-TTL appears as TTL in the menu), although you can choose to set it to Manual mode (you set the output). You can also use it with all the sync modes your camera offers: Front-curtain sync, Rear-curtain sync, Slow sync, and Red-Eye Reduction. To change the sync mode, press the Flash mode button located just below the Flash pop-up button. Rotating the Command dial while pressing the Flash mode button changes the mode. The selected mode appears on the LCD control panel.

Studio Strobes

Although the Nikon CLS allows you complete wireless control over lighting, it can be somewhat limited. The Speedlights are small, versatile, and portable, but they are limited in range, power, and options for accessories. Sometimes, there is no other option than to use a studio strobe, especially when lighting large subjects or when you need specific accessories to modify the light in a certain way.

A studio strobe has a much higher GN than a shoe-mounted Speedlight, which means more power. Studio strobes run on AC power instead of batteries, which means faster recycle times between flashes. Also, many different accessories and light modifiers are available for studio strobes.

There are two different types of studio strobes: standard pack and monolights. Standard pack and head strobes have a separate power pack and flash heads that are controlled centrally from the power pack. Monolights are flash heads that have a power pack built in, and you adjust them individually at each head. Monolights tend to be lower in power than standard strobes, but they are more portable and less expensive.

One of the downsides to using studio strobes is that you lose the advantage of i-TTL flash metering. Studio strobes are generally fired using a PC sync cord, which runs from the camera to the strobe, and which only tells the flash when to fire, not at what output level. You must calculate all the strobe settings.

Of course, there are flash meters that are designed to read the output of the strobe to give you a reading of the proper exposure. And you can always use the handy GN / D = A formula to determine the proper exposure. The D5000 doesn't have a PC sync terminal, and so you will need to purchase an additional accessory that fits in the camera's hot shoe. Nikon makes an inexpensive device called the AS-15.

One of the plus sides of using studio strobes is the continuous modeling light. Because the strobes are only lit for a fraction of a second, studio strobes are equipped with a constant light source (called a modeling light) that allows you to see what effect the strobe is going to have on the subject, although the modeling light isn't necessarily consistent with the actual light output of the flash tube.

Firing Your Studio Strobes Wirelessly

You can't use studio lighting setups completely wirelessly because you have to plug the lights in for power, and in the case of standard studio strobes, you must not only plug in the power pack but also connect the flash heads to the power pack. For the most part, studio strobes are fired using a sync cord, or using a hot-shoe sync device such as the Wein Safe Sync. This is the easiest and most affordable way of firing your studio flashes. Most monolights have a built-in optical sensor that allows the flash to be triggered by another flash. Most standard studio strobe power packs can also be fitted with an optical sensor. This allows you some freedom from the wires that connect your camera to the main flash unit.

More and more photographers these days use radio triggers. Radio triggers use a radio signal to fire the strobes when the shutter is released. Unlike the optical sensor, the radio trigger is not limited to "seeing" another flash to make it fire. Radio triggers can also fire from long distances and can even work from behind walls and around corners.

Radio trigger units have two parts: the transmitter and the receiver. The transmitter is attached to the camera and tells the receiver, which is connected to the strobe, to fire when the Shutter Release button is pressed. Some newer radio units are transceivers, meaning they're able to function as a transmitter or a receiver (not at the same time, of course), but you still need at least two of them to operate.

Radio triggers work very well and free you from being directly attached to your lights, but they can be very expensive. There are a few different manufacturers, but the most well known is Pocket Wizard. Pocket Wizard transceivers are fairly pricey, but they are built well and extremely reliable. Recently, there has been a proliferation of radio transmitters and receivers on eBay that are priced very low. I can't attest to how well they work, but a lot of folks on the Internet seem to like them. At around $30 for a kit with one receiver and one transmitter, you won't be losing much if it doesn't work well.

When looking for a studio lighting setup, you have thousands of different options. There are a lot of reputable manufacturers offering a lot of different types of lights. Your only limit is the amount of money you want to spend.

Standard studio strobes are the most powerful and most expensive option. With the standard strobes, you can usually attach up to six flash heads to the power pack, which provides a lot of lighting options. Of course, one power pack and two lights cost about $1,000 to start, not including stands, lighting modifiers (which I cover later in this chapter), and other accessories. If you opt for studio strobes, reputable manufacturers include Speedotron, Dynalite, and Profoto.

A more economical approach is to use monolights. Most of the manufacturers that make standard strobes also make monolights. Although they are lower in power than strobes that are powered by a power pack, they are also far more portable because they are lighter and smaller in size. You can outfit monolights with the same light modifiers as the bigger strobe units. I recommend going this route when purchasing lights for a small or home studio setup. You can get a complete setup with two 200-watt-second (ws) monolights (that's 400ws of combined power) with stands, umbrellas, and a carrying case for around $500; that's only a little more than you would pay for a 400ws power pack alone.

Flash Alternatives

There is a growing movement of amateur photographers who are using non-dedicated hot-shoe flashes to light their subjects. This movement is based on getting the flash off of the camera to create more professional-looking images (such as those you get when using studio lights), but is also centered on not spending a lot of money to achieve these results.

Basically, what these folks, called *Strobists*, are saying is that you don't need big, expensive studio lights or expensive dedicated flashes to achieve great images.

Small hot-shoe flashes are extremely portable and are powered by inexpensive AA batteries. You can find older-model flashes that don't have all of the features of the newer models at reasonable prices.

To get started with off-camera flash, you need a flash with two things: a PC sync terminal and a manual output power setting. If your flash doesn't have a PC sync terminal, you can buy a hot-shoe adaptor that has one on it. This adaptor slides onto the shoe of your flash and has a PC terminal on it that syncs with your flash.

The best flashes to use for this are the older Nikon Speedlights from the mid-80s to the mid-90s: the SB-24, SB-25, SB-26, and SB-28 Speedlights. These flashes are available at a fraction of the cost of the newer i-TTL SB-800 or SB-600. Unfortunately, with a greater number of people using the Strobist technique, the prices have increased a bit.

Given the number of people now using small hot-shoe flashes off-camera, manufacturers are making accessories to attach these flashes to stands, and other accessories to allow light modifiers to be added to them.

To learn more about the Strobist technique and find many tricks and tips, go to http://strobist.blogspot.com/.

When equipping your home or small studio with studio lighting, I recommend starting out with at least two strobes. With this setup, you can pretty easily light almost any subject. A three-light setup is ideal for most small home studios, with two lights for lighting the subject and one light for illuminating the background.

For those of you with a more limited budget, you can still achieve some excellent results using a single strobe head, especially when going for moody low-key lighting. The late Dean Collins was a skilled photographer and a master at lighting who could light some amazing scenes with just one strobe. I highly encourage anyone who is interested in photographic lighting to view some of his instructional videos.

Continuous Lighting

Continuous lighting is just what it sounds like: a light source that is constant. It is by far the easiest type of lighting to work with. Unlike natural lighting, continuous lighting is consistent and predictable. Even when using a strobe with modeling lights, you sometimes have to estimate what the final lighting will look like. With continuous lighting, "what you see is what you get." You can see the actual effects the lighting has on your subjects, and you can modify and change the lighting before you even press the Shutter Release button.

Continuous lights are an affordable alternative to using studio strobes. Because the light is constant and consistent, the learning curve is also less steep. With strobes, you need to experiment with the exposure or use a flash meter. With continuous lights, you can use the D5000's Matrix meter to yield excellent results.

As with other lighting systems, there are a lot of continuous light options. Here are a few of the more common ones:

✦ **Incandescent.** Incandescent, or tungsten, lights are the most common type of lights. Thomas Edison invented this type of light — your typical light bulb is a tungsten lamp. With tungsten lamps, an electrical current runs through a tungsten filament, heating it and causing it to emit light. This type of continuous lighting is the source of the name "hot lights."

✦ **Halogen.** Halogen lights, which are much brighter than typical tungsten lights, are actually very similar. They are considered a type of incandescent light. Halogen lights also employ a tungsten filament, but include a halogen vapor in the gas inside the lamp. The color temperature of halogen lamps is higher than the color temperature of standard tungsten lamps.

✦ **Fluorescent.** Fluorescent lighting is everywhere these days. It is in the majority of office buildings, stores, and even in your own house. In a fluorescent lamp, electrical energy changes a small amount of mercury into a gas. The electrons collide with the mercury gas atoms, causing them to release photons, which, in turn, cause the phosphor coating inside the lamp to glow. Because this reaction doesn't create much heat, fluorescent lamps are much cooler and more energy efficient than tungsten and halogen lamps. These lights are commonly used in TV lighting.

✦ **HMI.** HMI, or Hydrargyrum Medium-arc Iodide, lamps are probably the most expensive type of continuous lighting. The motion picture industry uses this type because of its consistent color temperature and the fact that it runs cooler than a tungsten lamp with the same power rating. These lamps operate by releasing an arc of electricity in an atmosphere of mercury vapor and halogenides.

Incandescent and halogen

Although incandescent and halogen lights cost less and make it easier to see what you're photographing, there are quite a few drawbacks to using these lights for serious photography work. First, they are hot. When a model has to sit under lamps for any length of time, he will get hot and start to sweat. This is also a problem with food photography. It can cause your food to change consistency or even to sweat — for example, cheese that has been refrigerated. Conversely, it can help keep hot food looking fresh and hot.

Second, although incandescent lights appear to be very bright to you and your subject, they actually produce less light than a standard flash unit. For example, a 200-watt tungsten light and a 200-watt-second strobe use the same amount of electricity per second, so they should be equally bright, right? Wrong. Because the flash discharges all 200 watts of energy in a fraction of a second, the flash is actually much, much brighter. Why does this matter? Because when you need a fast shutter speed or a small aperture, the strobe can give you more light in a shorter time.

An SB-600 gives you about 30 watt-seconds of light at full power. To get an equivalent amount of light at the maximum sync speed

of 1/250 second from a tungsten light, you would need a 7500-watt lamp! Of course, if your subject is static, you don't need to use a fast shutter speed; in this case, you can use one 30-watt light bulb for a 1-second exposure or a 60-watt lamp for a 1/2-second exposure.

Other disadvantages of using incandescent lights include the following:

✦ **Color temperature inconsistency.** The color temperature of the lamps changes as your household current varies and as the lamps get more and more use. The color temperature may be inconsistent from manufacturer to manufacturer and may even vary within the same types of bulbs.

✦ **Light modifiers are more expensive.** Because most continuous lights are hot, modifiers such as softboxes need to be made to withstand the heat; this makes them more expensive than the standard equipment intended to be used for strobes.

✦ **Short lamp life.** Incandescent lights tend to have a shorter life than flash tubes, and so you'll have to replace them more often.

Although incandescent lights have quite a few disadvantages, they are by far the most affordable type of lights you can buy. Many photographers who are starting out use inexpensive work lights that they can buy at any hardware store for less than $10. These lights use a standard light bulb and often have a reflector to direct the light; they also come with a clamp that you can use to attach them to a stand or anything else you have handy that might be stable.

Halogen work lamps, also readily available at any hardware store, offer a higher light output than a standard light, generally speaking. The downside is they are very hot, and the larger lights can be a bit unwieldy. You also may have to come up with some creative ways to get the lights in the position you want them. Some halogen work lamps come complete with a tripod stand. If you can afford it, I'd recommend buying these; they're easier to set up and less of an aggravation in the long run. The single halogen work lamps that are usually designed to sit on a table or some other support are readily available for less than $20; the double halogen work lamps with two 500-watt lights and a 6-foot tripod stand are usually available for less than $40.

If you're really serious about lighting with hot lights, you may want to invest in a photographic hot-light kit. These kits are widely available from any photography or video store. They usually come with lights, light stands, and sometimes with light modifiers such as umbrellas or softboxes for diffusing the light for a softer look. The kits can be relatively inexpensive, with two lights, two stands, and two umbrellas for around $100. Or you can buy much more elaborate setups ranging in price up to $2,000. I've searched the Internet for these kits and have found that the best deals are on eBay.

Fluorescent

Fluorescent lights have a lot of advantages over incandescent lights: They run at much lower temperatures and use much less electricity than standard incandescent lights. Fluorescent lights are also a much softer light source than incandescent lights.

In the past, fluorescent lights weren't considered viable for photographic applications because they cast a sickly green light on the subject. Today, most fluorescent lamps for use in photography are color-corrected to match both daylight and incandescent lights. Also, given that white balance is adjustable in the camera or in Adobe Photoshop with RAW files, using fluorescents has become much easier because you don't have to worry about color-correcting filters and special films.

These days, because more people are using fluorescent lights, light modifiers are more readily available. They allow you to control the light to make it softer or harder and directional or diffused.

Fluorescent light kits are readily available through most photography stores and online. These kits are a little more expensive than the incandescent light kits — an average kit with two light stands, reflectors, and bulbs costs about $160. Fluorescent kits aren't usually equipped with umbrellas or softboxes because the light is already fairly soft. You can buy these kinds of accessories, and there are kits available that come with softboxes and umbrellas, although they cost significantly more.

Unfortunately, there aren't many low-cost alternatives to buying a fluorescent light kit. The only real option is to use the clamp light I mentioned in the section about incandescent light and fit it with a fluorescent bulb that has a standard bulb base on it. These types of fluorescent bulbs are readily available at any store that sells light bulbs.

HMI

This type of continuous light is primarily used in the motion picture industry. HMI lamps burn extremely bright and are much more efficient than standard incandescent, halogen, or fluorescent lights. The light emitted is equal in color temperature to that of daylight.

Although I include them here for general information, these kits are usually too cost-prohibitive for use in average still-photography applications. For example, a one-light kit with a 24-watt light can start at more than $1,000, and an 18,000-watt kit can cost more than $30,000!

Light Modifiers

Light modifiers do exactly what their name says they do: they modify light. When you set up a photographic shot, in essence, you are building a scene using light. For some images, you may want a hard light that is very directional; for others, a soft, diffused light works better. Light modifiers allow you to control the light so that you can direct it where you need it, give it the quality the image calls for, and even add color or texture to the image.

Umbrellas

The most common type of light modifier is the umbrella. Photographic umbrellas are coated with a material to maximize reflectivity. They are used to diffuse and soften the light emitted from the light source, whether it's continuous or strobe lighting. There are three types of umbrellas to choose from:

✦ **Standard.** The most common type of umbrella has a black outside with the inside coated with a reflective material that is usually silver or gold in color. Standard umbrellas are designed so that you point the light source into the umbrella and bounce the light onto the subject, resulting in a non-directional, soft light source.

✦ **Shoot-through.** Some umbrellas are manufactured out of a one-piece, translucent, silvery nylon that enables you to shoot through the umbrella like a softbox. You can also use shoot-through umbrellas to bounce the light, as I previously mentioned.

✦ **Convertible.** This silver umbrella has a removable black cover on the outside. You can use a convertible umbrella to bounce light or as a shoot-through when you remove the outside covering.

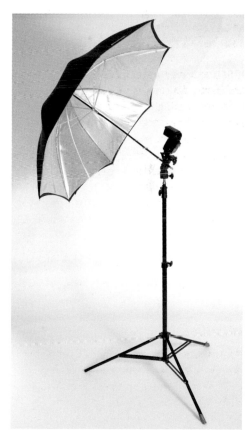

6.17 A Speedlight with a standard umbrella.

Photographic umbrellas come in various sizes, usually ranging from 27 inches all the way up to 12.5 feet. The size you use depends on the size of the subject and the degree of coverage you want. For standard headshots, portraits, and small to medium products, umbrellas ranging from 27 inches to about 40 inches supply plenty of coverage. For full-length portraits and larger products, a 60- to 72-inch umbrella is generally recommended. If you're photographing groups of people or especially large products, you'll need to go beyond the 72-inch umbrella.

The larger the umbrella is, the softer the light is that falls on the subject from the light source. It is also the case that the larger the umbrella is, the less light you have falling on your subject. Generally, the small to medium umbrellas lose about 1.5 to 2 stops of light. Larger umbrellas generally lose 2 or more stops of light because the light is being spread out over a larger area.

Smaller umbrellas tend to have a much more directional light than larger umbrellas. With all umbrellas, the closer your umbrella is to the subject, the more diffuse the light is.

Choosing the right umbrella is a matter of personal preference. Features to keep in mind when choosing your umbrella include its type, size, and portability. You also want to consider how it works with your light source. For example, regular and convertible umbrellas return more light to the subject when light is bounced from them, which can be advantageous, especially if you are using a Speedlight, which has less power than a studio strobe. Also, the less energy the Speedlight has to output, the more battery power you save. Conversely, shoot-through umbrellas lose more light through the back when bouncing, but they are generally more affordable than convertible umbrellas.

Softboxes

Like umbrellas, softboxes are used to diffuse and soften the light of a strobe or continuous light to create a more pleasing light effect. Softboxes range in size from small, 6-inch boxes that you mount directly onto the flash head, to large boxes that usually mount directly to a studio strobe.

The reason you may want to invest in a softbox rather than an umbrella for your studio is that it provides a more consistent and controllable light than an umbrella does. Softboxes are closed around the light source, thereby preventing unwanted light from bouncing back onto your subject. With the diffusion material, there is less of a chance of creating hotspots on your subject. A hotspot is an overly bright spot usually caused by bright or uneven lighting.

Softboxes are generally made for use with studio strobes and monolights, although special heat-resistant softboxes are made for use with hot lights. Softboxes attach to the light source with a device called a *speed ring*. Speed rings are specific to the type of lights to which they are meant to attach. If you are using a standard hot-shoe flash as your light source, some companies, such as Chimera (www.chimeralighting.com), manufacture a type of speed ring that mounts directly to the light stand and allows you to attach one or more Speedlights to the light stand, as well. You mount the speed ring to the stand, attach the softbox to the *speed ring,* attach the Speedlight with the flash head pointed into the softbox, and you're ready to go.

Softboxes are available in a multitude of shapes and sizes, ranging from squares and rectangles to ovals and octagons. Most photographers use the standard square or rectangular softboxes. However, some prefer to use oval or octagonal softboxes because they mimic umbrellas and give a more pleasing round shape to the catchlights in the subject's eyes. This is mostly a matter of personal preference. I usually use a medium-sized, rectangular softbox.

As with umbrellas, the size of the softbox you need depends on the subject you are photographing. You can take most softboxes apart and fold them up, and most of them come with a storage bag that you can use to transport them.

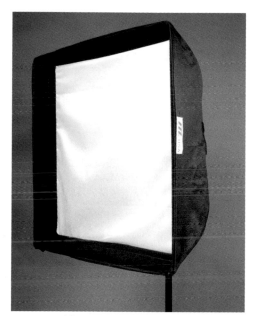

6.18 A softbox.

Diffusion panels

A diffusion panel is basically a frame made out of PVC pipe with reflective nylon stretched over it. Diffusion panels function similarly to softboxes, but you have a little more control over the quality of the light.

Diffusion panels are usually about 6 feet tall and have a base that allows them to stand without a light stand. You place the diffusion panel in front of the subject. You then place your light source behind the diffusion panel. You can move the light closer to the diffusion panel for more directional light or farther away for a softer, more even light. For a full-length portrait or a larger subject, you can place two or more lights behind the panel, achieving greater coverage with your lights.

You can use a diffusion panel as a reflector, bouncing the light from your light source onto the subject. You can purchase diffusion panels at most major camera stores at a fraction of the price of a good softbox. You can disassemble the PVC frame easily and pack it away into a small bag for storage or transport to and from location.

Tip   If you're feeling crafty, you can make a diffusion panel from items easily found in your local hardware and fabric stores. Numerous sites on the Internet offer advice on how to construct one.

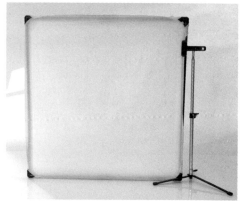

6.19 A diffusion panel.

Other light modifiers

There are many different types of light modifiers. The main types — umbrellas, softboxes, and diffusion panels — serve to diffuse the light by effectively increasing the size of the light source, thereby reducing contrast. In addition to these, other types of light modifiers, such as barn doors and snoots, are worth considering. They are also used to control the direction of the light to make it appear stronger or to focus it on a specific area of the subject. The following list includes some of the more common tools photographers use to direct the light from the light source.

✦ **Parabolic reflectors.** Most light sources come equipped with a parabolic reflector. They usually range from 6 to 10 inches in circumference, although you can buy larger ones. Without a reflector, the light from the bare bulb, whether it's a flash tube or an incandescent, scatters and lacks direction, resulting in the loss of usable light.

The reflector focuses the light into a more specific area, actually increasing the amount of usable light by 1 or 2 stops. Parabolic reflectors are commonly used in conjunction with other light modifiers, including umbrellas, barn doors, and grids. When you use an umbrella, you'll always use a reflector to direct the light into the umbrella, which diffuses the light. Using only a reflector gives the light a very hard quality that results in a lot of contrast.

✦ **Barn doors.** Barn doors are used to control the direction of light and to block stray light from entering the lens, which can result in lens flare. Blocking the light is also known as *flagging*. Barn doors are normally attached to the reflector and come in two types: 4-leaf and 2-leaf. Barn doors consist of panels that are attached to hinges, which allow you to open and close the doors to let light out or keep it in. Typically, barn doors are used when you want a hard light source to shine on a specific area of the subject but you don't want any stray light striking other parts of the subject or the camera lens.

✦ **Grids.** Grids, also known as grid spots or honeycombs, are used to create a light similar to a spotlight. A grid is a round disc with a honeycomb-shaped screen inside of it. When the light shines through it, it is focused to a particular degree, giving you a tight circle of light with a distinct fall-off at the edges.

There are different types of grids that control the spread of light. They run from a 5-degree grid to a 60-degree grid. The 5-degree grid has very small holes and is deep so that the light is focused down to a small bright spot. The higher the degree of the grid spot, the more spread out the spot becomes. Grids fit inside of the reflector, just in front of the lamp or flash tube. They are great to use as hair lights and to add a spot of light on the background to help the subject stand out.

✦ **Snoots.** A snoot creates a spotlight-like effect similar to the grid. A snoot is shaped like a funnel and it kind of works that way, too, funneling light into a specific area of the scene. The snoot usually has a brighter spot effect than a grid does. The snoot fits directly over the flash head.

✦ **Reflector.** A reflector doesn't directly modify the light coming from the light source, but it is used to reflect light onto the subject. Reflectors are usually white or silver, although some can be gold. Professional reflectors are usually round or oval disks with wire frames that can be easily folded up to a smaller size. You can make your own reflector by using white foam board that is available at any art supply store and at some photography stores. You can use the white board alone or cover it with silver or gold foil. In a pinch, almost anything white or silver, such as a lid from a Styrofoam cooler or even a white t-shirt, will work.

✦ **Gobos.** A gobo can be anything that "goes between" the light source and the subject or background, often to create a pattern or simulate a specific light source, such as a window. It is usually attached to a stand and placed a few feet in front of the light source. A common technique in film noir-type photography is to place venetian blinds between a light and the background to simulate sunlight shining through the blinds of the office window of a private eye. You can make gobos or purchase them from a photographic supply house.

Working with D-Movie

The D5000 has inherited a pretty special feature from the D90: the ability to use the Live View feature to record HD video. The D90 was a groundbreaking camera in this respect, and the D5000 follows right along in its footsteps.

First and foremost, this statement must be made: The D5000 is not a video camera. It's a still camera that just happens to record video by using the Live View feature. The D5000 is one of Nikon's dSLR cameras, and it's an excellent example of that. It has a 12-megapixel sensor, low noise at high ISO settings, and a fast continuous shutter speed — everything you could want from a dSLR. Why am I bringing this up? Because there are some people who aren't happy with the current video performance in dSLR cameras. These evaluations are being based on comparisons to dedicated video cameras. This is an unfair comparison, as the D5000 was designed primarily to shoot still photographs, and it does an excellent job accomplishing that. You wouldn't compare a still grab from a video camera to a high-res still image from the D5000, would you? Of course not. It's like comparing apples to oranges.

The D5000's Video mode is, for all practical purposes, fully automatic. Once you switch to Video mode, the camera controls all the settings. Shutter speed and ISO can't be adjusted at all, and the aperture setting is locked in once Live View is activated. The only way to manually adjust the exposure is by applying exposure compensation. There are some ways to get around the total lack of control, which are covered as you go through this chapter.

Here are some things the D5000 can do that dedicated video cameras can't:

✦ **Interchangeable lenses.** You can use almost every Nikon lens ever made on the D5000. While some video cameras take Nikon lenses, you need an expensive adapter, and you lose some resolution and the ability to get a very shallow depth of field.

✦ **Depth of field.** You can get a much more shallow depth of field than video when using a lens with a fast aperture, such as a 50mm f/1.4. Most video cameras have sensors that are much smaller than the sensor of the D5000, which gives them a much deeper depth of field.

✦ **Cleaner images.** The D5000's APS-C–sized sensor also allows the camera to record video with less noise at high sensitivities than most video cameras can.

So, although the D5000 doesn't have all the capabilities of a dedicated video camera, there are things that the D5000 can do better than video cameras.

About Video

Before getting into the basics of the D5000's Video mode, it's best to do a little exploration into the realm of video. Video capture functions much differently from still-photo capture. Of course, all photography is capturing light by using a sensor (or film), a lens, and a lightproof box (your camera). Video is just digitally capturing still images at a high frame rate and playing them back sequentially.

The D5000 can shoot video in three resolutions that can be set in the Shooting menu under the Movie settings option. You can choose a small video size of 320x216 pixels, which is shot using a 3:2 aspect ratio. This is the same ratio at which still images are recorded. This resolution is very small and best suited for filming small clips that are sent through e-mail. The next size, 640x424, is also shot using a 3:2 aspect ratio. This size

is good for posting on the Internet without using up too much bandwidth. The best setting to use is the HD setting of 1280x720 which is a 16:9 or cinematic ratio. This setting gives you the most resolution and can easily be watched on large HDTVs, offering a reasonable image quality.

Progressive versus interlaced

If you're familiar with HD, you've probably heard the terms progressive and interlaced. These terms are usually used in conjunction with the pixel resolution numbers of the HDTV or monitor (720p or 1080i, for example). To make things even more confusing, even the broadcast companies don't stick to one standard. Your D5000 also has an HDMI output setting (found in the setup menu) that lets you choose between progressive and interlaced resolutions.

So, what's the difference? It's actually quite simple. Interlaced video is displayed on your television by scanning in every other line that makes up the picture. First, the even lines are displayed and then the odd lines. This is done every 1/60 second. The way the human brain works allows this to appear as if it's being displayed all at once. This is how television has been displayed since the beginning. This method was used because the early cathode-ray tube televisions weren't fast enough to keep up with the information being sent through the signal.

Progressive scanning works by progressively displaying single lines of the image. The first line is displayed, then the second, the third, and so on. As with interlaced technology, all of this happens too fast for the human eye to detect the separate changes, and so everything appears to happen all at once.

Both of these types of video display can be used for HD viewing. Progressive video resolution is most commonly displayed at 720p and interlaced at 1080i. So far, none of the current broadcasters in the United States are using 1080p. The reason 1080p isn't commonly used is due to the high volume of information required to send a progressive signal of that resolution.

Because only half of the image is being sent at a time, 1080i is actually only broadcasting at 540 lines per second. So, although 1080i technically has a higher resolution, 720p has better image quality. Most of your standard HDTV programming is done in 1080i (mostly due to the smaller volume of information), but most sports are broadcast in 720p, which handles fast motion better. Neither is really better than the other, and each has it own specific strengths and weaknesses.

Frame rate

As mentioned earlier, video capture is simply recording still images, linking them together, and then playing them back one after another in sequence. This allows the still images to appear as if they're moving. An important part of video capture is frame rate. This is the rate at which the still images are recorded and is almost always expressed in terms of frames per second or, more commonly, fps. Most video cameras capture video at 30 or 60 fps. A rate of 30 fps is generally considered the best for smooth-looking video that doesn't appear jerky. While 30 fps is the standard, many videographers prefer to use a camera that shoots at 24 fps or cameras that use what's known as *pulldown* to convert 30 fps to 24 fps.

Why all this fuss over a few frames per second? Well, 24 fps is the standard that was set by filmmakers in the early years of movie-making. Shooting at 24 fps gives videos a quality that's similar to cinema, and a lot of filmmakers find this aesthetic more pleasing than the standard 30 fps of video capture.

The Nikon D5000 shoots video at 24 fps, giving you a cinematic feel from the start. Because the D5000 uses a progressive image sensor (all dSLR cameras do), you don't have the 24 fps pulldown that can cause artifacts in your movies.

Shutter

When shooting video with your D5000, the camera isn't using the mechanical shutter that it uses when making still exposures. The Video mode uses what's known as an electronic shutter. This electronic shutter isn't an actual physical shutter but is a feature of the sensor that tells the sensor when to activate to become sensitive to the photons of light striking it. When you press the Live View button, the camera flips up the reflex mirror and the mechanical shutter opens, exposing the sensor to light. If the sensor were continuously exposed to light, it would become overexposed very quickly (depending on the available light). To allow Live View to operate by providing a live feed of properly exposed images, the sensor must be turned on and off very rapidly.

What's more, there are two ways for this electronic shutter to work: global or rolling. Typically, on digital video cameras with a CCD sensor, you find a global shutter. This means that the sensor is exposed all at once, similar to the way the sensor would be exposed by using the mechanical shutter. As you know, the D5000 has a CMOS sensor. These types of sensors aren't normally equipped with global shutters but use a rolling shutter. The rolling shutter is used for the same reason that CMOS sensors are great energy-saving sensors. A global shutter could be used but would require more transistors, resulting in a more expensive sensor, not to mention higher noise.

A rolling shutter operates by exposing each row of pixels progressively (similar to HDTV reception discussed earlier) from top to bottom. In effect, it rolls the exposure down the sensor row by row. Unfortunately, this rolling shutter has a few unwanted artifacts that are inherent in its operation. These artifacts are usually most noticeable when the camera is making quick panning movements or the subject is moving from one side of the frame to the other. There are three types of artifacts common to the rolling shutter:

✦ **Skew.** This is the most common artifact. Skew causes objects in the video to appear as if they're leaning (or skewed). This artifact only appears when the camera is quickly panned. This artifact is cause by the image being progressively scanned. As just discussed, the rolling shutter exposes each single frame from the top down. When the camera is moved sideways while the frame is being exposed, the top of the subject is exposed on one side of the frame, and the bottom of the subject is on the other side of the frame.

✦ **Jello.** This video problem is closely related to skew and occurs when the camera is panned quickly back and forth. First, the video skews to one side and then the other, causing it to look like it's made of Jell-O; it looks as if the subject is wobbly. This is the most common problem you will encounter when shooting video with the D5000. Unfortunately, there's not much you can do about this problem. It's a symptom of the rolling shutter. Using a tripod can help to minimize it a bit.

✦ **Partial exposure.** This is caused by a brief flash of light, typically from a camera flash. As the shutter rolls down the frame, it's exposing for the ambient light. The brief flash duration causes part of the frame to be overexposed. This isn't a major problem, and you can expect to experience it at weddings or events where people are taking pictures with flash.

 Caution *Older fluorescent lights with low-frequency ballasts can cause video with a rolling shutter to flicker.*

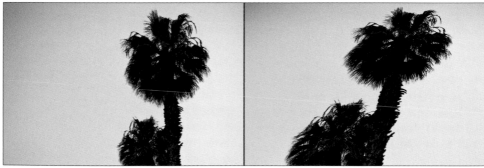

7.1 An example of video skew. The left side shows a still shot taken from video while the camera was static. The right side shows a still shot taken when the camera was panning.

Setting up D-Movie

Using D-Movie is quite simple. Simply press the Live View button on the back of the camera to activate Live View, and then press OK to start recording. It's as simple as that. However, there are some important things to consider before you start recording:

✦ **Quality.** The Quality setting determines what size your videos are. Sizes and their uses are covered earlier in this chapter. You set the Quality by going to the shooting menu, selecting the Movie settings option, selecting Quality, and then pressing OK. You have three choices: 1280x720 (16:9), 640x424 (3:2), or 320x216 (3:2).

✦ **Sound.** This option is also found under the Movie settings option. You can either record sound using the D5000's built-in microphone or you can turn the sound recording off.

✦ **Picture Control.** Just like your still images, the D5000 applies Picture Control settings to your movie. You can also create and use Custom Picture Controls that fit your specific application. For example, I created a Custom Picture Control called Raging Bull that uses the Monochrome Picture Control with added contrast and the yellow filter option. This gives me a black-and-white scene that's reminiscent of the Martin Scorsese film of the same name. Before you start recording your video, decide which Picture Control you want to use for your movie.

 For more information on Picture Controls, see Chapter 2. For more on the D5000 menus, see Chapter 3.

 Adding too much sharpening to a Picture Control can cause haloing in your movies.

✦ **Shooting mode.** Selecting a shooting mode is one of the most important parts of D-Movie. This is how you select your lens aperture. The mode you select determines the aperture that you shoot with for the entire clip. This is important for controlling depth of field. The Scene modes apply the same settings that they use for still photography, but they can be unpredictable. Because the shutter speed is controlled electronically, Shutter Priority mode isn't very useful either.

Using Programmed Auto is just taking a major risk with your aperture setting. Basically, that leaves you with the two most useful shooting modes: Aperture Priority and Manual. For all intents and purposes, these both operate exactly the same. Remember that the shutter is electronic and is completely controlled by the camera. The shutter speed that's displayed on the screen is for shooting stills in Live View and has no impact upon the movie. Basically, I recommend setting the camera to Manual mode when you record video.

 When in Live View mode with a CPU lens, the aperture actually only stops down to about a minimum of f/8 to allow enough light for Live View to work.

Recording

After you figure out all your settings and before you press the OK button to start recording, you want to get your shot in focus. You can do this by pressing the Shutter Release button halfway, as you normally would. When the AF point on the LCD is green, you're focused and ready to go. Press the OK button to start filming.

Once the camera is rolling, you have to do all the focusing manually. The camera pretty much runs things for you from then on. The only way to adjust the exposure while recording is to manually apply exposure compensation by pressing the Exposure Compensation button and then rotating the Command dial. You can dial in ±5 stops. The camera chooses the ISO settings for you. The rest is up to your imagination. You can make short clips of your kids running around that you can later e-mail to the grandparents or you can get creative with some software and produce a full-length feature film. You're the director.

Caution *When applying exposure compensation or making any sort of change that requires you to rotate a Command dial or even adjust the aperture ring on an MF lens, remember that the microphone is on the camera and that noise will be picked up. It may not sound loud at the time, but it will be extremely loud in your footage. The best bet is to get your settings right before filming starts to avoid this, or to turn the sound recording off.*

Tricks, Tips, and Workarounds

You probably bought a dSLR because you wanted flexibility and control that you just can't get with a compact digital camera. Now you have a D5000, but the Video mode wants to operate like a point-and-shoot camera. Is there a way to completely and manually control the D5000's settings when using the D-Movie mode? The short answer is no, but there are some ways to work around the camera settings by tricking it into choosing the settings that you prefer:

✦ **AE-L.** You've probably noticed that as you're filming, the video goes from light to dark as the lighting changes, depending on what the scene is. If you're filming in a high-contrast area, this can make your video look bad. The constant dimming and brightening of the video can be quite distracting. To stop your camera exposure from fluctuating, simply press the AE-L button. The best way to do this is to go to CSM f2, Assign AE-L/AF-L button, and set it to AE Lock (hold). This allows you to lock the exposure without holding the AE-L/AF-L button down.

You'll want to find a relatively neutral area in the scene and meter it by pointing the camera at it. Press the AE-L button to lock the exposure and record the video without fluctuations in your exposure. Be sure to press the AE-L button again to unlock the exposure meter. Even if you exit Live View mode, the exposure remains locked until the camera is turned off or goes to sleep.

✦ **Go fully manual.** In my opinion, to take full advantage of the D5000 video capabilities, you have to do something counterintuitive. Forsake all the newer lenses and get a non-CPU manual-focus lens. With a fully manual lens, you can adjust the aperture at any time during recording as well as close down to the actual minimum f-stop of the lens to maximize depth of field. The lens I use for most of my D5000 video work is a Nikkor-S 50mm f/1.4 AI from the 1960s. This lens is ultrasharp and can give you an extremely shallow depth of field when wide open or a deep focus when stopped down. You can find these lenses used for about $100 to $150. This lens is also an amazing portrait lens. Another good thing about using the older MF lenses for recording video is that these older lenses usually have a depth-of-field scale that can help you judge the focus range.

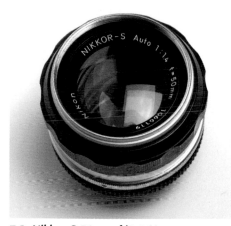

7.2 Nikkor-S 50mm f/1.4 AI.

✦ **ISO.** Unfortunately, there are no selectable ISO settings when recording video. This makes it difficult to control the amount of noise that your videos show. Before I get started with this trick, I need to point out that this isn't exact science. This is just an estimation of the settings that the camera may or may not use. When shooting video, the camera doesn't actually use an ISO setting but adjusts the signal gain. This is very similar to adjusting the ISO sensitivity. Looking at the footage, it's apparent that in

low light, the video appears noisier than video shot in bright light. This trick helps you to set the gain where you want it:

- **Select your camera settings.** Set the Quality, Sound, and Picture Control if needed. Set the camera to Aperture Priority or Manual. If you're using an MF, non-CPU lens, then set the shooting mode to Manual.

- **Set the scene.** Find the area or scene you're going to film. You need a constant light source, and the scene shouldn't have too much contrast or your exposures will be incorrect.

- **Set the aperture.** This step determines the ISO range the camera chooses. See Table 7.1 for settings.

- **Meter the scene.** This is important. Focus on an 18-percent gray card or a neutral object to take a meter reading. Don't do this step in Live View. Focus on the card or neutral object as if you were taking a picture normally.

- **Lock the exposure.** Use the AE-L/AF-L button to lock the exposure. The button should be set to AE Lock (hold). You can set this in CSM f2.

- **Activate Live View.** Press the Live View button. You're now ready to record your video by using the ISO range that you specified by the aperture setting.

The following table gives an approximation of the ISO sensitivity and noise levels in the video as they would relate to noise in still images.

Table 7.1
Aperture Settings

f/1.4–2.8	ISO 200–320
f/4–5.6	ISO 400–640
f/8–11	ISO 800–1200
f/16–32	ISO 1600+

 Note *Although when using a CPU lens the aperture doesn't stop down past f/8, when using a non-CPU lens you can stop down as far as the lens will allow.*

Video-editing Software

Because this is primarily a camera guide, I'm not going to go into all the different video-editing techniques that are available. That is a subject for another book. Editing allows you to combine different footage to make your video into a story, or you can simply cut out any extraneous footage. You may jump right in and make elaborate videos, or you may just film short clips to send to friends over e-mail.

There are many types of software that you can use to edit the D5000 video footage that you record. This software ranges in price from $1,300 for Apple Final Cut Studio 2 to free software, such as Avid Free DV. Personally, I use iMovie from Apple, which is fairly easy to learn. The reason I use this software is simply because it was already installed on my Mac when I bought it. There are many video-editing options, including the following:

✦ **Apple Final Cut Pro 6.** This program comes bundled inside of the Final Cut Studio 2 suite. This is the top-of-the-line video editing software that professional videographers use to edit their footage. It supports almost all video formats, including the AVI files of the D5000. This is a very intensive product that can do almost anything you can imagine.

✦ **Adobe Premiere CS4.** This is another high-end video-editing software package. With this software, you can edit multiple videos, add audio tracks, and apply color correction, among other options.

✦ **Adobe Premiere Elements.** This is a stripped-down, user-friendly version of Premiere meant for use by amateur filmmakers like you and me. This is supposed to be the best nonprofessional video-editing software available. You can add audio and narration, text, and titles. You can add special effects, transitions, and even picture-in-picture. Premiere Elements is very affordable at around $120.

✦ **iMovie.** Mac users get this application bundled with the operating system software. It's a very easy-to-use application that allows you to make cuts and paste together clips, add music from iTunes, add special effects, make simple color corrections, and add titles and text. This is a Mac-only application.

✦ **Windows Movie Maker.** This is the PC version of Mac's iMovie. This program is rated fairly well by PC users and does most of the same things as iMovie.

✦ **Sony Vegas.** This video-editing software comes in a few different versions for users of all different levels. The top-of-the-line Vegas Pro is comparable to Final Cut Pro or Premiere. The entry-level version is Vegas Movie Studio, which allows you to do all the standard editing. To take advantage of the D5000 HD video capabilities, you'll need to get the more advanced Vegas Movie Studio Platinum version, which allows you to export HD video.

Viewing and In-camera Editing

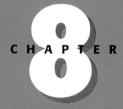
With the D5000's 2.7-inch VGA LCD monitor, you can view your images and even use the in-camera editing features, which allow you to save some time in post processing and give you the option to fine-tune your images for printing without ever having to download your images to a computer.

Nikon has upgraded the Retouch menu with some exciting new options that weren't available on previous cameras, such as the Perspective control feature. With all of these post-processing tools built right into the camera, it's entirely possible to do all of your image adjustments (including RAW image processing) from start to finish, connect the camera to a PictBridge-enabled printer, and print. This encompasses your entire workflow without touching a computer at all!

Viewing Your Images

The Nikon D5000 offers three different ways to view your images while the memory card is still inserted in the camera. You can view the images directly on the LCD monitor on the camera, you can hook your camera up to a standard TV using the Nikon EG-D2 audio/video cable that's included in the box, or you can connect the camera to an HDTV or HD monitor using a separate cable that you can buy from your local electronics store.

When viewing through an external device such as an HDTV, the view is the same as what would normally be displayed on the LCD monitor. The camera's buttons and dials function exactly the same way:

✦ **Press the Playback button to view the most recent photo or video.** To play the video, press OK.

✦ **Press the multi selector left or right to scroll through the images.** Press right to view the images in the order they were taken, and left to view them in reverse order. Rotating the main Command dial left and right also performs these same functions.

✦ **Press the multi selector up or down to view data.** By default, the camera displays shooting information that includes the brightness histogram, metering mode, shooting mode, shutter speed, ISO, focal length, exposure compensation (if any), WB color space, Picture Control, and Active D-Lighting settings (if any). The date and time, filename, and image quality are also displayed. You can display additional information, such as Highlights, RGB histograms, and more detailed data, by setting the Display mode option in the Playback menu. If the optional GPS device was used, then location and time details are also displayed on a separate page.

✦ **Press the Delete button (trash can icon) to erase an image or video from the memory card.** The camera asks for confirmation before permanently deleting the file.

✦ **Use the Protect button to prevent an image from being deleted.** The Protect button has a key icon on it. Press it once to protect the image, and press it again to unprotect the image. Note that the image will be erased when the card is formatted.

✦ **Use the Zoom Out button to view thumbnails.** Pressing this button from the default full-frame view gives you a 4-up view with one press, 9-up with two presses, and 72-up with three presses. Pressing the button a fourth time brings up a calendar view that displays images taken on a certain day. Use the multi selector to choose the date. Press the Zoom In button the appropriate amount of times to return to the default display.

✦ **Use the Zoom In button to inspect your images more closely.** From the default preview setting, you can press the button eight times to zoom in; the sixth step shows the image at 100 percent, and the last two steps appear pixelated. Use the multi selector to move around to different areas of the image. When viewing portraits, the camera has a face detection mode that allows you to zoom in directly on the face by scrolling the sub-command dial. When the camera detects a face in the frame, an icon appears in the lower-left corner of the image.

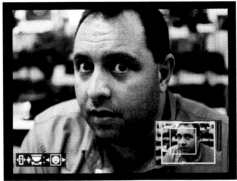

8.1 Face detection in Playback mode.

Before connecting the camera to your television, you need to set the video out mode. There are two different types of video interface, PAL and NTSC. By default, the camera (if you bought it in North America) is set to NTSC. These modes control how the electronic signal is processed. In NTSC mode, 30 frames are transmitted each second with each frame being made up of 525 scan lines. PAL mode transmits 25 frames per second with each frame being made up of 625 scan lines. These two different video modes are used in different parts of the world. Most of North and South America use the NTSC mode, while Asia and Europe use the PAL mode.

You probably live in North America, and so you want to set the video mode to NTSC. If you happen to live overseas, you probably want to set the video mode to PAL. If you're unsure whether your TV accepts NTSC or PAL, you should check the owner's manual of your TV.

To set the video mode, follow these steps:

1. **Turn the camera on.**

2. **Press the Menu button.**

3. **Use the multi selector to highlight the Setup menu.**

4. **Use the multi selector to highlight Video mode, and then press the OK button.**

5. **Use the multi selector to highlight NTSC (or PAL).**

6. **Press the OK button to save your settings.**

 Cross-Reference *For more information on playing back images, see Chapter 3.*

To connect your camera to a standard TV, follow these steps:

1. **Turn the camera off.** This can prevent damage to your camera's electronics from static electricity.

2. **Open the connector cover.** The connector cover is on the left side of the camera when the lens is facing away from you.

3. **Plug in the EG-D100 video cable.** The cable is available separately from Nikon. Plug the cable into the Video out jack. This is the connection at the top.

4. **Connect the EG-D100 to the input jack of your television or VCR.**

5. **Set your TV to the video channel.** This may differ, depending on your TV. See the owner's manual if you are unsure.

6. **Turn on the camera and press the Playback button.**

Connecting your camera to an HDTV or monitor is the same as connecting to a regular TV, with the exception that you must use a type C mini-pin HDMI cable that you can purchase at a local electronics store.

Downloading Images

After you've finished taking your pictures, you're probably going to want to download them to your computer for further image editing and tweaking, or so that you can post them to the Web or send them off to your friends and family.

Downloading your images is a fairly simple process, and there are a couple of different ways to do this. The most common way is to remove the memory card from the camera and insert it into a card reader that is connected to your computer. The other option is to use the USB cable supplied with the D5000 and connect the camera directly to the computer. Either option works just as well as the other, and it's mostly personal preference.

In the past, most Nikon dSLRs had an option that you could set the camera to appear on your computer as Mass Storage; in other words, when you plugged in your camera, it showed up the same as an external hard drive. For some reason, the Nikon D5000 has not included this option. What this means is that to download any images directly from the camera, you may have to use the Nikon Transfer software that is included on a CD with the camera.

I'm a Mac user, and with Mac OS X, the camera doesn't automatically show up when the camera is connected with a USB cable (it shows up in Nikon Transfer). I've been told that Windows automatically detects the camera with no problem. I, for one, have not been very pleased with this feature, although you may find it convenient. The Nikon Transfer software is very easy to learn and works well, but I prefer to manually download my images to folders that I have already created to help speed up my workflow. There are times that I forget my card reader, and so I need to plug the camera in directly, and using the Nikon software just adds another step for me to do. Again, this is a personal preference and I encourage you to use Nikon Transfer if you don't have a card reader or prefer to plug your camera directly into the computer (you really don't have any other choice).

Using Nikon Transfer

Before you download any images directly from the camera, you must first install Nikon Transfer to your computer. There is a CD included inside the box with your D5000. In addition to Nikon Transfer, the CD also contains Nikon's image-editing and -viewing software, Nikon View NX. You can use Nikon View NX to do most basic editing of your photos, such as contrast adjustments and red-eye removal.

After installing Nikon Transfer, as soon as your D5000 is connected to the computer and turned on, the application launches automatically. By default, Nikon Transfer is set up to create a new folder named Nikon Transfer, where your images will be saved. Nikon Transfer also automatically creates a numbered sub-folder each time new images are downloaded.

There are a number of different tabs in the Nikon Transfer main window that allow you to specify how Nikon Transfer deals with your files.

Source tab

The first tab is the Source tab. This allows you to set what type of media Nikon Transfer searches for. Clicking the "search for" drop-down menu allows you to set the program to recognize when a camera is attached or a removable disk has been connected. Both of these options can also be set at the same time. Choosing the camera option allows the program to recognize only when a camera has been connected. When using an external card reader, you want to set the removable disk option.

Embedded Info tab

This tab allows you to attach text information to the EXIF data of your image. EXIF stands for Exchangeable Image File. EXIF

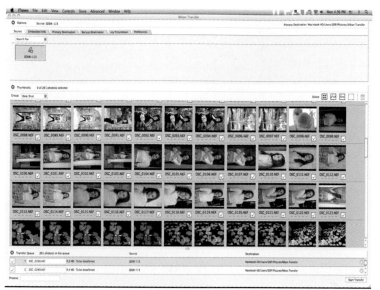

8.2 The Source tab in Nikon Transfer.

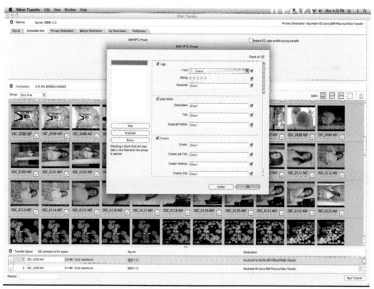

8.3 The Embedded Info editing screen.

data is embedded into your image file and has information such as the date and time, camera make and model, white balance settings, shutter speed and aperture, exposure and flash modes, and other information. The EXIF data can be read using programs such as Adobe Bridge and other image-editing software. Some photo-sharing Web sites like Flickr also allow you to view the EXIF data on images that are uploaded.

You can add all sorts of different information using the Embedded Info feature: a description of the photo, a title, your name and address, copyright information, and the location where the image was taken. You can also save a number of presets for saving different information.

Primary Destination tab

This tab allows you to choose where your images are downloaded. You can browse your hard drive to choose a specific destination or you can leave it at the default. There is also an option that allows you to customize the folder-naming sequence that Nikon Transfer uses.

Backup Destination tab

This tab allows you to automatically back up your images when transferring them. Backing up your images to an external hard drive is a good idea in case of a computer or hard drive failure. This feature works in much the same way as the Primary Destination tab.

Preferences tab

This tab allows you to customize how the program works and what it does with the files after transferring them. You can choose from a number of different options:

✦ **Launch automatically when device is attached.**

✦ **Disconnect automatically after transfer.**

✦ **Shut down computer automatically after transfer.**

✦ **Quit Nikon Transfer automatically after transfer.**

✦ **Synchronize camera date and time to computer when camera is connected.**

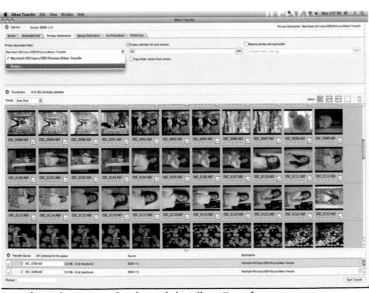

8.4 The Primary Destination tab in Nikon Transfer.

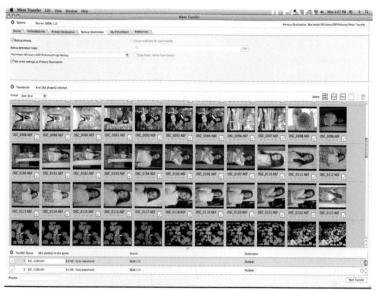

8.5 The Backup Destination tab in Nikon Transfer.

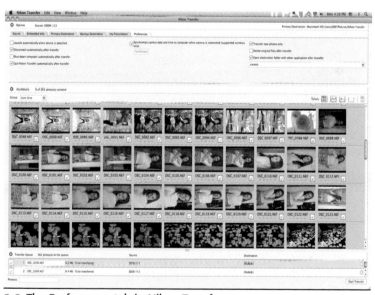

8.6 The Preferences tab in Nikon Transfer.

✦ **Transfer new photos only.**

✦ **Delete original files after transfer.**

✦ **Open destination folder with other application after transfer.**

Transferring your images

Once you have everything set the way you want it, transferring your images is a very simple process. All of the images on the memory card are displayed as thumbnails in the Nikon Transfer window; below the thumbnail is the image filename and a box that can be checked or unchecked. Simply click in the box to select the image.

When the checkmark appears in the box, the image is set to be transferred; if the box is empty, the image will not be copied. Once you have selected all of the images you want to transfer, simply click the button labeled Start Transfer, located on the bottom-right side of the window. The images are then copied to the specified destination.

The Retouch Menu

The Nikon D5000 has a very handy Retouch menu. The in-camera editing options in this menu make it simple for you to print straight from the camera without downloading your files to your computer or using any image-editing software.

One great feature of using the Retouch menu is that the camera saves the retouched image as a copy so that you don't lose the original image. This can be beneficial if you decide that you would rather edit the photo on your computer or if you simply aren't happy with the outcome. There are two ways to access the Retouch menu.

The first and quickest method is as follows:

1. **Press the Play button to enter Playback mode.** Your most recently taken image appears on the LCD screen.

2. **Use the multi selector to review your images.**

3. **When you see an image you want to retouch, press the OK button to display the Retouch menu options.**

4. **Use the multi selector to highlight the Retouch option you want to use.** Depending on the Retouch option you choose, you may have to select additional settings.

5. **Make adjustments if necessary.**

6. **Press the OK button to save.**

 Note *When the image review displays a video, pressing the OK button causes the video to play back.*

The second method is as follows:

1. **Press the Menu button to view menu options.**

2. **Use the multi selector to scroll down to the Retouch menu.** It's the fifth menu down and appears as an icon with a paintbrush.

3. **Press the multi selector right, and then use the multi selector up and down buttons to highlight the Retouch option you want to use.** Depending on the Retouch option you select, you may have to select additional settings. Once you have selected your option(s), thumbnails appear.

4. **Use the multi selector to select the image to retouch, and then press the OK button.**

5. **Make the necessary adjustments.**

6. **Press the OK button to save.**

Note   *Some Retouch menu options may not be available depending on the setting used when the image was taken, such as red-eye fix with a photo that wasn't taken with flash. If the feature isn't available, it is "grayed out" and you are not able to select it.*

Retouch Menu Options

There are a few options you can select when using the Retouch menu. The options vary from cropping your image to adjusting the color balance to taking red-eye out of your pictures.

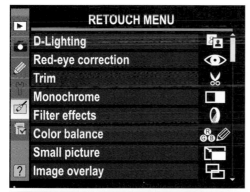

8.7 The Retouch menu.

D-Lighting

This option allows you to adjust the image by brightening the shadows. This is not the same as Active D-lighting. D-Lighting uses a curves adjustment to help bring out details in the shadow areas of an image. This option is for use with backlit subjects or images that may be slightly underexposed.

When the D-Lighting option is chosen from the Retouch menu, you can use the multi selector to choose a thumbnail and the Zoom In button to get a closer look at the image. Press the OK button to choose the image to retouch; two thumbnails are displayed, one the original image, and the other the image with D-Lighting applied.

You can press the multi selector up and down to select the amount of D-Lighting: Low, Normal, or High. The results can be viewed in real time and compared with the original before saving. Press the OK button to save, the Playback button to cancel, and the Zoom In button to view the full-frame image.

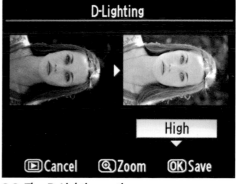

8.8 The D-Lighting option.

Red-eye correction

This option enables the camera to automatically correct for the red-eye effect that can sometimes be caused by using the flash on pictures taken of people. This option is only available on photos taken with flash. When choosing images to retouch from the Playback menu (by pressing the OK button during preview), this option is grayed out and cannot be selected if the camera detects that a flash was not used. When attempting to choose an image directly from the Retouch menu, a message is displayed stating that this image cannot be selected.

Once the image has been selected, press the OK button; the camera then automatically corrects the red-eye and saves a copy of the image to your CF card.

If an image is selected that flash was used on but there is no red-eye present, the camera displays a message stating that red-eye is not detected in the image, and no retouching is done.

Trim

This option allows you to crop your image to remove distracting elements or to crop more closely to the subject. You can also use the Zoom In and Zoom Out buttons to adjust the size of the crop. This allows you to crop more closely in or farther out, depending on your needs.

Use the multi selector to move the crop around the image so that you can center the crop on the part of the image that you think is most important.

When you are happy with the crop you have selected, press the OK button to save a copy of your cropped image, or press the Playback button to return to the main menu without saving.

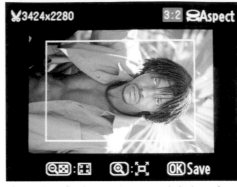

8.9 Using the in-camera crop (Trim) option.

Rotating the Command dial allows you to choose different aspect ratios for your crop. You can choose the aspect ratio to conform to different print sizes. The options are:

✦ **3:2.** This is the default crop size; this ratio is good for print sizes of 4x6, 8x12, and 12x18.

✦ **4:3.** This is the ratio for print sizes of 6x8 or 12x18.

✦ **5:4.** This is the standard size for 8x10 prints.

✦ **1:1.** This gives you a square crop.

✦ **16:9.** This is what's known as a cinematic crop. This is the ratio that movie screens and widescreen televisions use.

Monochrome

This option allows you to make a copy of your color image in a monochrome format.

There are three options:

✦ **Black-and-white.** This changes your image to shades of black, white, and gray.

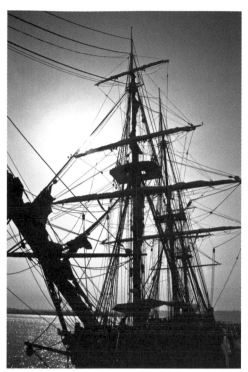

8.10 An image converted to black and white.

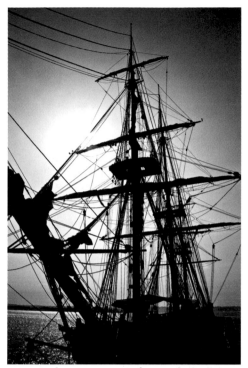

8.11 An image converted to sepia.

- ✦ **Sepia.** This gives your image the look of a black-and-white photo that has been sepia toned. Sepia toning is a traditional photographic process that gives the photo a reddish-brown tint.

- ✦ **Cyanotype.** This option gives your photo a blue or cyan tint. Cyanotypes are created from a form of processing film-based photographic images.

When using the Sepia or Cyanotype option, you can press the multi selector up and down to adjust the lightness or darkness of the effect.

Press the OK button to save a copy of the image, or press the Playback button to cancel without saving.

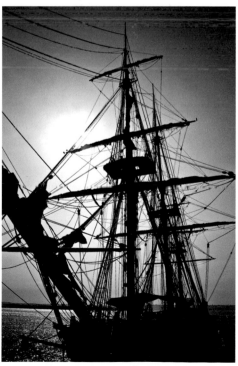

8.12 An image converted to cyanotype.

Filter effects

Filter effects allow you to simulate the use of certain filters over your lens to subtly modify the colors of your image. There are seven filter effects available:

✦ **Skylight.** A Skylight filter is used to absorb some of the UV rays emitted by the sun. The UV rays can give your image a slightly bluish tint. Using the Skylight filter effect causes your image to be less blue.

✦ **Warm filter.** A Warm filter adds a little orange to your image to give it a warmer hue. This filter effect can sometimes be useful when using flash because flash can sometimes cause your images to look a little too cool.

✦ **Red intensifier.** This filter adds a red colorcast to your image. You can press the multi selector up or down to lighten or darken the effect.

✦ **Green intensifier.** This filter adds a green colorcast to your image. You can press the multi selector up or down to lighten or darken the effect.

✦ **Blue intensifier.** This filter adds a blue colorcast to your image. You can press the multi selector up or down to lighten or darken the effect.

✦ **Cross screen.** This effect simulates the use of a star filter. A star filter creates a star-shaped pattern on the bright highlights in your image. If your image doesn't have any bright highlights, the effect will not be apparent. Once an image is selected for the Cross screen filter, you are shown a submenu with a few options that you can adjust. You can choose the number of points on the stars: 4, 6, or 8. You can also choose the amount; there are three settings, which give you more or fewer stars. You can choose three different angle settings, which control the angle at which the star is tilted. You also have three settings that control the length of the points on the stars.

✦ **Soft.** This filter applies a soft glow to your images. This effect is mostly used for portraiture but can also be used effectively for landscapes.

After choosing the desired filter effect, press the OK button to save a copy of your image with the effect added.

Color Balance

You can use the Color Balance option to create a copy of an image on which you have adjusted the color balance. Using this option, you can use the multi selector to add a color tint to your image. You can use this effect to neutralize an existing color tint or to add a color tint for artistic purposes.

Press the multi selector up to increase the amount of green, down to increase the amount of magenta, left to add blue, and right to add amber.

A color chart and color histograms are displayed along with an image preview so that you can see how the color balance affects your image. When you are satisfied with your image, press the OK button to save a copy.

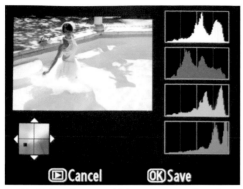

8.13 Color chart and histograms using the Color Balance option.

Small Picture

This is a handy option that allows you to make a copy of your images that are a smaller size. These smaller pictures are more suitable for e-mailing to friends and family.

The first thing you need to do when creating a small picture is to select the Choose size option from the Small Picture sub-menu. You have three sizes to choose from: 640x480, 320x240, or 160x120. After you have decided what size you want your small picture copies to be, go to the Select Picture option.

When the Select Picture option is chosen, the LCD displays thumbnails of all of the images in the current folder. To scroll through your images, press the multi selector left and right. To select or deselect an image, press the multi selector up and down. You can select as many images as you have on your memory card. When all of the images that you want to make a small copy of are selected, press the OK button to make the copies.

Image Overlay

This option allows you to combine two RAW images and save them as one. This option can only be accessed by entering the Retouch menu using the Menu button; you cannot access this option by pressing the OK button when in Playback mode.

 Note To use this option, you must have at least two RAW images saved to your memory card. This option is not available for use with JPEG or TIFF images.

To use this option, follow these steps:

1. **Press the Menu button to view the menu options.**

2. **Press the multi selector to scroll down to the Retouch menu, and press the multi selector right to enter the Retouch menu.**

3. **Press the multi selector up and down to highlight Image overlay.**

4. **Press the multi selector right; this** displays the Image overlay menu.

5. **Press the OK button to view RAW image thumbnails.** Use the multi selector to highlight the first RAW image to be used in the overlay. Press the OK button to select it.

6. **Adjust the exposure of Image one by pressing the multi selector up or down.** Press the OK button when the image is adjusted to your liking.

7. **Press the multi selector right to switch to Image 2.**

8. **Press the OK button to view RAW image thumbnails.** Use the multi selector to highlight the second RAW image to be used in the overlay. Press the OK button to select it.

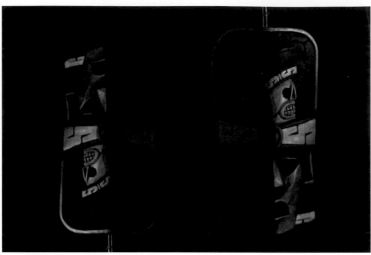

8.14 Two RAW images were combined using the Image Overlay option to produce this photo.

9. **Adjust the exposure of Image 2 by pressing the multi selector up or down.** Press the OK button when the image is adjusted to your liking.

10. **Press the multi selector right to highlight the Preview window.**

11. **Press the multi selector up or down to highlight *Overlay* to preview the image, or use the multi selector to highlight *Save* to save the image without previewing.**

NEF (RAW) Processing

This option allows you to do some basic editing to images saved in the RAW format without downloading them to a computer and using image-editing software. This option is limited in its function but allows you to fine-tune your image more precisely when printing straight from the camera or memory card.

You can save a copy of your image in JPEG format. You can choose the image quality

and size that the copy is saved as, adjust the white balance settings, fine-tune the exposure compensation, and select an Optimize image setting to be applied.

To apply RAW processing, follow these steps:

1. **Enter the NEF (RAW) Processing menu through the Retouch menu.** Press the OK button to view thumbnails of the image stored on your card. Only images saved in RAW format are displayed.

2. **Press the multi selector left and right to scroll through the thumbnails.** Press the OK button to select the highlighted image. This brings up a dialog box with the image adjustment sub-menu located to the right of the image you have selected.

3. **Press the multi selector up and down to highlight the adjustment you want to make.** You can select Image quality, Image size, White balance, Exposure compensation,

and Optimize image. The last option, EXE, sets the changes and saves a copy of the image in JPEG format at the size and quality that you have selected. The camera default saves the image as a Large, Fine JPEG. You can also use the Zoom In button to view a full-screen preview.

4. **When you have made your adjustments use the multi selector to highlight EXE and press the OK button to save changes, or press the Playback button to cancel without saving.**

Cross-Reference *For more information on image size, quality, white balance, and exposure compensation, see Chapter 2.*

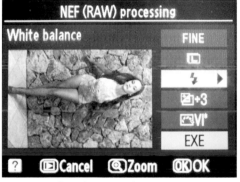

8.15 NEF (RAW) Processing menu screen.

Quick Retouch

Quick Retouch is the easiest option. The camera automatically adjusts the contrast and saturation, making your image brighter and more colorful, perfect for printing straight from the camera or memory card. In the event that your image is dark or backlit, the camera also automatically applies D-Lighting to help bring out details in the shadow areas of your picture.

Once your image has been selected for Quick Retouch, you have the option to choose how much of the effect is applied. You can choose from High, Normal, or Low. The LCD monitor displays a side-by-side comparison between the image as shot and retouched to give you a better idea of what the effect looks like.

Once you decide how much of the effect you want, press the OK button to save a copy of the retouched image, or you can press the Playback button to cancel without making any changes to your picture.

Straighten

This a fairly simple tool that allows you to straighten any images that you may have inadvertently shot at a bit of an angle. Select the image that you want to straighten and press the multi selector right to tilt the image to the right, or press the multi selector left to tilt the image to the left. The image is overlaid with a grid to assist you with the process. Press the OK button to save the changes, or press the Playback button to cancel.

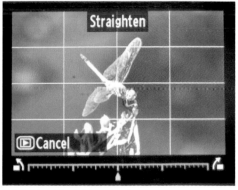

8.16 The Straighten tool.

Distortion Control

As discussed in Chapter 5, some lenses are plagued by distortion. Wide-angle lenses (or settings on a zoom lens) suffer from what is called barrel distortion, where the edges of the image seem to bulge out (like a barrel). Telephoto lenses suffer from the opposite effect. The edges seem to be sucked in; this is what's known as *pincushion distortion*.

Previously, in order to fix this lens distortion, you would need to fix the photo in an image editor such as Adobe Photoshop, Nikon Capture NX 2, or DxO Optics. Fortunately, this option is now included on-camera with the D5000. Although not as precise as an image editor for minor fixes, this option works pretty well.

There are two settings you can use with this menu option, Auto or Manual. The Auto setting automatically adjusts for the distortion, but allows you to fine-tune it a little to your taste by pressing the multi selector left or right. This option can only be used with certain lenses. Most D- and G-type lenses are supported, with the exception of the fisheyes and PC lenses. If the lens isn't supported, you will not be able to select the image when choosing the Auto option.

The Manual option can be used with any lens. Press the multi selector right to reduce barrel distortion, or left to counteract the effect of pincushion distortion.

Fisheye

This option applies a filter that simulates the spherical distortion that is the distinctive feature of the fisheye lens. Personally, I don't think the representation comes off very well and I'd recommend staying away from this feature.

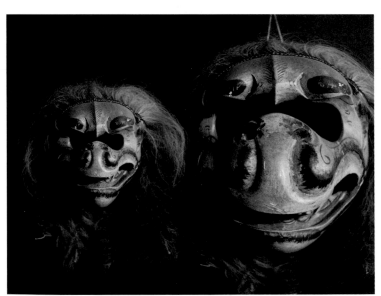

8.17 A before-and-after image using the Fisheye option.

Color Outline

The Color Outline feature takes the selected image and creates an outline copy that can be opened using image-editing software such as Adobe Photoshop or Corel Paint Shop Pro and colored in by hand. This option works best when used on an image with high contrast.

Perspective Control

Similar to the Distortion Control option, this feature allows you to make corrections to images that suffer from perspective distortion without the need for image-editing software. Perspective distortion can be seen when taking a picture looking up at a tall building. This is a very handy feature that you can use very easily to make minor perspective corrections.

Once you have selected an image to adjust, press the multi selector left, right, up, and down to make your adjustments.

Caution   *Applying Perspective Control causes the edges of the image to be cropped. The more correction is applied, the more of the image is cropped. Keep this in mind and loosely frame any images that you may want to use this feature on.*

Stop-motion Movie

This option allows you to link together up to 100 images to be shown in a series and saved as a movie (AVI) file. Stop motion is used in animation to make still objects appear as if they are moving, similar to cartoon animation. Basically, how it works is you take a picture of an object, move it slightly, take another picture, and so on. After these images are linked and played, the still object appears to move. The effect is sort of a crude, jerky animation. I don't find the need to use this option very often, but if you have some time and patience, I'm sure you could put together some very interesting short movies.

Some other ways to use this feature would be to shoot an action sequence, such as a skateboarder jumping a ramp, and link it together to show the motion, or even to put together a quick slide show of random images from your memory card. Follow these steps:

1. **After shooting a sequence of images, go to the Stop-Motion Movies option in the Retouch menu and press the OK button.** This brings you to a menu screen that gives you the following options: Create movie, Frame size, and Frame rate.

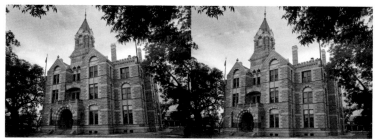

8.18 Before-and-after image of the Perspective Control feature.

2. **Select Frame size.** This allows you to choose how large the still frames in your movie are. The choices are:

   - **640x480.** This option stores your images at 640 pixels x 480 pixels. This is a suitable size for viewing on a small TV or computer monitor. This option results in a rather large file size.

   - **320x240.** This option is more suitable for posting to your Web site or to a site that hosts video such as YouTube or Flickr.

   - **160x120.** This gives you the smallest file size and is suitable for e-mailing.

3. **After you set your frame size, use the multi selector to scroll down to Frame rate and press the OK button.** This gives you the options for the frame rate. The frame rate, given in frames per second (fps), is how many still images are shown per second. There are four options:

   - **15 fps.** This is the highest option and generally speaking, 15 fps is about the minimum acceptable frame rate you can use before your movie appears jerky.

   - **10 fps.** This shows you ten images per second and appears somewhat jerky.

   - **6 fps.** This shows you six images per second. The video appears very jerky.

   - **3 fps.** This shows three images per second.

4. **After you choose your frame size and rate, use the multi selector to scroll up to Create movie, and press the OK button.** This brings you to a menu screen where you choose a starting image and a stopping image for your movie.

5. **Using the multi selector, choose the image you want to start on and press the OK button to select it.**

6. **Using the multi selector, choose the image you want to stop on and press the OK button to select it.**

7. **If you are happy with your choices, press the OK button again to save, or use the multi selector to highlight Edit, and then press OK to make new choices.**

8. **After you save your starting point, you are shown yet another menu from which you can select an option.** They are as follows:

   - **Save.** This option allows you to instantly save the stop-motion movie file to your memory card.

   - **Preview.** This allows you to view the stop-motion movie on your LCD monitor before saving to the memory card.

   - **Frame rate.** This allows you to adjust the frame rate as before: 15 fps, 10 fps, 6 fps, or 3 fps.

   - **Edit.** This allows you to change the starting and ending frame, as well as to choose to not show certain frames in the middle. To choose not to show middle frames, select the Middle Frame option, and then press the multi selector left and right to scroll through the thumbnails. Press the multi selector up and down to set the images to be shown or not. A small checkmark appears in the images to be shown; deselecting the image deletes it from playback (but not from the memory card).

Side-by-side Comparison

This option allows you to view a side-by-side comparison of the retouched image and the original copy of the image. This option can only be accessed by selecting an image that has been retouched.

To use this option, follow these steps:

1. **Press the Play button and use the multi selector to choose the retouched image to view.**

2. **Press the OK button to display the Retouch menu.**

3. **Use the multi selector to highlight Before and after, and then press the OK button.**

4. **Use the multi selector to highlight either the original or retouched image.** You can then use the Zoom In button to view the image more closely.

5. **Press the Play button to exit the Before and after comparison and return to Playback mode.**

Capturing Great Images with the Nikon D5000

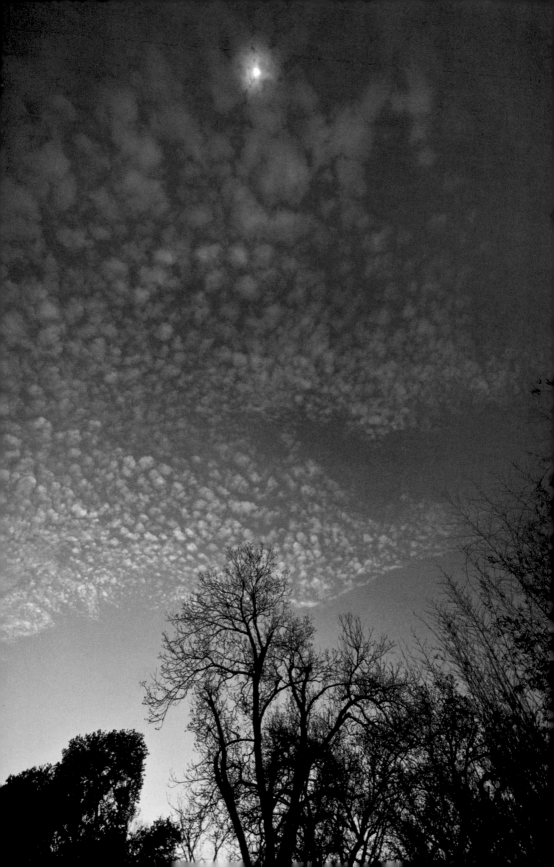

Action and Sports Photography

Nearly everyone likes photographs that portray some sort of exciting event unfolding. These types of photographs often bring you closer to an event or freeze the moment, allowing you to see the action in a way that's just not possible with the naked eye.

Action photography is usually equated with some kind of sport, although that's not always the case. Action photography can be done with any type of moving subject, from a pet running up the beach, to a child running the bases at their first Little League Baseball game, to a professional basketball player slam dunking the ball.

Preparing Your Shot

Probably the most essential skill for achieving great action shots is timing. To get a great shot, you need to get the peak of the action. In order to capture the action at its peak, it helps to be familiar with the sport. For example, when photographing a track event such as the 100-yard dash, you know that as the runners come off of the starting blocks, there will be strength and energy in their form. Of course, catching the winner crossing the finish line is also a great time for a shot.

The best way to get a feel for the sport you're photographing is quite simply to stand back and watch before you start shooting. Taking a few minutes to act as a spectator can allow you to see the rhythm of the action.

Another big part of capturing a great action shot is being in the right place at the right time. While this sounds like luck, it's not. Take basketball, for example; it's quite easy to be in the right place at the right time. With basketball, you know exactly where the action is going to be 95 percent of the time: right at the goal. With other sports it's not always quite as easy, but as I mentioned previously, watching for a while can give you an idea of where most of the action will be taking place.

Probably the most important camera setting for photographing action is the shutter speed. The shutter speed determines how the movement is shown in your photograph. For the most part, a fast shutter speed is used when photographing action. A fast shutter speed allows you to freeze the motion of the subject. Freezing the motion lets you do things like getting a nice sharp image of an athlete in motion.

Using a fast shutter speed isn't the only way to capture great action shots. Using a slow shutter speed can sometimes be exactly what you need to bring out the movement in an action shot. For example, when shooting any type of motorsports, it's very common for a photographer to use a slow shutter speed to introduce some blurring into the image to illustrate movement.

Panning

For figures 9.1 and 9.2, I was photographing the horse races at a nearby track. As you probably know, horses are extremely fast, and in order to capture the action, I had to employ a few different techniques here for each picture. I used a fast shutter speed and panning, as well as a slow shutter speed and panning. If you're not familiar with panning, it is a technique in which you follow your subject along the same plane that it is traveling. Generally, you would pan horizontally, but you can also pan vertically, although this can be more difficult.

Panning reduces the relative speed of the subject in relation to the camera, thereby allowing you freeze the motion of the subject more easily than if you held the camera still and snapped the shot while the subject moved through the frame.

Panning with a fast shutter speed

Using a fast shutter speed on a shot like figure 9.1 allows you to completely freeze all of the action in the scene, which allows you to see that all four of the horse's hooves are off of the ground at once. This was actually only conjecture until Eadweard Muybridge proved it. In the late 1800s, Muybridge was the first person to undertake high-speed photography, and he also invented the first mechanically tripped shutter.

For figure 9.1, I set the camera to Shutter Priority and set the shutter speed to a relatively fast 1/800 second. This allowed me to completely freeze all movement of the horse and jockey. Because the day was overcast, there wasn't a lot of contrast to the scene, and so I set the camera to Matrix metering, which works quite well in lighting such as this.

Panning with a slow shutter speed

Panning is most effective when used in conjunction with a relatively slow shutter speed. Because the speed of the subject is effectively reduced by the camera movement, you can use a slower shutter speed to freeze the action. In addition to this, the background is effectively moving faster, and so the slow shutter speed causes the background to have motion blur. The background blur gives your image the illusion of movement and also helps to isolate the subject from the background.

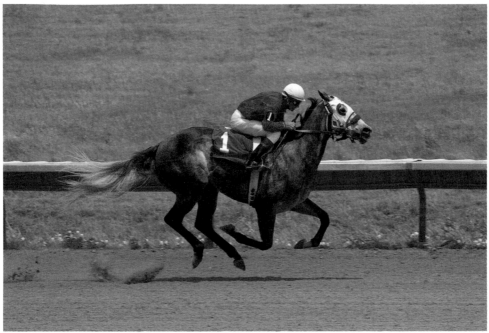

9.1 In this shot, I used a fast shutter speed to freeze the motion.

For figure 9.2, I wanted to show movement in a different way; still using Shutter Priority, I slowed the shutter speed down to 1/50 second. Using a monopod to steady my heavy 70-200mm zoom lens, I focused on the jockey in the green jersey and panned along with him.

When I snapped the shot, the jockey and the body of the horse remained in relatively sharp focus because I was moving the lens along with them while the horse's legs, which were moving much faster and in different directions, were rendered as a blur. This blur, along with the motion blur in the background, gives the image a sense of movement in a completely different way than in figure 9.1. This shows you the power of varying your shutter speed in capturing action shots.

In horse racing, you can use either a fast or slow shutter speed to show movement. Some sports require one or the other. For example, auto racing is best done using a relatively slow shutter speed. I say 'relatively' because for most sports, a fast shutter speed is generally 1/250 second or faster. In auto racing, 1/250 second is relatively slow.

When photographing racing cars that are moving at 100+mph, using a fast shutter speed sounds like an obvious choice, right? Wrong. Using a fast shutter speed freezes all of the movement of the car including the tires, which are the fastest-moving part of the car. Freezing the motion of the tires causes the car to look like it's sitting parked on the track.

Using a slower shutter speed and panning with the vehicle allows you to capture the movement of the wheels, giving them a blur that adds the illusion of movement in your still photograph. In figure 9.3, I employed a slow shutter speed of 1/160 second using Shutter Priority.

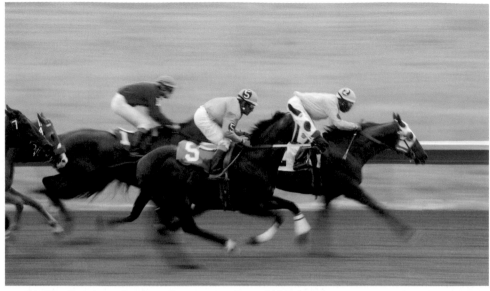

9.2 In this shot, I used a slow shutter speed to add blur to show movement.

Using Speedlights

For figure 9.4, I used a completely different technique to freeze action: Speedlights. I used flash to light this skateboarder, but I also kept the background in mind when choosing my settings.

Although it was nearing dusk, there was still enough light in the sky to give it a normal dull-blue appearance. I was looking to get a very dynamic image, and I wanted to under-expose the background to make the sky more dramatic and to give the image a darker nighttime appearance.

When setting up for the shot in figure 9.4, I knew I wanted an extreme perspective dis-tortion to give the image more impact, so I used a Nikon 10.5mm fisheye lens. The extreme wide angle of this lens gives it a really deep depth of field, so achieving focus with this lens is simple.

I pre-focused on the edge of the ramp before the skateboarder approached. To get the extreme perspective distortion I was looking for, I had to get really close. I put my lens very near to the coping and hoped that he wouldn't slip, sending the skateboard into my camera (and face). When I took this shot, that skateboard wheel was literally six inches in front of my lens.

Caution *Be careful when using wide-angle lenses when photographing mov-ing subjects. Wide-angle lenses make things look farther away than they really are when looking through the viewfinder. What looks like feet to you may actually be inches.*

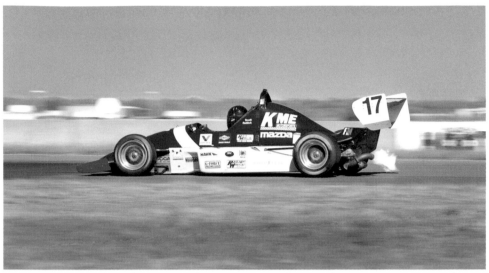

9.3 I employed a slow shutter speed of 1/160 second using Shutter Priority. I panned along with the car to freeze the motion, but the faster-moving wheels are rendered as blurs.

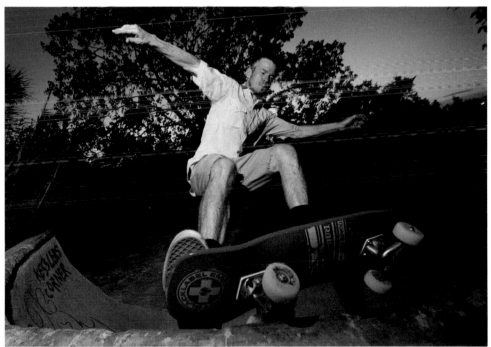

9.4 Overexposing the subject and underexposing the background can create interesting results.

I first set my camera to Spot meter. I then aimed the lens at the brightest spot in the sky, which was just over the horizon. I took the reading, then I subtracted two stops from it, and I had the exposure I was looking for, which was 1/60 second at f/5.6, which I set in Manual exposure. This is a relatively slow shutter speed for action shots, but I wasn't worried because I was using a Speedlight. The short duration of the flash is often enough to freeze your subject in motion.

I used two flashes to achieve this shot: an SU-800 as a commander and an SB-800 as a remote. I set the SB-800 to function as a remote on Group A and used the AS-19 Speedlight stand to hold it. I positioned the SB-800 on the lip of the ramp, near the center off to the left of the camera. I used the built-in wide-angle diffuser to soften the light just a bit and to give the flash a little more coverage.

Caution

Before using flash on action shots, be sure to get permission from the athlete. Using a flash may blind them, which can lead to disastrous results.

The first couple of shots I took with straight TTL weren't quite bright enough to make the skateboarder really stand out, and so I adjusted the FEC on the SU-800 to +2 exposure value (EV). This gave me just the amount of light that I was looking for, exposing my subject perfectly while the background was underexposed, and giving it dramatic colors.

Flower and Plant Photography

Flowers and plants have inspired artists down through the centuries. Many artists choose flowers and plants not only because of their beauty but also presumably because you don't have to pay them to model!

Many famous artists such as Vincent van Gogh have found inspiration in the beauty of plants, and some of his most treasured paintings are the Sunflowers series, Irises, and the many paintings he did in Arles, France, of the wheat fields and cypress trees.

It's not only painters who have derived inspiration from plants and flowers; many photographers down through the years have also used plants and flowers as subjects. Edward Weston regularly photographed different succulents such as the agave cactus, as well as many other plants, including fruits and vegetables. His image of the pepper, shot in 1930, is one of his most famous works.

Preparing Your Shot

One of the great things about photographing plants and flowers, as opposed to other living things, is that you have almost unlimited control with them. If they are potted or cut, you can place them wherever you want, trim off any excess foliage, sit them under a hot lighting setup, and you never hear them complain.

Some other great things about photographing plants and flowers are the almost unlimited variety of colors and textures you can find them in. From reds and blues to purples and yellows, the color combinations are almost infinite.

Plants and flowers are abundant, whether purchased or wild, and so there is no shortage of subjects. Even in the dead of winter, you can easily find plants to take photos of. They don't have to be in bloom to have an interesting texture or tone. Sometimes the best images of trees are taken after they have shed all of their foliage.

Flower and plant photography also offers a great way to show off your macro skills. Flowers especially seem to look great when photographed close up.

You don't have to limit flower and plant photography to the outdoors. You can easily go to the local florist and pick up a bouquet of flowers, set them up, and take photos of them. After you're done, you can give them to someone special as an added bonus!

Backlit Lotus

While at a botanical garden, I noticed the way the sun was shining through a lotus flower, making it glow. If you walk around and look at the interesting colors of the local flora, you may notice interesting features.

Pay close attention to the way the light interacts with different plants. A lot of the time, it is undesirable to have a backlit subject, but the light coming through a transparent flower petal can add a different quality of beauty to an already beautiful flower, as in figure 10.1.

The complementary colors of green and magenta give this image an added boost. Pay attention to the color scheme of the background and subject. Try to avoid having your subject and background be a similar color.

For the shot in figure 10.1, I was just wandering around taking snapshots, and so I had my camera set to Programmed Auto. When I snapped this shot, I was focused more on the composition than the settings. I was using the 18-105mm VR kit lens from my D90, and I zoomed out to 105mm, so I knew that, being fairly close to the subject, I would get a fairly shallow depth of field with the aperture that the camera selected.

Had I not been happy with the camera's exposure settings, I could have simply engaged the Flexible Program by rotating the Command dial until the desired aperture was set.

Because I was at the botanical gardens photographing flora to get a nice, saturated tone for the image, I set the Picture Control to Landscape, which gives a boost to the greens in particular.

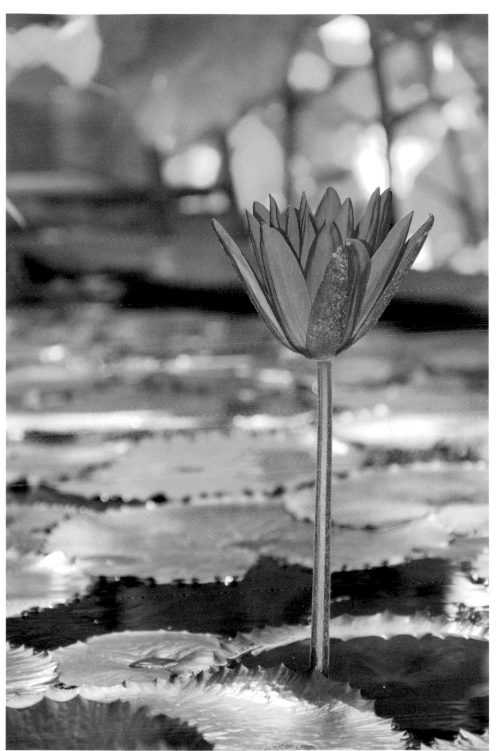

10.1 Backlighting gives a nice glow to this lotus flower.

Dried Seeds

Plants don't have to be brightly colored or even alive to make a good photograph, as demonstrated in figure 10.2. While taking a stroll at Edgewater Metro Park in Cleveland in the spring, I noticed these dead thistle seed pods.

As with figure 10.1, I was interested in the way the sun backlit the plants, which gave them a bit of glow, separating them from the background.

For the shot in figure 10.2, I set the camera to Aperture Priority mode to take advantage of the wide aperture of the Nikon 35mm f/1.8G, so that I could get a nice, shallow depth of field; this further separated the thistles from the background, which had a similar color.

The lighting was fairly even, nearing late afternoon, and so I chose to use Matrix metering. I dialed in -1.3 exposure compensation to help the colors pop and to keep the thistles fairly dark.

Setting minus exposure compensation also allowed me to keep the sky a deeper shade of blue. Using the camera's metering exposure settings would have resulted in the sky being much paler. I also set the Picture Control to Landscape, which boosts greens and blues.

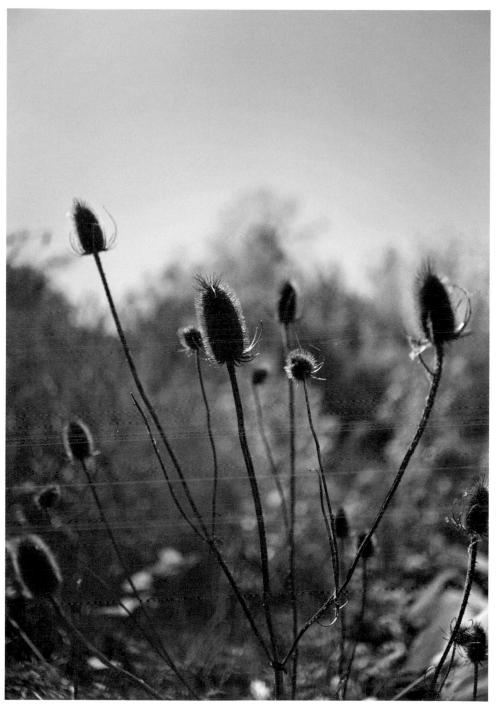

10.2 Taking photos of plants doesn't necessarily require a lengthy setup. Strolling around in nature is often the most you need to do. Just keep your eyes open for odd juxtapositions and interesting angles.

Macro Photography

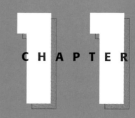

One of the most popular and interesting types of photography has to be macro photography. It is also referred to as close-up photography, although technically speaking, you don't necessarily need to be to close up to get a macro shot.

Macro photography often involves images of insects because most insects are so small that photographing them any other way doesn't allow you to see the details that you can get with macro photography. That being said, of course, insects aren't the only things you can take macro photos of. Macro photography is used for making many different types of images, from small product and food shots to abstract close-ups of all different types of subjects.

Preparing Your Shot

To do macro photography, you need to be able to focus closely enough so that the image your lens projects on the sensor of your camera is the exact same size as the subject that you are photographing. The relative size of the actual subject to the projected image is defined in terms of a ratio. So if your image size is the same as the subject size, you have a ratio of 1:1.

Strictly speaking, the true definition of a macro image is one that has a ratio of 1:1 or better. These days, however, the marketing gurus at the camera and lens manufacturing companies have broadened the definition of macro lens to encompass any lens that allows you get a ratio of 1:2, or half size.

Nikon's macro lenses are termed "Micro-Nikkor."

Generally speaking, the most difficult aspect of macro photography is getting your entire subject in focus. The closer you get to an object, the less depth of field you get, and it can be difficult to maintain focus. When your lens is less than an inch from the face of a bug, just breathing in is sometimes enough to lose focus on the area that you want to capture (or to scare the bug off). For this reason, you usually want to use the smallest aperture you can (depending on the lighting situation) and still maintain focus. I say "usually" because a shallow depth of field can also be very useful in bringing attention to a specific detail.

Tools of the Trade

There are many different ways to take macro shots of your favorite subjects. You can spend a lot of money on a top-of-the-line dedicated macro lens or you can go the inexpensive route of using close-up filters or reversing rings on a lens you already have.

Lenses

The preferred and probably best method is to purchase a lens specifically designed for this purpose. Nikon makes two highly regarded macro lenses that work well with the D5000: the 60mm f/2.8G and the 105mm f/2.8G VR. Both of these lenses have the AF-S motor, and so they autofocus perfectly. Personally, I use the 105mm lens and I find it superb, not only for macro photography, but also for many other types of photography.

Macro lenses allow you to focus very close to the subject, which is how you get a reproduction ratio of 1:1 or better. Using a good,

dedicated macro lens is going to get you the best results by far.

Close-up filters

Another inexpensive alternative to a macro lens is a *close-up filter*. A close-up filter is like a magnifying glass for your lens. It screws onto the end of your lens and allows you to get closer to your subject. There are a variety of different magnifications, and they can be *stacked,* or screwed together, to increase the magnification even more.

As with any filter, there are cheap ones and more expensive ones. Using cheap close-up filters can reduce the sharpness of your images because the quality of the glass isn't quite as good as the glass of the lens elements. This reduction in sharpness becomes more obvious when stacking filters. Buying the more expensive filters is still cheaper than buying a macro lens, and the quality of your images will definitely be better.

Extension tubes

An extension tube is exactly what it sounds like: it's a tube that extends your lens. An extension tube attaches between the lens and the camera body and gives your lens a closer focusing distance, allowing you to reduce the distance between the lens and your subject. Extension tubes are widely available and easy to use. Although manufacturers make both autofocus tubes and those that require you to focus manually, there are no extension tubes with an AF-S motor, and so even tubes labeled as AF need to be manually focused with the D5000.

A drawback to using extension tubes is that they effectively reduce the aperture of the lens they're attached to, causing you to lose a bit of light. Extension tubes come in various lengths, and some of them can be stacked or used in conjunction with each other. Unless you don't mind manually focusing, until an extension tube with AF-S is available, I recommend sticking to one of the other options in this chapter.

Reversing rings

Reversing rings are adapters that have a lens mount on one side and filter threads on the other. The filter threads are screwed into the front of a normal lens like a filter, and you attach the lens mount to the camera body. The lens is then mounted to the camera backward. This allows you to closely focus on your subject. One thing to be careful of when using reversing rings is damaging the rear element of your lens; special care should be taken when using one of these.

Not all lenses work well with reversing rings. The best lenses to use are fixed focal-length lenses that have aperture rings for adjusting the f-stop. Zoom lenses simply don't work well, nor do lenses that have no aperture control (such as the kit lens). If you're thinking about going this route, the best option for a lens is to get an inexpensive MF lens like a 50mm f/1.8. This lens can also work very well for the Video mode.

Another thing to remember is that when using a reversing ring, your camera will have no CPU contact to the lens; therefore, you will have to shoot in manual exposure.

Tripod

Arguably one of the most important tools in the macro photographer's toolkit is the tripod. As I mentioned before, sometimes even the small motion of breathing in and out is enough to shift focus on your subject

when the lens is very close. To remedy this, simply stick your camera on a tripod. This ensures that the focus is maintained exactly where you want it. Of course, a tripod only works if the subject is stationary; it can be quite difficult to chase down small animals and try to get them to stand still in front of your tripod-mounted camera.

A tripod is also great to counteract camera shake. As you magnify the subject, any camera movement is also magnified. Even the smallest amount of shaking from your hands or any vibration is enough to cause blur in your images. VR lenses can also help with this, but as you get closer to your subject, the VR function has less of an effect.

Flash

To get enough depth of field, you often need to stop down the aperture to the point that you don't have enough light to make the shot without having a very long exposure, high ISO settings, or in the worst case, both. If you have a moving subject or are hand-holding your camera, using a slow shutter speed isn't an option. The only other option is to add some light.

Nikon and a few other manufacturers make macro flash kits, which attach to the end of your lens to evenly illuminate your subject; this allows you to get maximum depth of field by providing enough light so that you can use a small aperture. The Nikon kit is the R1-C1 and is pretty expensive, costing nearly as much as the D5000 camera body itself, but it is an excellent kit. I have also found a very inexpensive unit, the Phoenix 46N ring flash. It costs about $100 and functions with i-TTL, albeit with pretty limited features. For the price, the Phoenix works exceptionally well and I don't have any problems recommending this simple macro flash unit.

Manual Focus with Macro

Although autofocus is a great help in most photography, there are times when it's beneficial to focus manually. There are quite a few photographers who swear that manual focus is the only way to do macro photography. Personally, I find that AF is a great benefit with macro photography, especially when trying to catch small, fleeting critters, but there are many instances where only manual focus will do.

As I discussed earlier, the closer you focus on a subject, the less depth of field you have at any aperture. For this reason, the point of focus is extremely important. For instance, when photographing an insect's face, if the point of focus is just a little bit off, the eyes of the insect will be out of focus while just behind them will be sharp. As with any portrait, even those of non-humans, the eyes should be sharp.

When photographing up close, it's best to pick the spot that you feel is most important to the image and focus on that (eyes, for instance). When using AF, the best way to do this is to use a single point, but even then, you are relying on the AF module, which may not always be exact. Simply switching to Manual and using your own eyes to determine that your point of focus is exact can be the best method to ensure that your image comes out exactly as you want it.

That being said, another option for inexpensive macro photography is a manual focus lens. Nikon has a few older MF macro lenses that are very sharp and much less expensive than the newer AF-S versions. You can also look into other options. I have an excellent Pentax M-42 screw-mount macro lens (Macro-Takumar 50mm f/4) that I found for next to nothing. With an inexpensive M-42 to Nikon F-mount adaptor that I got on eBay, I have a great macro setup that gives me a 4:1 ratio. So don't overlook the benefits of taking control and manually focusing. After all, the camera is your tool; make it work for you, not against you.

Using Ring Flashes

For the simple shot in figure 11.1, I used the Phoenix ring flash mentioned previously. Ring flashes are circular and are attached to the end of the lens with an adapter. Putting the flash around the lens allows the light to surround the optical axis of the lens. This gives a very flat light that allows you to see the fine detail in a macro shot. This type of lighting can often appear flat, especially when the subject is close in color to the background. While this can be great for technical photography (think circuit boards) and simple product photography (think eBay), for artistic purposes this type of lighting can lack depth and drama. One way you can add interest and depth to an image when using a ring flash is to use a contrasting background or one with complementary colors.

For figure 11.1, I simply placed the light skull on a dark surface; this gave the image the contrast and depth it needed while retaining nice, even lighting.

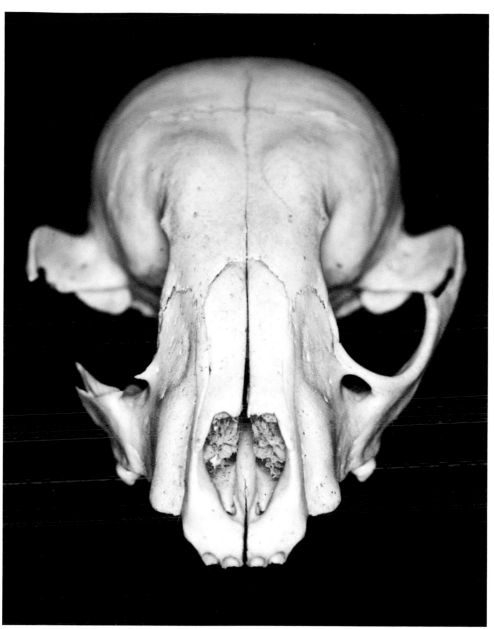

11.1 For this macro shot, I used a ring flash.

Because figure 11.1 was a fairly simple and straightforward shot, all of my settings were quite simple. First of all, I started out in Aperture Priority mode because I knew that the close focus that the shot required would give me an extremely shallow depth of field. I set the aperture for f/16, and you can see that I'm still losing depth of field about half-way up the skull. For this image, losing some depth of field is okay because most of the detail is in the front part of the skull. For your own images, you might want to stop down further to be sure that the whole subject is in focus, or even open the aperture up a bit to focus on a small part of the image to draw attention to it.

For the flash, I simply used the default TTL settings; no FEC was needed. If you don't have (or don't want to buy) a ring flash and you have an additional Speedlight such as the SB-400, SB-600, SB-800, or SB-900, you can get your light on axis by using an inexpensive, off-camera TTL flash cord such as the Nikon SC-27. This cord allows you to hold the Speedlight next to the lens for softer lighting (remember, the closer the light source is to the subject, the softer the light). I often use this technique because the one-sided light adds a nice depth to some images.

Outdoor Macro

For figure 11.2, a much simpler setup was used. I simply went out with my camera and Nikon 105mm f/2.8 VR macro lens and scouted around, looking for any insects that came across my path. Often this is the easiest way to find interesting subjects for macro photography.

Unfortunately, when photographing outdoors, the lighting is far from perfect most of the time. During the brightest part of the day,

the sun is often too bright, giving your images a lot of contrast, which can result in blown-out highlights and/or blocked-up shadows. When the lighting is the best for outdoor photography (early morning or evening and overcast days), there often isn't enough light to allow you either a small aperture setting to ensure a deep depth of field or a fast shutter speed to combat camera shake.

There are a few different ways you can get around these problems. In bright light, you can use Spot metering to ensure that the highlight detail is retained while letting the shadows go completely black. Advanced D-Lighting can also help in this situation. You can have a friend hold a diffuser in front of the subject (although this may frighten your subject off). You can also use a bit of fill flash to reduce contrast.

When the light is lower, you can increase your ISO sensitivity (which may give you more noise). You can open up your aperture and use selective focus on your image or you can use flash, as described earlier in this chapter.

When shooting figure 11.2, it was near high noon and the bright Texas sun wasn't the best lighting option, but it was the best I could do at the time and I don't often find colorful dragonflies like this one in the area I was hiking in.

Using Matrix metering, I was getting unsatisfactory exposures. As described earlier, the highlights were completely blown out. I switched to Spot metering and metered on the brightest part of the dragonfly. This brought my highlights in so that there was detail on the dragonfly's abdomen. Although the shadows of the background were slightly underexposed, this gave me a nicely saturated background that allowed the dragonfly to "pop" from the background.

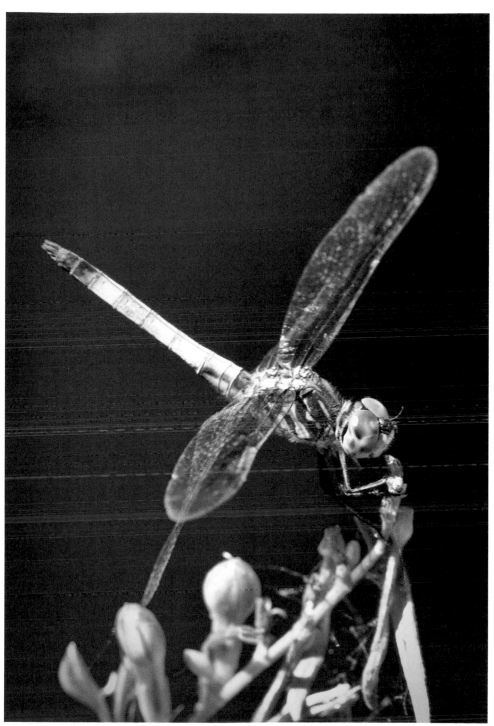

11.2 An outdoor macro shot.

Because I was photographing a moving subject, I had switched the camera to AF-C, or Continuous AF, to ensure that even if the dragonfly or I moved a bit, the camera would continue to focus on the subject.

When handholding macro photography, I recommend using AF-C because even the slightest movement can throw your focus out, and allowing the AF to adjust for your movements will get you sharper images. If you're using a tripod and photographing a non-moving subject, using AF-A (Auto) or Single AF is advised.

While the D5000 has the Close-up Advanced scene mode, I hesitate to recommend it for the settings it locks you into. The camera automatically selects Matrix metering, which you cannot change in the scene mode. As I explained earlier, there are many times when Matrix metering isn't the best option.

Night and Lowlight Photography

When the sun sets and the light becomes low, a whole new world of photography opens up. You can capture many different aspects and portray the world in a different light, so to speak. Taking photographs in low light brings a whole different set of challenges that are not present when you take pictures during the day. The exposures become significantly longer, making it difficult to handhold your camera and get sharp images. Your first instinct may be to use the flash to add light to the scene, but as soon as you do this, the image loses its nighttime charm.

Preparing Your Shot

Almost any type of photography can be accomplished in low light, from landscapes to portraits. Each type of photography has slightly different techniques and accessories, but the goal is the same: to get enough light to make a good exposure and to capture the delicate interplay between light and dark.

Concerts

The type of low-light photography that I deal with the most is concert photography. This type of photography can be the most difficult to deal with. The lighting is erratic at best and can throw your meter off, resulting in over- or under-exposed images.

The performers are often moving around, necessitating a fast shutter speed to freeze them, but the light is low and so the ISO needs to be increased in order to get a fast enough shutter speed. This represents all of the worst shooting conditions that you encounter in photography rolled up into one!

Yes, this type of photography is challenging, but that's what makes it fun. Getting the quintessential shot of your favorite performer when the odds are against you is where the thrill of concert photography lies.

A good way to get started with concert photography is to find out when a favorite band or performer is playing and bring your camera. Smaller clubs are usually better places to take good close-up photos, simply because you are more likely to have closer access to the performers.

Most local bands, performers, and regional touring acts don't mind having their photos taken. You can also offer to e-mail the performers some images to use on their Web site. This is beneficial for both them and you, as a lot of people will see your photos. I spent a lot of time honing my craft in smaller clubs and venues for lesser-known bands before I had a good enough portfolio to show to the agency that now gets me access to the national touring acts at the larger venues.

Tip   *A good way to get your foot in the door is to offer to photograph bands for local or regional publications.*

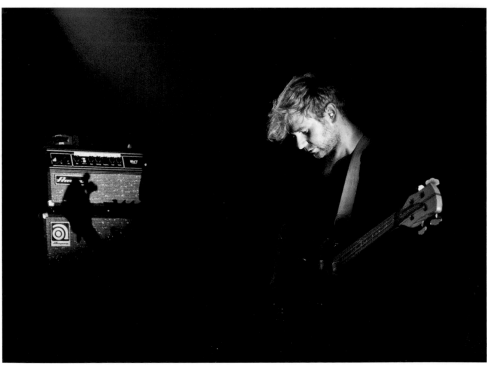

12.1 The exposure for this shot was metered based on the performer's face, allowing the background to go dark, which draws attention to the subject.

For the most part, with concert photography the lighting comes from the stage lights. If you're shooting at a larger venue or concert, usually the stage lighting is wonderful and you can get amazing images using relatively low ISO settings. The stage-lighting engineers are paid to make the performers look good and you're essentially piggybacking off of their expertise; of course, you are in charge of the composition.

Sometimes when photographing in places with less-than-perfect lighting, I need to increase the ISO to 3200; with some previous cameras I've owned, this would have rendered the shots barely usable; not with the D5000. At ISO 3200, images from the D5000 are perfectly usable and amazingly low in noise. For these situations, I have started using the Auto ISO feature. I know that sometimes I may need to use ISO 3200 for some shots, but not all of them.

I didn't want to waste my time switching ISO settings all through the show, and so I set the ISO sensitivity auto control to On/Maximum sensitivity 3200/Minimum shutter speed 1/250 second. You can set the Auto ISO in the Shooting menu under the ISO sensitivity settings option. Using a minimum shutter speed of 1/250 second allows me to handhold the camera, and freezes the action of the band members so that they aren't blurry.

For lighting situations such as the one in figure 12.1, I usually use spot metering to set the exposure for the performer's face because I'm not usually concerned about the background. Often it's preferable to lose detail in the background because it brings out the subject of the image much better.

I occasionally switch to Matrix metering when I want to include some background details in the image or if the lighting is constant, but for flashing and moving lights, I recommend staying away from Matrix metering because the moving lights thoroughly confuse the metering system, resulting in widely varying exposures.

Most of the time, the lighting is fairly dim and you need to shoot with the widest aperture available, and setting the camera to Aperture Priority allows you to set the aperture and let the camera decide the shutter speed. Using a wide aperture also allows you to throw the background out of focus to get rid of distracting elements in the background.

Because performers are usually in motion, even if it's just the motion of strumming a guitar, I always set the focus mode to Continuous AF (AF-C) with the AF-area mode set to Dynamic. This allows the camera to track the performer if they should happen to move in the frame.

This type of photography is ideally done with a fast lens of f/2.8 or better. This allows you to keep your ISO settings relatively low for the best image quality. Unfortunately, at this time there are few affordable options for fast lenses that allow the D5000 to AF. The one exception is the new Nikon 35mm f/1.8G. This is a good normal lens and will get you good shots as long as you're not too far away.

A standard-focal-length zoom lens is what I recommend for this type of photography, the Nikon 17-55mm f/2.8 being the preferred lens. The kit lens can be used, but you'll be pushing the limits of the ISO settings to get a fast enough shutter speed.

If you can get close enough to the stage, using an ultra-wide angle lens can add a great effect to your concert images. The ultra-wide view adds an interesting perspective and allows your images to stand out from the pack, as shown in figure 12.2.

Nightlife

One of the easiest ways to do night photography is simply to grab a tripod and venture out into the night. Set up the camera on the tripod and shoot! The tripod stabilizes your camera so that you don't have to worry about camera shake with long exposures.

You can use the long exposures to create special effects like the streaks of light from moving vehicles. One of my favorite things to do when I visit any city is to photograph the skyline at night. The multitudes of different-colored lights make these pictures vibrant and interesting. Even though these are shot in the dark, there is actually plenty of light to be found. Cities take on a different and more interesting character when photographed at night.

It's best to get a nice, sturdy tripod for this type of work. A ball head on the tripod is also great for quickly composing your images.

Generally, when doing this type of photography, I use manual exposure and I bracket my exposures. Bracketing allows me to be sure that I get the exact exposure that I'm looking for, and if necessary, I can combine elements of different exposures. For my base exposure, I set the metering mode to Matrix and look at the light meter in the viewfinder.

I generally start my exposure settings where the meter says that it's 1 stop under-

exposed. I find that this is generally pretty close to the right exposure. I bracket five frames at 1/2-stop intervals from my base exposure. You can use smaller or larger increments and bracket more frames if you'd like more or less latitude in your exposures.

When doing night photography such as this, I generally use small apertures and long shutter speeds. The long shutter speeds allow anything that might be moving in the scene to not register.

For example, when photographing a city street scene using a shutter speed of 30 seconds, a person walking through the scene would register as long as they kept moving. This also allows you to capture streaks from any moving light sources such as a car or truck headlights.

I also like to use long shutter speeds because most metropolitan cites are located near a river or lake and the reflection of the city in the water gets a glasslike appearance with the longer exposure.

I use small apertures for two specific reasons. The first is that smaller apertures require longer shutter speeds to make an exposure. Second, when using a small aperture, any points of light that are in the scene are rendered as starbursts, as seen in figure 12.4. This is due to the diffraction of the light from the aperture blades, and the smaller the aperture, the more pronounced the points are. Unfortunately, diffraction also causes the image to lose a little sharpness. For this reason, I recommend stopping down no further than f/16.

One thing to watch for when doing night photography with long exposures is lens flare. This is especially prevalent if you are using an ultra-wide angle lens.

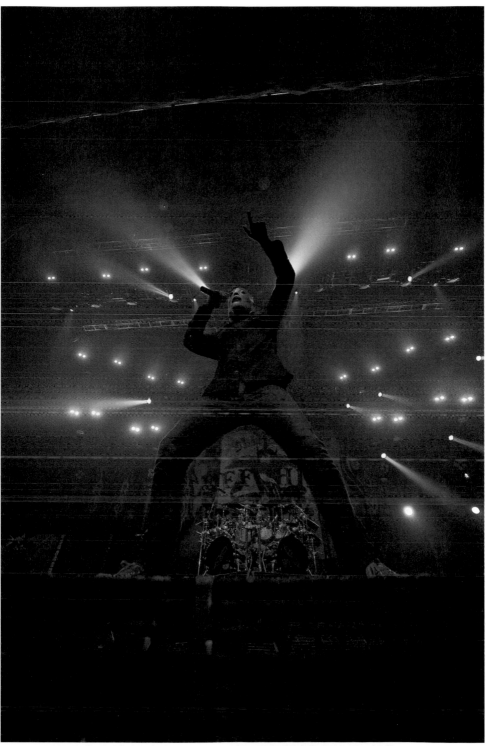

12.2 A 10mm ultrawide angle-lens was used to give this shot a surreal effect.

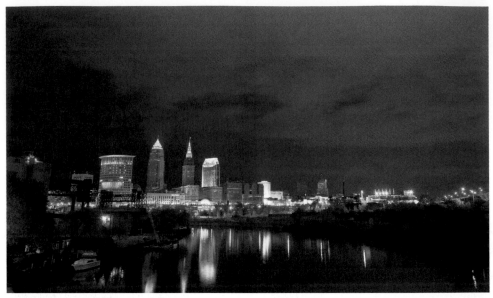

12.3 Cleveland skyline at night.

In figure 12.4, I used a Nikon 10-24mm lens, and you can see that there is lens flare all over the image caused by the various bright points of light and exacerbated by the long exposure time making it more visible. Using a slower shutter speed makes lens flare of this type less noticeable.

If you find yourself without a tripod, don't fret. The D5000 is excellent in low light when using high ISO sensitivity settings. Couple that with the VR on the kit lens, and shooting most still subjects in the darkness is easy.

You can also use wide-angle settings when shooting handheld in low light. Wide-angle settings are easier to handhold at longer shutter speeds without camera shake.

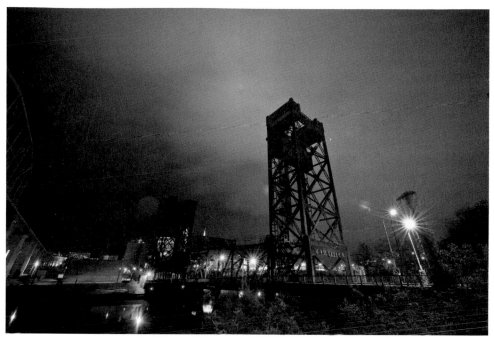

12.4 Columbus Ave. Bridge in Cleveland, Ohio, at night.

Portrait Photography

Portrait photography can be one of the easiest or one of the most challenging types of photography. Almost anyone with a camera can do it, and yet it can be a complicated endeavor. Sometimes, simply pointing a camera at someone and snapping a picture can create an interesting portrait; other times, elaborate lighting setups may be needed to create a mood or to add drama to your subject.

A portrait, simply stated, is the likeness of a person — usually the subject's face — whether it is a drawing, a painting, or a photograph. However, a good portrait should go farther than that. It should go beyond simply showing your subject's likeness and delve a bit deeper, hopefully also revealing some of your subject's character or emotion.

Preparing Your Shot

There are many things to consider when setting out to shoot a portrait. Assuming you've already got a subject, first you need to decide on the setting. The setting is the background and surroundings, the place where you'll be shooting the photograph. Different settings can evoke different kinds of moods. A dark setting, for example, will give your image a more somber or serious mood, while a lighter background can often suggest a brighter or more playful mood. Keep in mind that your subject may also have some ideas about how they want the images to turn out. Always try to keep an open mind and be ready to try some other ideas that you may not have considered.

There are many different ways to evoke a certain mood or ambience in a portrait image. Lighting and background are the principal ways to achieve an effect, but there are also other ways. For example, your camera settings or post-processing effects can play a big role. Shooting the image in black and white can give your portrait an evocative feeling. You can shoot your image so that the colors are more vivid, giving your photo a lively, vibrant effect, or simply tone the colors down for a more ethereal look.

There are two main types of lighting: broad and short. *Broad lighting* occurs when your main light is illuminating the side of the subject that is facing towards you. *Short lighting* occurs when your main light is illuminating the side of the subject that is facing away from you. Broad lighting works best with people who have narrow, angular faces, while short lighting works best with people who have broader faces.

Studio

With studio portraits, the lighting and background are controlled to a much greater extent than with a standard indoor portrait. The studio portrait is entirely dependent on the lighting and background to set the tone of the image.

The most important part of a studio setting is the lighting setup. Directionality and tone are a big part of studio lighting, and close attention must be paid to both. There are quite a few things to keep in mind when setting up for a studio portrait; here are a few to consider:

✦ **What kind of tone are you looking for?** Do you want the portrait to be bright and playful or somber and moody? These elements must be considered, and the appropriate lighting and backgrounds must be set up.

✦ **Do you want to use props?** Sometimes having a prop in the shot can add interest to an otherwise bland portrait.

✦ **What kind of background is best for your shot?** The background is crucial to the mood and/or setting of the shot. For example, when shooting a high-key portrait, you must have a vibrant background. You can also use props in the background to evoke a feeling or specific place. Some photographers go so far as to build sets to achieve their shots, similar to a movie set.

✦ **What type of lighting will achieve your mood?** Do you want hard light for an edgy look or soft lighting for a nice, smooth appearance? Do you need a hair light or some other type of accent light?

Setup

Studio portraits often require the most thought and planning of all the different types of portraits. Before setting out to do this portrait, we discussed what types of images the subject needed, as well as what types of lighting she wanted. We decided to do low-key portraits with a single light to add a little mystery to the image.

This type of photography also requires the most equipment; lights, stands, reflectors, backgrounds, and props are just a few of the things you may need. For example, for figure 13.1, I used a 200-watt second strobe set up at camera left on a boom stand, bounced from a 36-inch umbrella, for the main light. A reflector, which was attached to a stand using a reflector holder, was used to add a little fill on the left.

To fire the studio-type strobe, it was necessary to use a Wein Safe Sync. This device

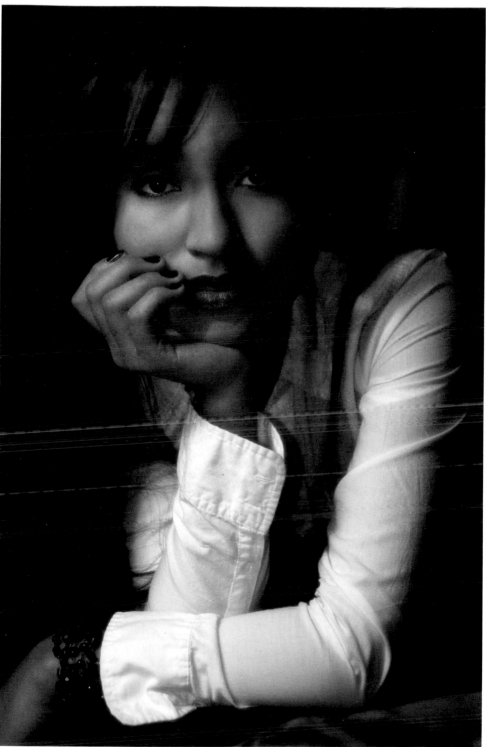

13.1 For this studio portrait, we planned for a low-key look.

slides into the D5000 hot shoe. The Safe Sync has a PC terminal connection, which is connected using a PC sync cord, which in turn connects to another terminal on the strobe. When the Shutter Release button is pressed, the strobe is triggered.

 Cross-Reference *For more information on lighting and accessories, see Chapter 6.*

Camera settings

When using studio strobes, it's best to use your camera in the Manual exposure mode. This allows you to directly choose which settings to apply. Using strobes requires an accessory flash meter, or you can use the GN / D = A equation that is discussed in Chapter 6.

Indoor

When shooting portraits indoors, there often isn't enough light to make a correct exposure without using flash or some other sort of additional lighting. Although the built-in flash on the D5000 sometimes works very well, especially outdoors, I find that when I try to use it for an indoor portrait, the person ends up looking like a deer caught in headlights. This type of lighting is very unnatural-looking and doesn't lend itself well to portraiture. It works fine for snapshots, but your goal here is to get beyond taking snapshots and move up to making quality images.

A better option than using the built-in flash is using a shoe-mounted Speedlight such as an SB-900. As with the built-in flash, photographing your subject with the Speedlight pointed straight at him or her is unadvisable.

When using one of the shoe-mounted Speedlights, the best bet is to bounce the flash off the ceiling or a nearby wall to soften the flash. Ideally, you should use the flash

off-camera, utilizing the wireless capabilities of the D5000's built-in flash and Nikon's Creative Lighting System (CLS).

By far the easiest way to achieve a more natural-looking portrait indoors is to simply move your subject close to a window. This gives you more light to work with, and the window acts as a diffuser, softening the light and giving your subject a nice glow.

Setup

While on assignment to shoot musician and author Martin Atkins (see figure 13.2) giving a presentation, I had a chance to shoot some quick portraits before his speech. It just so happened that he was near the entrance door to the lecture hall, and so I had him step out into the hallway, which contained mostly large windows. The windows gave a nice, soft light with a very defined highlight edge, which added to the ambience of the portrait.

Camera settings

As usual, when shooting portraits, I used Aperture Priority and opened the lens all the way up. The lens I was using was the Micro-Nikkor 105mm f/2.8 VR. Although this is a macro lens, I find that it doubles as an excellent portrait lens as well.

The camera was set to spot metering so that the shadow side of the subject's face was properly exposed. I let the background blow out to add a little flare to the shot.

Sometimes, breaking the rules can yield great results. Although the light looks fairly bright in the shot, in reality it was fairly dark and I had to increase the ISO setting to 3200 to get a shutter speed of 1/200 second to avoid any motion blur from the subject moving.

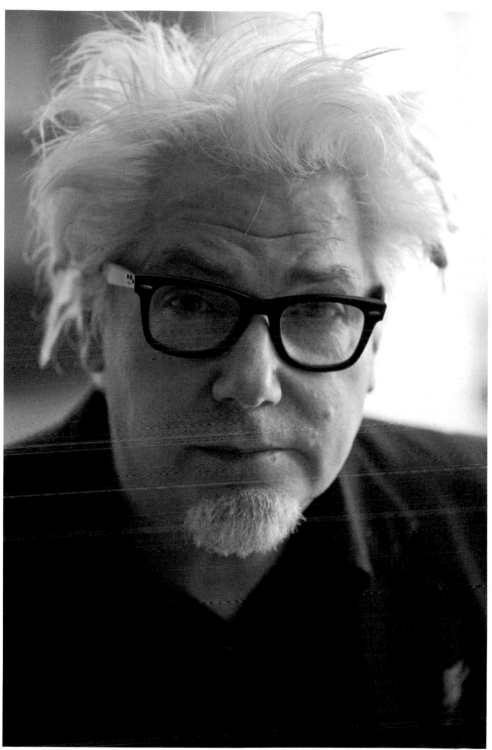

13.2 For this portrait, the subject was placed next to a window.

Outdoor

When you shoot portraits outdoors, the problems that you encounter are usually the exact opposite of the problems you have when you shoot indoors. For example, the light tends to be too bright, causing the shadows on your subject to be too dark. This results in an image with too much contrast.

In order to combat this contrast problem, you can use your flash. Although this may sound counterintuitive, using the flash in the bright sunlight fills in the dark shadows, resulting in a more evenly exposed image. This technique is known as *fill flash*.

Another way to combat images that have too much contrast when you're shooting outdoors is to have someone hold a diffusion panel over your model or move your model into a shaded area such as under a tree or a porch. This helps block the direct sunlight, providing you with a nice, soft light for your portrait.

 Cross-Reference *For more information on fill flash, see Chapter 6.*

Setup

In figure 13.3, I found myself shooting some impromptu portraits of musician Kristin Diable. It was in the middle of the afternoon with the sun high in the sky and not a cloud in sight.

Often when faced with this type of situation, I'll use a diffusion panel to soften the sunlight, but in this case I didn't have my panel with me, nor did I have anyone to hold the panel even if I did. The next easiest thing to do was to bring her under the roof at the front of the venue where she had performed.

By keeping her close to the edge of the overhang, I was able to get a fairly directional yet soft light. This allowed me to add some dimension and contour to her face. Placing her further back under the overhang would have diffused the light even more, giving me shadowless light, which can lack character and definition.

A beautiful portrait doesn't need to have an elaborate lighting setup. This portrait rivals any studio portrait I could have done, and it only took me a few seconds to set up.

Camera settings

As usual, when shooting portraits, I had my camera set to Aperture Priority with the aperture of my 50mm f/1.4G lens set to f/2.8 to be sure that I carried focus throughout her whole face. Sometimes, when using a very wide aperture, you can have one eye in focus and one out of focus. However, this can be distracting to the viewer and should generally be avoided.

The 50mm is a great lens choice for portraits on the camera, with the 1.5x crop factor landing the equivalent focal length in at 75mm, which is pretty close to the standard portrait focal length of 85mm on a full frame camera.

The metering was set to Center-weighted, as I was mainly concerned with the exposure on her face. Spot metering would have either made the shadows too dark or the highlights too bright. Center-weighted metering allowed me to get a proper exposure on the face.

The Portrait Scene mode is also an obvious setting choice when attempting any portraits. This mode generally opens the aperture to most lenses' widest setting, the exception being the 50mm f/1.4G — at no time could I get the camera to set an aperture wider than f/2.8 when set to Portrait mode.

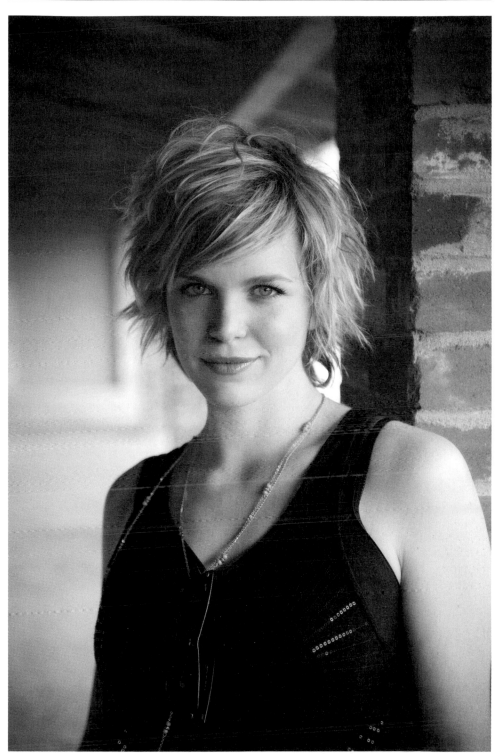

13.3 An outdoor portrait.

The Portrait Scene mode is also smart enough to pop up the built-in flash when in low light and also when in bright light to provide fill flash. When using the Portrait mode in low light, I would definitely recommend using a diffuser to soften the flash output or switching over to Night Portrait mode, which will likely yield better results.

Still-life and Product Photography

CHAPTER

14

For all practical purposes, product and still-life photography are the same; you are basically taking a photo of an object or a group of objects. Lighting is the key to making these images work. You can set a tone using creative lighting to convey the feeling of the subject. You can also use lighting to show texture, color, and form to turn a dull image into a great one. For example, becoming good at this type of photography can help you sell your items on eBay. When your product looks good, it's more likely to sell at a higher price.

Preparing Your Shot

There are two main qualities of lighting: hard light and soft light. You must know when to use each type in order to get the right quality of light for your subject. For the most part, when lighting objects, you want a soft, diffused light, as hard lighting often creates harsh shadows, giving a rather unpleasant look. Of course, hard lighting can also be useful. Hard light highlights the textures in an object, whereas diffused lighting plays down the texture. The key is determining when to use which type.

The background is another important consideration when photographing products or still-life scenes. Having an uncluttered background that showcases your subject is often best, although you may want to show the particular item in a scene, such as photographing a piece of fruit on a cutting board with a knife in a kitchen.

When shooting products or still-life scenes, you have different options when it comes to lighting. You can choose to use available lighting or you can use some sort of secondary lighting such as flash or continuous lighting. When it comes to using flash, I wholeheartedly recommend using Nikon Speedlights wirelessly off-camera. Using the built-in flash or on-camera flash does not yield the best results.

Sometimes the shadow areas need some filling in. You can do this by using a second light as fill or by using a fill card. A *fill card* is a piece of white foam board or poster board used to bounce some light from the main light back into the shadows, which lightens them a bit. When using two or more lights, be sure that your fill light isn't too bright, or it can cause you to have two shadows. Remember, the key to good lighting is to emulate the natural lighting of the sun.

Using Available Light

For available light, I recommend using the tried-and-true method of window lighting. Light filtering through the window is almost always very soft and diffuse, which is pleasing to the eye and complements the subject well. This is often the best way to light subjects such as food. More often than not, I find that if I'm shooting food on location, the best shots are usually with window light. For figure 14.1, I simply placed this cupcake on a table near a window for the main light and used a small reflector to fill the shadows in a little bit. Apart from the lighting, I used the leading lines from the table to draw the viewer's eye up through the image.

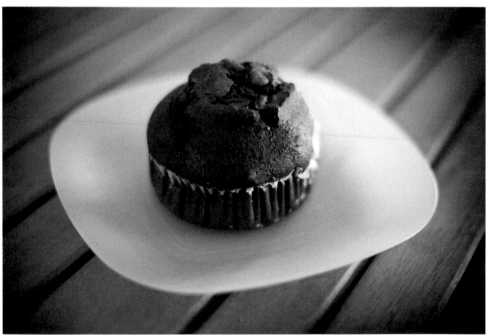

14.1 This food product shot was lit using simple window lighting.

For this shot, I simply set the camera to Matrix metering using Aperture Priority. I opened up the aperture to f/1.4 and adjusted the ISO up to 800 until I achieved a shutter speed of 1/40 second, about the bare minimum for handholding this shot while using a 50mm f/1.4 lens.

Of course, one of the easiest settings to use when photographing a food setup is the Food scene mode. This mode boosts the saturation and contrast of your food images. Other Advanced scene modes that can come in handy for product or still-life shots are the High Key and Low Key scene modes. The High Key mode is great for photographing subjects on a bright background, and the Low Key mode is great for objects on a black background.

Product and still-life lighting doesn't need to be complicated or difficult. As for composition, I focused on the microphone, which is, of course, the main subject; I wanted to give a vintage vibe to go along with the vintage-styled microphone, and so I placed an old hollow-body guitar in the background.

I wanted the microphone to be the center of attention, and so I used a shallow depth of field to throw the background out of focus.

For figure 14.2, I set the camera to Matrix metering using Aperture Priority. I opened up the aperture to f/1.4 and adjusted the ISO up to 3200. This gave me a shutter speed of 1/500 second, which ensured that there was no camera shake and that the microphone was in sharp focsus.

Using Continuous Lighting

One of the easiest ways to light a product or still life is to use continuous lighting. When using continuous lighting, WYSIWYG (what you see is what you get). This makes it very simple to light your subject.

If you don't like the lighting pattern, you can move the lights and instantly see the change. There are a few different types of continuous lights, some of which are covered in Chapter 6.

In figure 14.2, I simply used an inexpensive clamp light that I bought at a hardware store for about $5. I clamped it to a light stand and moved it until I got the highlight where I wanted it (you can also see a blue highlight from the sun shining in a window).

Using Speedlights

Figure 14.3 shows a more ambitious approach to lighting. This guitar and amplifier combo was shot using three Nikon Speedlights and various modifiers and accessories.

The Speedlights were controlled using an SU-800 with an SB-900 set to Group A, SB-800 set to Group B, and SB-600 set to Group C. For the main light, I used the SB-900 mounted on a stand with a shoot-through umbrella. This Speedlight was placed to the right of the subjects, and Group A was set to TTL on the commander.

Because the fronts of the subjects were in deep shadow using only a single light, I used an SB-800 to add some fill. I set the Speedlight to Group B so that I could control it independently from the main light. I

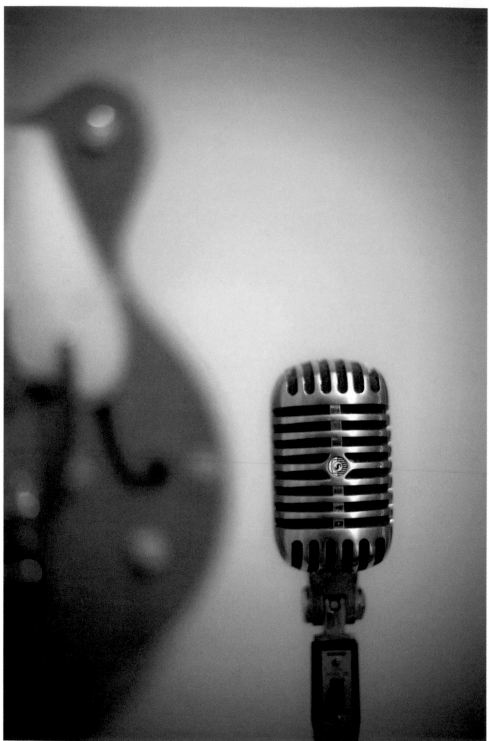

14.2 This microphone was lit with a single continuous light.

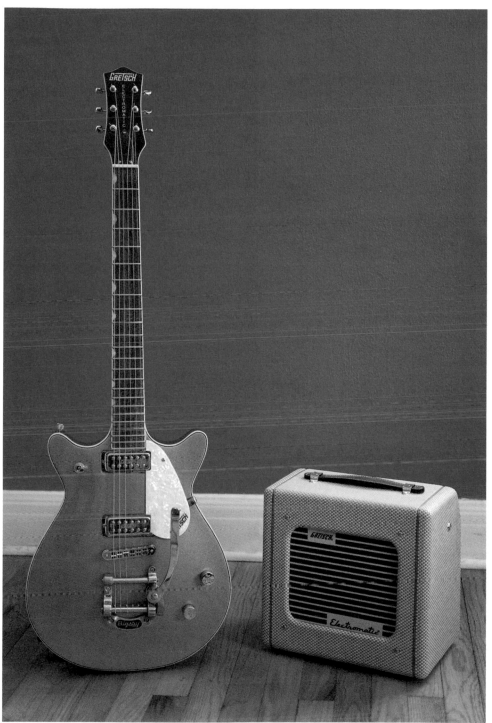

14.3 Multiple Speedlights were used to light this product shot.

set the SB-800 on a stand and aimed it into a reflector to bounce the light for a diffused fill. Group B was set to TTL on the commander, and I dialed down the FEC to -2EV to make the area a little darker to make sure that there was dimension in the image, giving it a more 3-D feel instead of looking flat and lifeless.

The lighting on the subjects was nice, but the background was too dark. I set the SB-600 on Group C to the right of the subjects just behind them, and pointed it straight up to bounce the light off of the ceiling, filling in the background. Group C was set to TTL and the FEC was dialed down to -3EV so as not to compete with the other lights.

Generally when I'm working with any type of strobes, I switch the camera to Manual exposure. In this instance, I set the shutter speed to the normal sync speed of 1/60 second (you don't really need to use the top sync speed unless you're shooting outdoors and need to be sure that the sunlight doesn't add to your exposure).

Using a 28-70mm f/2.8 lens set to 52mm, I opened up the aperture to f/2.8 to avoid showing the texture of the wall in the background, thus softening the background.

Urban and Rural Landscape Photography

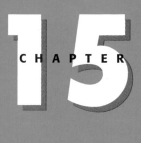
With landscape photography, the intent is to represent a specific scene from a certain viewpoint. For the most part, animals and people aren't included in the composition, and so the focus is solely on the view. Landscape is a very popular type of photography because anyone can do it. There are many famous landscape photographers, the most famous of whom is probably Ansel Adams.

Preparing Your Shot

Landscape photography can incorporate any type of environment — desert scenes, mountains, lakes, forests, skylines, or just about any terrain. You can take landscape photos just about anywhere, and one nice thing about them is that you can return to the same spot, even as little as a couple of hours later, and the scene will look different according to the position of the sun and the quality of the light. You can also return to the same scene months later and find a completely different scene due to the change in seasons.

There are three distinct styles of landscape photography:

✦   **Representational.** This is a straight landscape, the "what you see is what you get" approach. That is not to say that this is a simple snapshot; it requires great attention to details such as composition, lighting, and weather.

✦ **Impressionistic.** With this type of landscape photo, the image looks less real due to filters or special photographic techniques such as long exposures. These techniques can give the image a mysterious or otherworldly quality.

✦ **Abstract.** With this type of landscape photo, the image may or may not resemble the actual subject. The compositional elements of shape and form are more important than an actual representation of the scene.

One of the most important parts of capturing a good landscape image is knowing about quality of light. Simply defined, quality of light is the way the light interacts with the subject. There are many different terms to define the various qualities of light, such as soft or diffused light, hard light, and so on, but for the purposes of landscape photography, the most important part is knowing how the light interacts with the landscape at certain times of day.

For the most part, the best time to photograph a landscape is just after the sun rises and right before the sun sets. The sunlight at those times of day is refracted by the atmosphere and bounces off of low-lying clouds, resulting in a sunlight color that is different, and more pleasing to the eye, than it is at high noon. This time of day is often referred to as the golden hour by photographers due to the color and quality of the light at this time.

This isn't to say you can't take a good landscape photo at high noon; you absolutely can. Sometimes, especially when you're on vacation, you don't have a choice about when to take the photo, so by all means take one. If there is a particularly beautiful location that you have easy access to, spend some time and watch how the light reacts with the terrain.

Urban

For the urban landscape in figure 15.1, I simply used my 50mm f/1.4 prime lens, composed the image, and shot. Because the light was pretty bright, I didn't need to worry about camera shake. The shutter speed of 1/400 second was more than enough to counteract any camera shake. When the light is dimmer, you may need to use a tripod to ensure a sharp image.

 For more information on shooting skylines at night, see Chapter 12.

My camera settings for the image in figure 15.1 were quite simple. I used Aperture Priority so that I could select a small aperture of f/11 for a deep depth of field. The light was relatively uniform, and so I chose Matrix metering. The darkness of the cityscape caused the sky to be a bit overexposed, and so a -0.7EV of exposure compensation was added.

I set my WB to Auto, but when I opened the image in Adobe Photoshop, I could tell that the WB wasn't quite right. This is one reason why I generally shoot RAW. If you're not comfortable or simply prefer not to shoot RAW, then you may want to try WB bracketing to ensure that you get the correct WB.

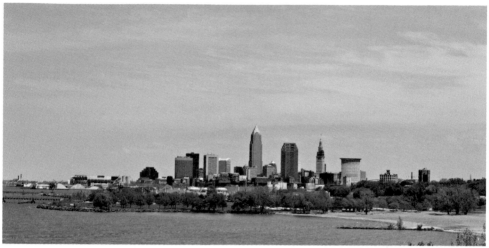

15.1 Cleveland, Ohio, skyline from Edgewater Metro Park.

Silhouettes

One very cool way to shoot a landscape photo is to pick a prominent feature in the scene and silhouette it against the backdrop of the sky. This gives you a bold and striking image with saturated colors and a dark subject that pops from the background.

Of course, you can use the Silhouette advanced scene mode to get this effect, but I believe it's better to know how to get the image yourself rather than relying on the camera to do all the work for you.

The process is actually very simple, but it yields results that will really impress your friends and family.

Follow these steps:

1. **Set your camera to Spot meter.** You can do this in the Quick Settings menu. When you have Spot metering selected, find the brightest point in the scene and put your focus point on that spot.

2. **Lock the exposure using the AE-L button.** In CSM f2, set the AE-L/ AF-L button to AE lock only or to AE lock Hold.

3. **Compose your image.** Focus on the most prominent feature in the scene. In the image shown here, I focused on the large cactus in the foreground.

4. **Take your shot.** Review your shot on the LCD. If it doesn't work out, follow these steps again, being sure that you have metered on the absolute brightest spot in the scene.

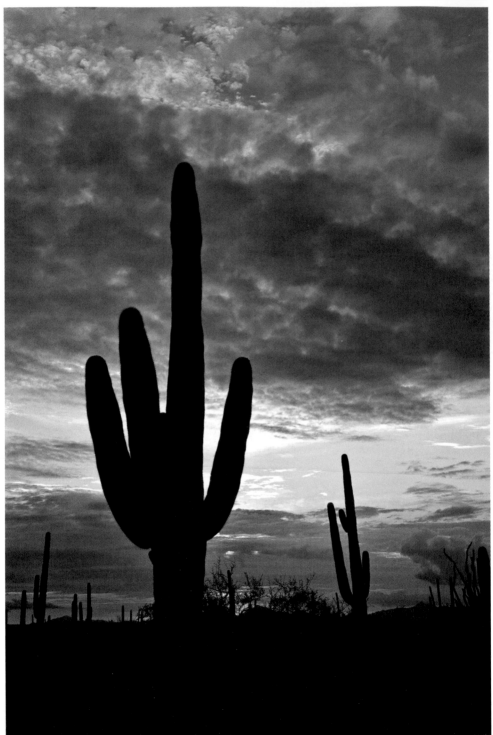

15.2 Silhouette photography is best done when the light is fairly low, such as at sunset or dawn.

Desert

Figure 15.3 was shot on a recent trip to one of my favorite places, White Sands, New Mexico. With its shimmering white sand and vast expanses of sky, you can get images of sweeping vistas for representational landscapes, or you can concentrate on small details such as the patterns of the wind-blown sand for abstract landscape images such as that depicted in figure 15.4.

Generally, when shooting landscapes, I like to use a tripod so that I can use a small aperture to be sure to get plenty of depth of field; however, in this situation, I didn't have one with me because trudging around in the sand under the sun all day is exhausting enough without dragging a lot of extra gear.

When I shot figure 15.3, it was just as the sun was dipping below the horizon at dusk (the golden hour, remember?), and although there was enough light to make a decent exposure while handholding the camera, I needed to use a wide aperture to get a fast enough shutter speed to avoid camera shake.

Now, you always hear, "wide apertures for shallow depth of field," and this is generally true; depth of field is determined not only by aperture but also by your distance from the subject you are focusing upon as well as the focal length of the lens you're using. In this instance, using a 17mm lens and focusing on the horizon allowed me to have a deep depth of field while using a very wide aperture of f/2.8.

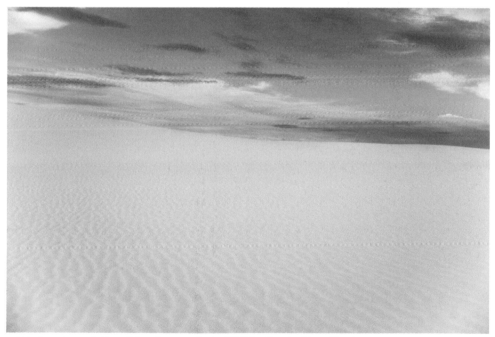

15.3 A representational landscape shot of White Sands, New Mexico.

15.4 An abstract landscape shot of White Sands, New Mexico.

Generally, when shooting landscapes, you want to get a very deep depth of field, and so choosing the right aperture is the most important thing. For this reason, when shooting landscapes, I generally set my camera to Aperture Priority so that I can control how much depth of field I get. Depending on the scene, I'll sometimes shoot in manual exposure as well, often bracketing my exposures.

When shooting bright expanses such as these shots at White Sands, your camera's exposure meter will be fooled. The overabundance of white in the scene causes the camera to see the scene as too bright, and so it underexposes your image, causing the sand or snow to appear a dull, dingy grey. In order to combat this, you need to add +1 to +2EV of exposure compensation or you can manually set the exposure by setting it to where the exposure meter reads 1 or 2 stops over. This ensures that your whites are bright, just as they look in real life. When using the Beach/Snow advanced scene mode, this is precisely what the scene mode tells the camera to do.

Appendixes

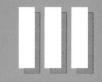

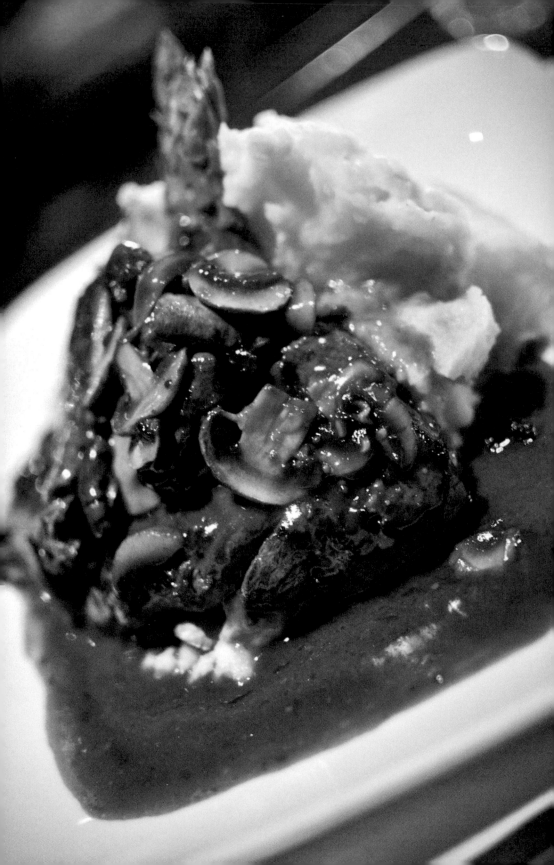

Accessories

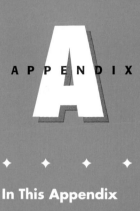
There are a number of accessories and additional equip-ment that are available for the Nikon D5000. These accessories range from batteries and flashes to tripods and camera bags. They can enhance your shooting experience by providing you with options that aren't immediately available with the purchase of the camera alone.

ML-L3 Wireless Remote Control

This relatively inexpensive and handy little device is used to wirelessly trigger the D5000 shutter release by using the infra-red sensor located on the front of the camera. To use this feature, set the camera's Drive mode to Remote (you can choose from Quick Response Remote or Delayed Remote). Point the remote at the camera and then press the button.

This remote is great for triggering the camera when you want to do self-portraits or if you want to get in the picture when doing a group portrait. This remote is also very useful in reduc-ing camera shake when doing long exposures with the cam-era mounted on a tripod.

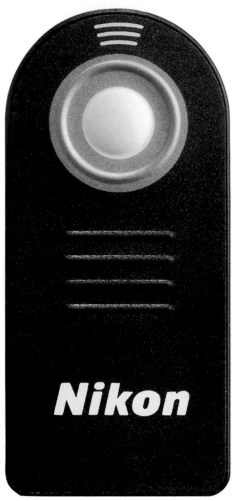

computer — for example, if you shoot only small products and your camera doesn't often leave the studio.

Caution *The EH-5A cannot be used without the EP-5 AC adapter connector.*

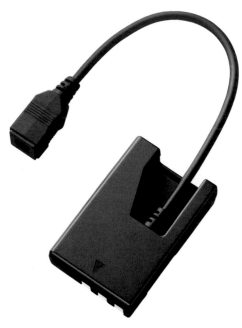

Image courtesy of Nikon Inc.
A.2 The EP-5 AC adapter connector.

Image courtesy of Nikon Inc.
A.1 The ML-L3 wireless remote control.

GP-1 GPS Unit

This GPS unit mounts to your camera's hot shoe or to the camera strap by using the supplied adapter, and connects to the camera through the accessory terminal on the side of the camera.

 Note *The Bulb setting is unavailable when the camera is set to one of the remote Drive modes.*

EH-5A AC Adapter

This handy gadget allows you to power your D5000 using standard AC input. This is great for people who mostly shoot tethered to the

This device allows you to automatically geo-tag your image with the latitude and longitude your image was taken at. Using Nikon's View NX version 1.2, you can match up your images with maps.

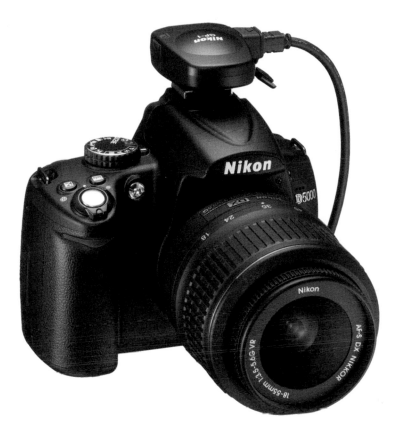

Image courtesy of Nikon Inc.
A.3 The D5000 with the GP 1 GPS unit.

Tripods

One of the most important accessories you can have for your camera, whether you're a professional or just a hobbyist, is a tripod. The tripod allows you to get sharper images by eliminating the shake caused by hand-holding the camera in low-light situations.

A tripod can also allow you to use a lower ISO, thereby reducing the camera noise and resulting in an image with better resolution.

There are literally hundreds of types of tripods available, ranging in size from less than 6 inches up to 6 feet or more. In general, the heavier the tripod is, the better it is at keeping the camera steady.

The D5000 is a fairly heavy camera, so I definitely recommend purchasing a heavy-duty tripod; otherwise, the weight of the camera can cause the tripod to shake, leaving you right back where you started with a shaky camera.

There are many different features available on tripods, but the standard features include the following:

✦ **Height.** This is an important feature. The tripod should be the right height for the specific application for which you are using it. If you are shooting landscapes most of the time and you are 6 feet tall, using a 4-foot-tall tripod will force you to bend over to look into the viewfinder to compose your image. This may not be the optimal-size tripod for you.

✦ **Head.** Tripods have several different types of heads. The most common type of head is the pan/tilt head. This type allows you to rotate, or pan, with a moving subject and also allows you to tilt the camera for angled or vertical shots. The other common type of head on a tripod is the ball head. The ball head is the most versatile, as it can tilt and rotate quickly into nearly any position.

✦ **Plate.** The plate attaches the camera to the tripod. The D5000 has a threaded socket on the bottom. Tripods have a type of bolt that screws into these sockets, and this bolt is on the plate. Most decent tripods have what is called a *quick release* plate. You can remove a quick release plate from the tripod and attach it to the camera, and then reattach it to the tripod with a locking mechanism.

If you're going to be taking the camera on and off of the tripod frequently, this is the most time-efficient type of plate to use. The other type of plate, which is on some inexpensive tripods, is the standard type of plate. This plate is attached directly to the head of the tripod. It still has the screw bolt that attaches the camera to the plate, but it is much more time-consuming to use when you plan to take the camera on and off a lot.

You must screw the camera to the plate every time you want to use the tripod, and you must unscrew it when you want to remove it from the tripod.

When to use a tripod

There are many situations when using a tripod is ideal, and the most obvious is when it's dark or lighting is poor. However, using a tripod even when there is ample light can help keep your image sharp. The following are just a few situations where you may want to use a tripod:

✦ **When the light is low.** Your camera needs a longer shutter speed to get the proper exposure if there isn't much available light. The problem is, when the shutter speed becomes longer, you need steadier hands to get sharp exposures. Attaching your camera to a tripod eliminates camera shake.

✦ **When the camera is zoomed in.** When you are using a long focal-length lens, the shaking of your hands is more exaggerated due to the higher magnification of the scene and can cause your images to be blurry, even in moderate light.

✦ **When shooting landscapes.** Landscape shots, especially when you're using the Landscape scene mode, require a smaller aperture to get maximum depth of field to ensure that the whole scene is in focus. When the camera is using a smaller aperture, the shutter speed can be long enough to cause camera shake, even when the day is bright.

✦ **When shooting close up.** When the camera is very close to a subject, camera shake can also be magnified. When you're shooting close-ups or macro shots, it may also be preferable to use a smaller aperture to increase depth of field, thus lengthening the shutter speed.

Which tripod is right for you?

Considering that there are so many different types of tripods, choosing one can be a daunting experience. There are many different features and functions available in a tripod; here are some things to think about when you're purchasing one:

✦ **Price.** Tripods can range in price from as little as $5 to as much as $500 or more. Obviously, the more a tripod costs, the more features and stability it's going to have. Look closely at your needs when deciding what price level to focus on.

✦ **Features.** There are dozens of different features available in any given tripod. Some tripods have a quick-release plate, some have a ball head, some are small, and some are large. Again, you have to decide what your specific needs are.

✦ **Weight.** This can be a very important factor when deciding which tripod to purchase. If you are going to use the tripod mostly in your home, a heavy tripod may not be a problem.

On the other hand, if you plan on hiking, a seven-pound tripod can be an encumbrance after awhile. Some manufacturers make carbon-fiber tripods. While these tripods are very stable, they are also extremely lightweight. On the downside, carbon-fiber tripods are also very expensive.

Monopods

An option you may want to consider is a monopod instead of a tripod. A monopod connects to the camera the same way as a tripod, but it only has one leg. Monopods are excellent for shooting sports and action with long lenses, because they allow you the freedom to move, along with support to keep your camera steady.

Camera Bags and Cases

Another important accessory to consider is the bag or carrying case you choose for your camera. These can provide protection not only from the elements but also from impact. Camera bags and cases exist for any kind of use you can imagine, from simple cases to prevent scratches to elaborate camera bags that can hold everything you may need for a week's vacation. Some of the bag and case types available include the following:

✦ **Hard cases.** These are some of the best cases you can get. Pelican Products, Inc., offers hard cases that are watertight, crushproof, and dustproof. They are unconditionally guaranteed forever. If you are hard on your cameras or do a lot of outdoor activities, you can't go wrong with these. Recently, Pelican has started to offer soft camera bags; obviously, they aren't waterproof and crushproof, but they are excellent bags, nonetheless.

✦ **Shoulder bags.** These are the standard camera bags you can find at any camera shop. They come in a multitude of sizes to fit almost any amount of equipment you can carry. Reputable makers include Tamrac, Domke, and Lowepro. Look them up on the Web to compare the various styles and sizes.

✦ **Backpacks.** Some camera cases are made to be worn on your back just like a standard backpack. These also come in different sizes and styles, and some even offer laptop-carrying capabilities. The type of camera backpack I use when traveling is a Naneu Pro Alpha. It's designed to look like a military pack, and so thieves don't know you're carrying camera equipment.

When traveling, I usually pack it up with two Nikon dSLR camera bodies, two COOLPIX cameras, a wide-angle zoom, a long telephoto, three or four prime lenses, two Speedlights, a reflector disk, a 12-inch Apple PowerBook, and all of the plugs, batteries, and other accessories that go along with my gear. And, with all that equipment packed away, there is space left over for a lunch. Lowepro and Tamrac also make some very excellent backpacks.

✦ **Messenger bags.** Recently, more camera bag manufacturers have started to offer messenger bags, which resemble the types of bags that a bike messenger uses. They have one strap that goes over your shoulder and across your chest. The bag sits on your back like a backpack.

The good thing about these bags is that you can just grab them and pull them around to the front for easy access to your gear. With a backpack, you have to take it off to get to your camera. I also have one of these bags for when I'm traveling light. My messenger bag is the Echo made by Naneu Pro.

Glossary

Active D-Lighting A camera setting that preserves highlight and shadow details in high-contrast scenes with a wide dynamic range.

AE (Auto-Exposure) A general-purpose shooting mode where the camera selects the aperture and/or shutter speed according to the camera's built-in light meter. See also *Shutter Priority* and *Aperture Priority*.

AE/AF (Auto-Exposure/Autofocus) lock A camera control that lets you lock the current metered exposure and/or autofocus setting prior to taking a photo. This allows you to meter an off-center subject, and then recompose the shot while retaining the proper exposure for the subject. The function of this button can be altered in the Custom Settings menu (CSM f7).

AF-assist illuminator An LED light that is emitted in low-light or low-contrast situations. The AF-assist illuminator provides enough light for the camera's autofocus to work in low light.

AF-S See *Single Autofocus*.

ambient lighting Lighting that naturally exists in a scene.

angle of view The area of a scene that a lens can capture, determined by the focal length of the lens. Lenses with a shorter focal length have a wider angle of view than lenses with a longer focal length.

aperture The lens opening through which light passes. The designation for each step in the aperture is called the f-stop. The smaller the f-stop (or f/number), the larger the actual opening of the aperture; the higher-numbered f-stops designate smaller apertures, which let in less light. The f/number is the ratio of the focal length to the aperture diameter.

Aperture Priority A camera setting where you choose the aperture, and the camera automatically adjusts the shutter speed according to the camera's metered readings. Aperture Priority is often used by the photographer to control depth of field.

aspect ratio The proportions of an image as printed, displayed on a monitor, or captured by a digital camera.

autofocus The capability of a camera to determine the proper focus of the subject automatically.

backlighting A lighting effect produced when the main light source is located behind the subject. Backlighting can be used to create a silhouette effect or to illuminate translucent objects. See also *frontlighting* and *sidelighting*.

barrel distortion An aberration in a lens in which the lines at the edges and sides of the image are bowed outward. This distortion is usually found in shorter focal-length (wide-angle) lenses.

bounce flash Pointing the flash head in an upward position or toward a wall so that it bounces off another surface before reaching the subject. This softens the light that illuminates the subject. Bouncing the light often eliminates shadows and provides a smoother light for portraits.

bracketing A photographic technique in which you vary the exposure of your subject over two or more frames. By doing this, you ensure a proper exposure in difficult lighting situations where your camera's meter can be fooled.

broad lighting A lighting effect produced when your main light is illuminating the side of the subject that is facing toward you.

camera shake The movement of the camera, usually at slower shutter speeds, which produces a blurred image.

catchlights Highlights that appear in the subject's eyes.

center-weighted meter A light-measuring device that emphasizes the area in the middle of the frame when you're calculating the correct exposure for an image.

colored gel filters Colored, translucent filters that are placed over a flash head or light to change the color of the light emitted on the subject. Colored gels can be used to add a colored hue to an image. Gels are often used to change the color of a white background when shooting portraits or still lifes, by placing the gel over the flash head and firing the flash at the background.

compression Reducing the size of a file by digital encoding, using fewer bits of information to represent the original. Some compression schemes, such as JPEG, operate by discarding some image information, while others, such as RAW with lossless compression, preserve all the detail in the original.

Continuous Autofocus (AF-C) A camera setting that allows the camera to continually focus on a moving subject.

contrast The range between the lightest and darkest tones in an image. In a high-contrast image, the shades fall at the extremes of the range between white and black. In a low-contrast image, the tones are closer together.

D-Lighting A function within the camera that can fix the underexposure that often happens to images that are backlit or in deep shadow. This is accomplished by adjusting the levels of the image after it has been captured. It is not to be confused with Active D-Lighting.

D-movie Nikon's term for using the video mode of the D5000.

dedicated flash An electronic flash unit, such as the Nikon SB-900, SB-800, SB-600, or SB-400, designed to work with the automatic exposure features of a specific camera.

default settings The factory settings of the camera.

depth of field (DOF) The portion of a scene from foreground to background that appears sharp in the image.

diffuse lighting A soft, low-contrast lighting.

digital SLR (dSLR) A single-lens reflex camera with interchangeable lenses and a digital image sensor.

DX Nikon's designation for dSLRs with an APS-C sized sensor, and the lenses made for use with this sensor size.

equivalent focal length A DX-format digital camera's focal length, which is translated into the corresponding values for 35mm film or FX format.

exposure The amount of light allowed to reach the film or sensor, determined by the intensity of the light, the amount admitted by the aperture of the lens, and the length of time determined by the shutter speed.

fill lighting In photography, the lighting used to illuminate shadows. Reflectors or additional incandescent lighting or electronic flash can be used to brighten shadows. One common technique when shooting outdoors is to use the camera's flash as a fill.

FX Nikon's designation for dSLRs using a sensor that is equal in size to a frame of 35mm film.

exposure compensation A technique for adjusting the exposure indicated by a photographic exposure meter, in consideration of factors that may cause the indicated exposure to result in a less-than-optimal image.

exposure modes Camera settings that let you take photos in Aperture Priority mode, Shutter Priority mode, Manual mode, and Automatic mode. In Aperture Priority mode, the shutter speed is automatically set according to the chosen aperture (f-stop) setting. In Shutter Priority mode, the aperture is automatically set according to the chosen shutter speed. In Manual mode, both aperture and shutter speeds are set by the photographer, bypassing the camera's metered reading. In Automatic mode, the camera selects the aperture and shutter speed. Some cameras also offer Scene modes, which are automatic modes that adjust the settings to predetermined parameters, such as a wide aperture for Portrait scene mode and a high shutter speed for Sports scene mode.

fill flash A lighting technique where the Speedlight provides enough light to illuminate the subject in order to eliminate shadows. Using a flash for outdoor portraits often brightens the subject in conditions where the camera meters light from a broader scene. See also *Speedlight*.

flash An external light source that produces an almost instant flash of light to illuminate a scene. Also known as electronic flash.

Flash Exposure Compensation Adjusting the flash output by +/− 3 stops in 1/3-stop increments. If images are too dark (underexposed), you can use Flash Exposure Compensation to increase the flash output. If images are too bright (overexposed), you can use Flash Exposure Compensation to reduce the flash output. Sometimes abbreviated FEC.

flash modes Modes that enable you to control the output of the flash by using different parameters. Some of these modes include Red-Eye Reduction and Slow sync.

flash output level The output level of the flash as determined by one of the flash modes used.

front-curtain sync Front-curtain sync causes the flash to fire at the beginning of the period when the shutter is completely open, in the instant that the first curtain of the focal plane shutter finishes its movement across the film or sensor plane. This is the default setting. See also *rear-curtain sync.*

frontlighting The illumination coming from the direction of the camera. See also *backlighting* and *sidelighting.*

f-stop See *aperture.*

full-frame sensor A digital camera's imaging sensor that is the same size as a frame of 35mm film (24mmx36mm).

histogram A graphic representation of the range of tones in an image.

hot shoe The slot located on the top of the camera where the flash connects. The hot shoe is considered hot because it has electronic contacts that allow communication between the flash and the camera.

ISO sensitivity The ISO (International Organization for Standardization) setting on the camera indicates the light sensitivity. Film cameras need to be set to the ISO speed of the film being used (such as ISO 100, 200, or 400 film), whereas a digital camera can be set to any available ISO setting. In digital cameras, lower ISO settings provide better-quality images with less image noise; however, the lower the ISO setting, the more exposure time is needed.

JPEG (Joint Photographic Experts Group) An image format that compresses the image data from the camera to achieve a smaller file size. The compression algorithm discards some of the detail when saving the image. The degree of compression can be adjusted, allowing a selectable tradeoff between storage size and image quality. JPEG/Exif is the most common image format used by digital cameras and other photographic image-capture devices.

Kelvin A unit of measurement of color temperature based on a theoretical black body that glows a specific color when heated to a certain temperature. The sun is approximately 5500 K.

lag time The length of time between when the Shutter Release button is pressed and the shutter is actually released; the lag time on the D5000 is so short that it is almost imperceptible. Compact digital cameras are notorious for having long lag times, which can cause you to miss important shots.

LCD (liquid crystal display) A screen on the back of a camera that displays the camera's images.

leading line An element in a composition that leads the viewer's eye toward the subject.

lens flare An effect caused by stray light reflecting off of the many glass elements of a lens. Lens shades typically prevent lens flare, but sometimes you can choose to use it creatively by purposely introducing flare into your image.

lighting ratio The proportion between the amount of light falling on the subject from the main light and the secondary light. An example would be a 2:1 ratio in which one light is twice as bright as the other.

macro lens A lens with the capability to focus at a very close range, enabling extreme close-up photographs.

manual exposure Bypassing the camera's internal light meter settings in favor of setting the shutter and aperture manually. Manual exposure is beneficial in difficult lighting situations where the camera's meter does not provide correct results. When you switch to manual settings, you may need to review a series of photos on the digital camera's LCD to determine the correct exposure.

Matrix metering The Matrix meter (Nikon exclusive) reads the brightness and contrast throughout the entire frame and matches those readings against a database of images (over 30,000 in most Nikon cameras) to determine the best metering pattern to be used to calculate the exposure.

metering Measuring the amount of light by using the camera's internal light meter.

mirror lock-up A function of the camera that allows the mirror, which reflects the image to the viewfinder, to be retracted without the shutter being released. This happens in order to reduce vibration from the mirror moving or to allow sensor cleaning (when the shutter is open).

NEF (Nikon Electronic File) The name of Nikon's RAW file format.

noise Pixels with randomly distributed color values in a digital image. Noise in digital photographs tends to be more pronounced with low-light conditions and long exposures, particularly when you set your camera to a higher ISO setting.

noise reduction A technology used to decrease the amount of random information in a digital picture, usually caused by long exposures and high ISO settings.

pincushion distortion An aberration in a lens in which the lines at the edges and sides of the image are bowed inward. This distortion is usually found in longer focal-length (telephoto) lenses.

Programmed Auto (P) A camera mode where the shutter speed and aperture are set automatically when the subject is focused.

RAW An image file format that contains the unprocessed camera data as it was captured. Using this format allows you to change image parameters such as white balance saturation and sharpening after the image is downloaded. Processing RAW files such as Nikon's NEF requires special software, such as Adobe Camera Raw (available in Photoshop), Adobe Lightroom, or Nikon's Capture NX 2 or View NX.

rear-curtain sync Rear-curtain sync causes the flash to fire at the end of the exposure, an instant before the second or rear curtain of the focal plane shutter begins to move. With slow shutter speeds, this feature can create a blur effect from the ambient light, which appears as patterns that follow a moving subject with the subject shown sharply frozen at the end of the blur trail. This setting is usually used in conjunction with longer shutter speeds. See also *front-curtain sync.*

red-eye An effect from flash photography that appears to make a person's eyes glow red, or an animal's yellow or green. It's caused by light bouncing from the retina of the eye and is most noticeable in dimly lit situations (when the irises are wide open), and when the electronic flash is close to the lens and, therefore, prone to reflect the light directly back.

Red-Eye Reduction A flash mode controlled by a camera setting that is used to prevent the subject's eyes from appearing red in color. The Speedlight fires multiple flashes just before the shutter is opened. See also *Speedlight.*

self-timer A mechanism that delays the opening of the shutter for a few seconds after the Shutter Release button has been pressed.

short lighting A lighting effect that occurs when your main light is illuminating the side of the subject that is facing away from you.

shutter A mechanism that allows light to pass to the sensor for a specified amount of time.

Shutter Priority A camera mode where you set the desired shutter speed, and the camera automatically sets the aperture for you. It's best used when you're shooting action shots to freeze motion of the subject using fast shutter speeds.

Shutter Release button A button that, when pressed, causes the camera to take a picture.

shutter speed The length of time the shutter is open to allow light to fall onto the imaging sensor. The shutter speed is measured in seconds or, more commonly, fractions of seconds.

sidelighting Lighting that comes directly from the left or the right of the subject. See also *frontlighting* and *backlighting.*

Single Autofocus (AF-S) A focus setting that locks the focus on the subject when the Shutter Release button is half-pressed. This allows you to focus on the subject and recompose the image without losing focus as long as the Shutter Release button is half-pressed.

Slow sync A flash mode that allows the camera's shutter to stay open for a longer time to allow the ambient light to be recorded. The background receives more exposure, which gives the image a more natural appearance.

Speedlight A Nikon-specific term for its flashes.

spot meter A metering system in which the exposure is based on a small area of the image; usually the spot is linked to the AF point.

TIFF (Tagged Image File Format) A type of file storage format that has no compression, and, therefore, no loss of image detail. TIFFs can be very large image files.

TTL (Through-the-Lens) A metering system where the light is measured directly though the lens.

tungsten light The light from a standard household light bulb.

vanishing point The point at which parallel lines converge and seem to disappear.

Vibration Reduction (VR) A function of the camera in which the lens elements are shifted to reduce the effects of camera shake.

white balance A setting used to compensate for the differences in color temperature common in different light sources. For example, a typical tungsten light bulb is very yellow-orange, so the camera adds blue to the image to ensure that the light looks like standard white light.

Index

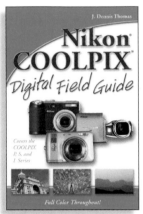
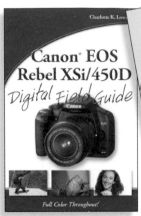
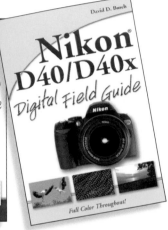
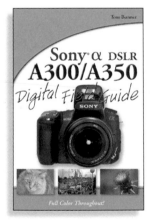
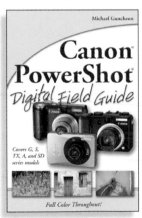
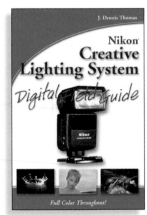